EARLY ANIMAL DOMESTICATION AND ITS CULTURAL CONTEXT

MASCA Research Papers in Science and Archaeology

Series Editor,

Kathleen Ryan

MASCA Research Papers in Science and Archaeology

Special Supplement to Volume 6, 1989

EARLY ANIMAL DOMESTICATION AND ITS CULTURAL CONTEXT

edited by

Pam J. Crabtree,
Douglas Campana,
and
Kathleen Ryan

MASCA, The University Museum of Archaeology and Anthropology
University of Pennsylvania, Philadelphia
1989

Published by
The Museum Applied Science Center for Archaeology (MASCA)
The University Museum of Archaeology and Anthropology
University of Pennsylvania,
33rd and Spruce Streets, Philadelphia, PA 19104-6324

ISSN 1048-5325

To the Memory of

Dexter Perkins, Jr. and Patricia Daly

Cover:
Scene from 'Scarlet Ware' vase from Tell Agrab,
Diyala valley, Iraq, ca. 3100 B.C.
Drawing by Jennifer R. Houser, after Stuart Piggott,
The Dawn of Civilization, p. 69. McGraw Hill, New York.

CONTENTS

DEXTER PERKINS, JR., 1927-1983

Ralph S. Solecki

Department of Anthropology, Texas A & M University, College Station, TX 77843-4352

Dexter Perkins, Jr., was born in 1927, the son of a famous historian. He was straight Harvard (B.A. 1949; Ph.D. 1959). The title of his doctoral dissertation is as singular as Dexter himself. It was called "The Post-Cranial Skeleton of the Caprinae: Comparative Anatomy and Changes under Domestication." He claimed that he did not bother with the cranium because its study was "too easy."

Comparing notes with Dexter's former students and colleagues, we have assembled a kind of history of his professional activities. Dexter evidently never saw fit to compile a full bibliographic statement of himself.

We have a couple of glimpses of his work at the Peabody Museum, Cambridge, during his student days. Charles Reed writes (pers. comm.) that when he went to visit Barbara Lawrence in the summer of 1955, he found her Peabody office and laboratory empty of people. But on the table were laid out the skeletons of all the mammals which Reed had become familiar with in his investigations in Iraq. The bones were not simply laid out. They were arranged as though someone was studying them. This person turned out to be Dexter Perkins, Jr., who was doing his doctoral research on caprids. About the same time, Philip Smith first met Dexter in Hallam Movius's laboratory, also in the Peabody Museum. Dexter very obligingly identified for Smith the faunal material which Henry Field had collected along with some flints on his rambles in Saudi Arabia.

In my visitors log at the Smithsonian Institution where I was then curator of Old World Archaeology in the National Museum, I recorded that a Dr. Dexter Perkins, Jr., had paid me a visit in 1959. He had read about our work in Iraq (I believe it was in a newspaper report). He asked me if he could join us in the field. Since we did not have a palaeozoologist then on our Shanidar team, it appeared to be a good idea to enlist Dexter's aid. He was 32 years old then, had just completed his doctorate, and was quite eager and ready to do field work. His experi-ence was limited (he had been a teaching assistant in the Department of Zoology at Harvard in 1952-53), but his willingness and enthusiasm satisfied me. So in 1960 began Dexter's first field trip to the Near East to an archaeological site. He somehow managed to find the site on his own, overcoming language and travel barriers. Characteristic of his thoughtfulness, he had packed in most welcome delicacies and a fat jar of peanut butter. Shanidar, situated in a then relatively remote part of northern Iraq, far from paved roads and all amenities of civilization, did not seem to faze Dexter a bit. Reflecting back on this, perhaps he supposed that the situation was simply the normal lot of an archaeologist. The work at Shanidar Cave, and the nearby later period site of Zawi Chemi Shanidar which Rose Solecki dug, yielded important faunal material for Dexter's researches in that field. It was of keen interest to him, because as it happened, the material was directly concerned with his doctoral researches.

Dexter filled in as an archaeologist at Shanidar Cave in the 1960 season, when the number of human skeletal finds became so numerous that our staff manpower (Dale Stewart, Jacques Bordaz, and myself) was stretched to the limit. Rose also had her hands full at her site on the river terrace under the brow of the police post where we lived.

That season must have whetted Dexter's appetite for field work, because in the next decade and a half he logged more field assignments in the Near East on expeditions than is usually possible for one person. He would get himself appointed as an expedition member with regular status, or he would volunteer his service. Independent income from his family carried him over where grants did not cover costs, and this was rather frequent.

We were unable to return to do field work at Shanidar the next year or succeeding years because of the troubles in northern Iraq. Our next trip together was to be to the Sudan, where Dexter served as the palaeozoologist-archaeologist on our team from 1961 to 1963. He served in the same capacity on our expedition to Syria (Yabroud) in

1964. I am afraid that the fauna from this site was not as interesting to Dexter as that from Shanidar. The bones consisted of the older Pleistocene fauna, associated with early Middle Palaeolithic deposits. But it was on this expedition that Dexter met Pat Daly, later to become his wife.

Pat Daly was his field companion on a number of Dexter's trips in the late 60s. He weaned her away from stone age archaeology and from doing lithics illustration for us to become a convert to faunal analysis. Together they wrote a number of professional papers, including "A Hunters' Village in Neolithic Turkey" (Scientific American 1968), which as I recall introduced the term "schlepp effect" into faunal studies parlance.

It was in the middle of the 1960s that Dexter truly became a peripatetic in the professional sense. Through association with Jacques Bordaz, who was then with New York University, Dexter joined the N.Y.U. team to Suberde in Turkey in 1964 and 1965. He worked with two British expeditions in the Near East during the first half of the 1960s. He was with James Mellaart at Çatal Hüyük, Turkey, in 1963, 1964, and 1965, and arranged to work with Diana Kirkbride at Beidha, Jordan, in 1964. These expeditions were sponsored, respectively, by the Institute of Archaeology, University of London, and the British School of Archaeology at Jerusalem and Oxford University.

Dexter, whose path had crossed again with Phil Smith's in the Sudan in 1962, read about Phil's work at Ganj Dareh in Iran in 1965 via the New York Times. He wrote to Phil asking if he could study the fauna. Phil agreed, sending the collections to Dexter in New York. Brian Hesse, one of the graduate students in Dexter's faunal class at Columbia University, was given the task of studying the material for his doctoral dissertation. Similarly, Howard Hecker, another of Dexter's Columbia students, was given the Beidha faunal material to study.

In 1965, possibly through the old school tie, Dexter joined Louis Dupree's expedition to Afghanistan, which was sponsored by the American Museum of Natural History and the American Field School of Afghanistan. We invited Dexter to join the Columbia University field expedition again in 1968, this time to Azerbaijan, Iran. There was really not too much of interest for Dexter professionally on this expedition; however he did serve the expedition as archaeologist on surveys during the slack periods. That same year he participated in Kenan Erim's work on New York University's excavations at Aphrodisias, Turkey.

The next decade, the 1970s, proved to be the turning point in Dexter's career. He was appointed Research Associate at the Peabody Museum in Harvard in 1970, and attended Peabody affairs frequently. Dexter and Pat spent about three months with C.C. Lamberg-Karlovsky at Tepe Yahya in 1971. They were the first scientists to start the systematic study of the Tepe Yahya fauna. Among the Harvard students with whom Dexter had contact was Richard Meadow, who was a member of the Yahya expedition. Also in 1971, we know that Dexter attended the International Council for Archaeozoology in Budapest.

We do not know what Dexter did in 1972 or 1973 in the way of field work, but he was out again with Pat Daly at his side in 1974 on a quick motor tour of Near East sites. He spent a few days with Phil Smith at Ganj Dareh in Iran. Smith gave him permission to undertake the study of the Ganj Dareh faunal collection. Dexter also undertook the study of the fauna from the palaeolithic site of Ghar-i-Khar, Iran, which Smith had sounded near Bisitun in 1965. Smith says (pers. comm.) that "Dexter's report was mislaid or lost or perhaps was not completed." Brian Hesse later studied the small faunal collection which Smith had retained in Montreal.

In 1974, Dexter became gravely ill and had to be hospitalized, and Pat Daly stubbornly fought his doctors to save him until he pulled through. In his recovery, he appeared to have lost some of his old stamina. Pat and Dexter were married the next year. He became very ill again in November 1977, the same year that Pat Daly died. He broke contact with the Peabody Museum after Pat died, and withdrew to his family home in Harvard, Massachusetts.

We have a hiatus of three years (1978-1981) in his field trips abroad. During this period, he was engaged in turning out archaeozoologists at Columbia University and the University of Pennsylvania. We had arranged to have Dexter teach a course in archaeozoology in the Department of Anthropology, Columbia University in 1971, 1973, 1977, and 1979. Throughout his association with the department, he held the title of Research Associate. As I recall, his classes were overflowing with students eager to learn. He appeared to inject a bit of humor into his lectures, judging from the bursts of laughter frequently emanating from his classroom. Dexter's students who completed their doctorates under his supervision included Allan S. Gilbert (1979), Douglas Campana (1980), Brian Hesse (1978), Howard Hecker (1975), and Tom McGovern (1979). Paula Wapnish earned her degree in another department at Columbia, and Anne Jensen left Columbia to continue her work at Bryn Mawr College.

Instruction in the study of faunal analysis came to the University of Pennsylvania when Dexter Perkins and Pat Daly taught Anthropology 515 together there, first in the spring of 1974, and then in the spring of 1977. Dexter taught the course again in 1979 and 1981. His teaching assistant was Pam Crabtree, who took over the course after his death. In his years of teaching at the University of Pennsylvania, as at Columbia, he inspired students to commitments to faunal studies for their dissertation work. Those at the University of Pennsylvania included David

Anthony (1985), Gil Stein (1987), David Geddes (1981), and Pam Crabtree (1982). The class enrollment at Penn was so high he had to turn students away.

In 1982, Dexter attended the International Council for Archaeozoology meetings in London, while on his way to study Egyptian tomb paintings depicting animals. This was his last field trip. Other than that, the declining health of his parents kept Dexter close to his Massachusetts home during the later years of the 70s into the early 80s. Dexter Perkins, Sr., particularly, was hospitalized for a long time. The old man's obituary appeared in the news-papers shortly after Dexter's unexpected death.

Although Dexter gave the impression of being a "loner," in retrospect, he sought team work in research. In his own way, perhaps more in person than by the printed word, he has affected the professional lives of numbers of young developing scientists in anthropology. The very production of this volume is proof of his worth and the regard in which he is held by his former students and his colleagues. It is a fitting memorial to one of the newer advocates of the discipline of archaeozoology. We have all profited from knowing Dexter Perkins, Jr.

THE CONTRIBUTIONS OF DEXTER PERKINS, JR. AND PATRICIA DALY TO ZOOARCHAEOLOGICAL STUDIES AND THEIR IMPLICATIONS FOR CONTEMPORARY FAUNAL RESEARCH

Pam J. Crabtree

Anthropology Department, New York University, 25 Waverly Place, New York, NY 10003

Douglas V. Campana

285 Lawrenceville-Pennington Rd., Trenton, NJ 08638

Introduction

This volume is dedicated to the memory of Dexter Perkins, Jr. and Patricia Daly, who together made numerous important contributions to the study of early animal domestication in the Middle East and to the development of zooarchaeological method. Perhaps their most important contributions were pedagogical. They actively promoted the *archaeological* study of animal bone remains as a means of reconstructing ancient economic patterns. During the 1970s they trained an entire generation of graduate students at Columbia University and the University of Pennsylvania in the study of faunal analysis. Many of these former students have gone on to write dissertations and to develop careers in archaeological faunal analysis. Perkins and Daly also actively collaborated with specialists in other disciplines, including Burton Singer in statistics and Isabella Drew in geology. They brought the results of these researchers' efforts to the attention of the archaeological community. Dexter Perkins, Jr. and Pat Daly were instrumental in establishing zooarchaeology as a recognized subdiscipline within archaeology. They helped move faunal analyses out of the back pages of site reports and into the archaeological mainstream.

In this review we plan to examine Pat and Dexter's contributions to zooarchaeology. In particular, we want to examine their role in the study of animal domestication in the Middle East, their contributions in the development of zooarchaeological method, and their views concerning the place of faunal analysis in archaeological interpretation. We hope to show how Perkins and Daly's pioneering work has affected both the goals and the methods of contemporary zooarchaeological research.

The study of early animal domestication in the Middle East

The transition from hunting and gathering to food production is one of the most significant developments in all of human prehistory, since it led to profound changes in population, settlement patterns, and technology. Faunal analysis can play an important role in the study of this transition, since we can use animal remains to study the process of animal domestication. This process has been most intensively studied in the ancient Near East, and it is in the Near East that most of Perkins and Daly's research was carried out.

In studying the beginnings of animal domestication in the Near East, Perkins and Daly were concerned with two basic questions: (1) How can a domestic animal be identified archaeologically? In other words, how do we distinguish wild from domestic forms? and (2) How can we describe the *process* of animal domestication in the Middle East?

The identification of animal domestication in the archaeological record

One of the first scholars to address the question of how animal domestication could be identified in the archaeological record was Robert Dyson (1953). Dyson argued that domestication could be defined in two ways. An animal may be considered culturally domesticated if it breeds in captivity and is some significant use to a human community (Dyson 1953:661). Osteological domestication, on the other hand, is defined by the existence of observable morphological differences between a domestic animal and its wild progenitor. Dyson noted that cultural domestication must necessarily precede osteological domestication. In this seminal article, Dyson contrasted what Hecker (1982:218) has termed the exclusivist and inclusivist positions regarding the definition of animal domestication. Exclusivists take an essentially zoological or taxonomic approach to animal domestication. The zoological approach emphasizes "man's creation of reproductively isolated populations" (Jarman and Wilkinson 1972:83). For example, Bökönyi (1969:219) has defined animal domestication as "…the capture and taming by man of a species with particular behavioral characteristics, their removal from their natural living areas and breeding community, and their maintenance under controlled breeding conditions…" In the zooarchaeological record, zoological or osteological domestication can be recognized by certain morphological changes such as a reduction in animal size and changes in the size and shape of the horn cores of animals such as sheep and goats (Davis 1987:134-140). Morphological changes would be the only criteria that would be acceptable to the exclusivist, since an exclusivist would define "a domestic species osteologically as one that is so different in its hard anatomy from its wild ancestor that a zoologist would consider it a new species" (Perkins and Daly 1974:77).

A more inclusivist definition of animal domestication could include a wide range of man/animal relationships (Higgs and Jarman 1969), not all of which would necessarily lead to changes in the animal's morphology (cf. Hecker 1982). We do not know how long animals must breed in captivity before morphological changes are apparent on the animals' skeletons. Bökönyi (1969) has suggested that only a few generations would be necessary, while Ducos (1969) argues that a much longer time is required for morphological changes to be visible on the animal's skeleton. If we assume, as Dyson did, that there is a time lag between the beginnings of cultural domestication and the appearance of morphological changes on the skeleton, then we need to consider alternative criteria for animal domestication. Dyson (1953:662) suggested that changes in species ratios and in age profiles, in addition to artifactual evidence, could cautiously be used as indicators of cultural domestication.

Perkins and Daly explicitly addressed this problem in 1974 in a review article on the beginnings of food production in the Near East. They noted that the zoological distinction between wild and domestic animals may not be useful to the archaeologist since "in the earliest stages of domestication such changes may not have taken place or may have been so slight as to be undetectable…" (Perkins

and Daly 1974:77). They suggest instead that "a domestic animal…is one that breeds in captivity and is of significant economic importance" (Perkins and Daly 1974:80). Following Dyson, they would accept a broader range of archaeological evidence for animal domestication.

Archaeological evidence for cultural control may be artifactual (harnesses for draft animals, for example, or graphic and plastic art showing animals in domestic situations) or from the analysis of the bones themselves showing the age-grade composition of the population to be different from that of a wild group (Perkins and Daly 1974:80).

Perkins faced this same problem in his analysis of the fauna from Zawi Chemi Shanidar (Perkins 1964) in Iraq. The site of Zawi Chemi Shanidar in Iraqi Kurdistan, excavated by Rose L. Solecki (1981), is probably one of the best known archaeological sites in the ancient Near East. In his analysis of the fauna from Zawi Chemi Shanidar, Perkins found that the sheep and goat bones were morphologically wild. He suggested (Perkins 1964:1565), following Dyson, that "an increase in the number of specimens from a potentially domesticable species, coupled with an increase in the number of immature specimens from that species, implies cultural control (that is, domestication)." Perkins argued that the fauna from Zawi Chemi Shanidar showed an increased reliance on sheep in the upper levels and an increased proportion of immature sheep. He concluded that:

Presumably domestic sheep, morphologically identical to their wild ancestors, were introduced from some other region. Domestication of a species prior to the onset of osteological change has long been postulated by archaeologists, but the data from Zawi Chemi Shanidar and Shanidar Cave are the first direct evidence of this important stage in the beginnings of animal husbandry (Perkins 1964:1566).

Although widely cited in introductory textbooks (see, for example, Fagan 1986:234), Perkins' conclusions have not gone unchallenged. They have been challenged on statistical and on broader methodological grounds. One of the main problems with Perkins' analysis of the Zawi Chemi Shanidar fauna is the issue of sample size and statistical significance. Uerpmann (1979:76), for example, notes that the apparent increase in the proportion of sheep bones in the *upper* levels of Zawi Chemi Shanidar is not statistically significant. Reed and Perkins (1984:14), however, note that the differences in the proportions of juveniles between the Baradostian (Late Upper Paleolithic) levels at Shanidar Cave and the Protoneolithic deposits at Shanidar Cave and Zawi Chemi Shanidar are statistically significant. Similarly, Bökönyi (1969:222), following an unpublished paper by Hopkins (1967), notes that the relatively small sample of Mousterian sheep from

Shanidar Cave also shows a high proportion of juvenile mortalities and suggests that it is unlikely that sheep were domesticated during the Middle Paleolithic. Reed and Perkins (1984:13) agree, but argue that the Mousterian sample is so small (n=7) that reliable conclusions cannot be drawn from it.

The major challenge, however, to Perkins' interpretation of the Zawi Chemi Shanidar fauna has been to his use of kill patterns or harvest profiles to infer animal domestication. Collier and White (1976) examined the population structures of a wide variety of wild ungulates and found substantial intraspecific and interspecific variations in the age and sex composition of these herds. They conclude that "when the only evidence for domestication is a high proportion of immature animals, there is no evidence for domestication" (Collier and White 1976:101).

Should we then stop using changes in harvest profiles as possible indicators of animal domestication? There are certainly good economic reasons why early herders may have slaughtered a high proportion of juvenile animals. Since the rate of growth of most animals decreases rapidly with age, older animals become increasingly expensive to keep (Hesse 1982:405). One can obtain a maximum meat yield for a given amount of fodder if one slaughters an animal shortly before it reaches maturity (Davis 1987:150).

Collier and White's criticism, however, rests on the assumption that the proportion of juvenile animals found in wild herds is so variable that it should not be used as a criterion for animal domestication. As Hesse (1982:409) points out, their criticism does not take into account the nature of the Near Eastern midden deposits from which the archaeological faunal samples are drawn. While the age composition of a single herd can vary considerably as a result of seasonal or other local factors, archaeological faunal assemblages from habitation sites do not generally represent a single hunting or culling episode. Hesse (1982:409) notes that "samples drawn from midden deposits are likely to 'average out' short-term or local variations in the availability of different age classes."

The main obstacle to the use of age profiles as an indicator of early animal domestication is that a number of factors, in addition to cultural control, can influence the age and sex composition of an animal herd. Hunting pressure can lead to the culling of an increased number of juvenile animals (Elder 1965). Since the age composition of many animal herds changes seasonally, alternations in seasonal hunting and settlement patterns can also lead to changes in harvest profiles (Davis 1983). If we are going to use changes in harvest profiles as possible indications of animal domestication, we must be sure that these changes in kill patterns cannot be reasonably attributed to other causes.

Age profiles, however, have been successfully used to identify early goat domestication in Iran (see, for example, Flannery 1969 and Hesse 1978, 1984). The case for domes-

tication is strengthened when information on sex can be combined with ageing data. For example, Hesse (1984) was able to show both age and sex changes in the harvest profiles of goats from Ganj Dareh between the earliest non-architectural phase and the later occupation phases. The earlier faunal assemblage contains "a combination of mostly adult females, males under a year of age, and a relatively large fraction of very young animals" (Hesse 1984:258). He suggests that this may represent the culling of a wild goat nursery herd. In contrast, the architectural phases show a slightly increased survivorship for males, a decreased survivorship for adult females, and a decrease in the proportion of very young individuals. This age and sex harvest profile is not typical of wild goat herds; it is more characteristic of domestic goats raised for their meat.

Unfortunately, we do not have this kind of information for the Zawi Chemi Shanidar faunal sample. Given the small size of the faunal assemblage from Zawi Chemi Shanidar and the absence of any evidence for morphological change (Uerpmann 1979:100-101), the case for domestic sheep at Shanidar should be regarded as unproven at this time (Davis 1987:151).

Although the case for domestic sheep at Zawi Chemi Shanidar cannot be proved on the basis of the available evidence, Perkins' use of age profiles as a criterion for domestication stimulated a wide range of zooarchaeological studies. Perkins and Daly (1974:80) suggested that,

As a hunter/predator, man apparently did not make any purposeful selection of particular age groups in the animals he hunted... [H]unters, unlike animal predators, take all age groups, including a high percentage of adults. But the evidence indicates that the earliest stock raisers in the Near East selected more immature animals than adults to be killed, thus maintaining an adult breeding population.

This kind of assertion stimulated two kinds of important archaeological research. First, archaeologists needed to know something about the dynamics of wild ungulate populations. What was the age and sex structure of these populations, and how variable were these populations on an annual or seasonal basis? (see, for example, Simmons and Ilany 1975-77; Collier and White 1976). Second, archaeologists needed to know more about human hunting practices. Are humans non-selective hunters, or do they selectively cull certain age and sex classes of animals? These questions have stimulated research into the hunting behavior of modern hunter-gatherers and into the archaeology of hunter-gatherers, an area of research that was comparatively neglected until about 20 years ago (Higgs and Jarman 1969).

It was the search for evidence of animal domestication, in the absence of evidence for gross morphological changes, that led Perkins and Daly, in collaboration with Isabella

Drew, to investigate the possibility that changes in bone microstructure might be used to identify early animal husbandry (Drew et al. 1971; Daly et al. 1973). They argued, "Examination of the bones in standard petrographic thin-section and x-ray diffractometer studies indicate that these are well-defined characteristics that distinguish specimens of wild bone from those of domestic animals" (Drew et al. 1971:280). Based on a comparison of the faunal remains from the sites of Erbaba and Suberde in Turkey, they suggested that wild and domestic bones showed differences in the orientation of their hydroxyapatite crystals. They argued that the crystallites tend to be more randomly oriented in the bones of wild animals.

A major criticism of their method has come from J.P.N. Watson (1975; see also Zeder 1978) who suggested that the apparent differences between the wild Suberde and domestic Erbaba specimens may result from differences in collagen preservation rather than differences in the orientation of the hydroxyapatite crystals. In his paper in this volume, Allan Gilbert reviews the history of research on bone microstructure and the initial critiques of Drew et al.'s research. Gilbert describes his own ongoing research on bone microstructure and its implications for the use of bone microstructure to distinguish wild from domestic animals.

The pattern of animal domestication

The determination of whether a particular faunal assemblage includes hunted or herded animals is simply a means to an end. The real goal of zooarchaeological studies of animal domestication is the study of the domestication *process*. In 1974 Perkins and Daly suggested that in the Near East cattle, sheep, and goats were each initially domesticated for their meat. They noted, however, that each of these domesticates provides valuable secondary products such as wool, milk, and hides. They suggested (Perkins and Daly 1974:82) that the desire for these secondary products may have served as an incentive for the acquisition of multiple domesticates (see also Perkins 1973a:280).

In their 1974 article, Perkins and Daly anticipated by nearly a decade the interest in the "secondary products revolution" that was sparked by Sherratt's (1981) study of the effects of the spread of the plow on animal husbandry in the Old World. In contrast with Perkins and Daly, Sherratt (1981:263) argued that the secondary products revolution was a relatively late development, intimately linked to the introduction of the plow and the beginnings of the use of animals for traction. Sherratt suggested, based on archaeological evidence for plows, plow marks, and wheeled vehicles, that these developments did not appear in the Old World until the fourth millennium B.C.

The evidence for the introduction of dairy and wool production at this time is less clear cut. Historical and pictorial evidence certainly indicates that the use of domestic animals for milk and wool production was well established by the late fourth millennium in the Near East. In Europe, evidence from the Swiss Lake villages indicates a shift from the use of flax to the use of wool for textiles in the late third millennium (Sherratt 1981:283). These changes are paralleled by changes in the style of clothing fasteners during the Early Bronze Age.

The origins of the secondary products revolution, and of dairying in particular, may have a much greater antiquity. On the basis of both faunal and artifactual evidence, Bogucki (1984, 1986) has suggested that cattle may have been kept primarily for their milk during the earliest phases of the Neolithic in temperate Europe. Faunal assemblages from Linear Pottery sites are dominated by cattle, including many calves. A substantial proportion of the adult cattle were females. This kind of harvest profile is expected from a dairy herd (Legge 1981). Linear Pottery sites have also produced many fragments of ceramic sieves which may have been used as cheese strainers (Bogucki 1986:55). While Bogucki's findings do not contradict Sherratt's evidence for the intensified use of animal secondary products in the Old World beginning in the fourth millennium B.C. (Bogucki 1984:27), they do suggest a great antiquity for the beginnings of the secondary products revolution. Perkins and Daly's (1974) suggestion that the desire for secondary products may have encouraged the adoption of multiple domesticates needs to be tested using archaeological data from a wide variety of sites in the Near East and Europe.

Zooarchaeological methods

Measures of taxonomic abundance

While Perkins and Daly were interested in the study of animal domestication in the Middle East, they were also concerned with the broader problems of zooarchaeological method, and in particular with the vexing problem of the estimation of the relative importance of the different animal species within a faunal assemblage. As Perkins (1973b:367) noted,

The most important objective of the analysis of faunal remains from archaeological sites is the determination of the importance of animals, either wild or domestic, as a food source, and the relative importance of each individual species.

An examination of the recent literature of quantitative zooarchaeology (see, for example, Grayson 1979, 1984; Klein and Cruz-Uribe 1984; Gautier 1984; Ducos 1984; Lie 1980) shows that the way we estimate taxonomic abundance is still a critical methodological problem for contemporary zooarchaeology.

While Perkins and Daly may not have solved all the problems associated with the estimation of taxonomic abundance, no one else has been able to propose a universally accepted solution, either. For example, two major books on zooarchaeological quantification appeared in 1984. In one, Grayson (1984:92) advocated the use of the NISP as a measure of taxonomic abundance, while in the other Klein and Cruz-Uribe (1984:37) favored the MNI for most intersample comparisons. It is probably fair to say that at this time there is no single quantitative technique that can adequately and unambiguously measure the relative proportions of the animal species present at an archaeological site. Perkins and Daly, however, have made a valuable contribution to this ongoing debate.

Perkins and Daly are most closely associated with the development of the Relative Frequency method of quantification (Perkins 1973b; see also Hesse and Perkins 1974), but it is clear that their approach to the problem of taxonomic abundance developed over time. In 1969 Daly (1969:150) advocated the use of the Minimum Number of Individuals technique, following White (1953). She also suggested that the Minimum Numbers be corrected for the ages of the individuals concerned, a position subsequently advocated by Chaplin (1971:70-75).

At the first ICAZ (International Council for Archaeozoology) meeting in Budapest, however, Perkins (1973b) took a somewhat different approach. He rejected the use of the NISP (number of identified specimens per taxon) on three grounds. First he noted that the number of bones in an animal skeleton is not a constant. This is a valid objection to the NISP, but this problem can be easily controlled by correcting for anatomical complexity (Gilbert and Singer 1982; see also Grayson 1984:25).

Second, Perkins (1973b:368) noted that "the pattern of bone survival may not be the same for all species." Perkins suggested that this problem had not been adequately investigated. This is a problem that plagues all attempts to estimate taxonomic abundance. Subsequent research has shown that archaeological context can have a pronounced effect on the pattern of bone survival for different species. For example, Meadow (1975, 1978) found significant differences in the proportions of pigs and caprines between the interior and exterior contexts at the Iranian Neolithic site of Hajii Firuz. Similarly, Maltby (1981:165) found marked differences in the proportions of cattle and sheep/goats from the pit and ditch contexts at the late prehistoric site of Winnall Down in England. It should be noted, however, that these problems will also affect estimates of taxonomic abundance based on Minimum Numbers of Individuals.

Perkins' third criticism of the NISP is perhaps the most important. He noted that butchering techniques for different species may differ. He cites the example of the "schlepp effect" (Perkins and Daly 1968), i.e. the differential butchery and transport of large and small animal carcasses by hunters. As Grayson (1984:25-26) has shown, this criticism points to the main problem in the use of the NISP, "the

effects of the lack of independence among the units being counted." In other words, we do not know whether the bones counted by the NISP came from the same individual or not.[1]

The use of the MNI has been advocated as a means of overcoming this problem of interdependence. Perkins, however, also objected to the use of the MNI. He argued (Perkins 1973b:369) that in many cases analysts have confused the MNI with the actual number of individuals killed at a site. The degree to which the MNI may underestimate the actual number of individuals killed at a site was forcefully demonstrated by Guilday (1970). Guilday examined the faunal remains from the 18th century A.D. site of Fort Ligonier in Pennsylvania. Using the MNI, he calculated the amount of meat that would have been available to the soldiers at Fort Ligonier and found that it would have sustained the entire garrison of the fort for only a single day.

Perkins (1973b:368) also noted that estimates of taxonomic abundance based on the Minimum Number of Individuals can be variable and unreliable for small sample sizes. While this is certainly a valid criticism, it fails to address the basic problem with the MNI statistic, which is the affect of aggregation (see Grayson 1984:27-48 for a discussion of the effects of aggregation on the MNI). What this means in practice is that MNIs behave unpredictably when individual archaeological contexts are combined into larger analytical units.[2]

As an alternative to the use of MNI and NISP, Perkins advocated the use of the Relative Frequency statistic. Perkins (1973b:367) assumed that each bone or fragment came from a different individual. In so doing, he essentially assumed away the problem of interdependence. This may be a problematic assumption for many faunal collections. It is also a difficult one to test, since there is no unequivocal way to determine whether or not two non-articulating bones originally came from the same individual. Similarly, Klein and Cruz-Uribe (1984:37) have criticized Perkins for making "unwarranted assumptions about the postdepositional history of a fossil assemblage" and then building these assumptions into the measurement method.

Perkins then corrected his raw anatomical frequencies for skeletal complexity, producing a relative frequency. In his initial formulation of the method (Perkins 1973b), the relative frequencies for all anatomical elements for each species are then averaged. Comparisons of these average relative frequencies allows the analyst to measure the relative taxonomic abundance of the species in question. The implicit assumption that underlies the method is that the true taxonomic abundance of a species is measured by the average abundance of the different anatomical elements. This is very different from the assumption which underlies the MNI. This statistic is based on the assumption that the most common anatomical element most accurately reflects the taxonomic abundance of a particular species.

In a later paper, Perkins made this implicit assumption explicit. Hesse and Perkins (1974:151) suggested that over- and under-represented elements could be eliminated from relative frequency computations. This raises the important question of whether the most common anatomical elements in a faunal assemblage are truly over-represented. It may be fair to say that an element is over-represented when it is imported into the site for an industrial or other non-food purpose. An example would be the importation of male goat horn cores into the medieval city of Dorestad in the Netherlands (Prummel 1982:121). These horn cores apparently represent waste from a horn-working industry, and inclusion of them in any estimation of taxonomic abundance would certainly over-estimate the proportion of goats in the Dorestad diet. In most other circumstances, the notion that certain anatomical elements are over-represented is problematic. For example, Payne (1972, 1975) has shown that when archaeological deposits are not wet-sieved, the smaller anatomical elements of medium-sized mammals such as sheep and goats may be systematically lost. He argues (Payne 1975) that the MNI statistic may be the most useful indicator of taxonomic abundance in these cases since it is based on the most commonly represented element. He would argue that what we are seeing in an archaeological faunal assemblage is varying degrees of under-representation. Other taphonomic factors, such as the destruction of bones by dogs (Brain 1967; Guilday 1971; Payne and Munson 1985) may have similar effects on anatomical distributions.

While the use of the Relative Frequency statistic did not solve all the problems inherent in the use of MNI and NISP for estimating taxonomic abundance, Perkins' work did serve to stimulate debate on the problems of zooarchaeological quantification. It also stimulated experimental studies on the behavior of MNI, NISP, and RF (Gilbert and Singer 1982; Gilbert et al. 1982) which are critical to our understanding of the behavior of these methods in relationship to sample size. These experimental studies indicated that the MNI and the NISP statistics "do not universally provide accurate and precise reconstructions of original species ratios even when applied to fully representative samples" (Gilbert et al. 1982:92).

Patterns of assemblage variability

The most important contribution that Perkins and Daly made to the problems of zooarchaeological quantification was their recognition that faunal analysts had to address the problems of assemblage formation when they attempted to estimate the relative importance of the various animal species in a faunal assemblage. They were among the first to recognize that faunal assemblages have been extensively modified by both human and non-human activities, drawing attention to the problems that we today would term taphonomy and site formation process. For example, in 1969 Daly (1969:148) suggested that zooarchaeologists should address the "*pattern* of bone survival, as this is an excellent example of cultural factors imposed on natural ones." In calling attention to this problem, Daly recognized the need to examine the ways in which the archaeological record is transformed by both human and non-human agencies (see, for example, Schiffer 1972, 1976).

The position adopted by Perkins and Daly is that much of the variability that we see in the zooarchaeological record is the result of human behavior, rather than of non-human agencies. Daly (1969:146-147) suggested that,

In an archaeological site bones from food animals are the direct result of human activity: selective hunting, specific butchering techniques, and in the case of domestic animals, morphological modification of the animal itself.

It was this essentially cultural approach that Perkins and Daly brought to the analysis of the faunal assemblage from the Neolithic hunters' village of Suberde in Turkey (Perkins and Daly 1968).

In their analysis of about 14,000 identified pieces of animal bone from Suberde, Perkins and Daly found very different body part distributions for the sheep/goat and the cattle bones. For the cattle, foot bones were much more common than upper limb bones, while foot and limb bones were nearly equally common among the sheep and goats. On the basis of ethnographic analogy, they argued that the meaty upper limb bones of the cattle were stripped of meat and left at the kill site. The foot bones, they suggested, remained attached to the hide and served as handles which were used to drag the animals back to the camp site. They termed this pattern the "schlepp effect" after the German verb *schleppen*, "to drag" (Perkins and Daly 1968:104).

Although Perkins and Daly's interpretation of the Suberde faunal assemblage has been widely accepted (see, for example, Schiffer 1976:21), it was roundly criticized by Binford (1981:184-185) as an example of post hoc accomodation.[3] Binford (1981:194) criticized Perkins and Daly and others for their assumption that faunal assemblage variability resulted from differential butchery practices and from the differential transport and abandonment of anatomical parts, i.e. from anthropogenic causes. He argues that bone preservation is not uniform but differential, and that "…assemblages generally have multiple causes" (Binford 1981:245). While Binford's criticism that Perkins and Daly did not adequately examine non-human causes of assemblage variability is probably valid, it leaves us with an unanswered question. What factors other than butchery and differential bone transport could produce the body part distributions seen at Suberde?

The study of the possible causes of variations in body part distributions is central to contemporary zoo-archaeology. To give just a few examples, Brain (1981) has examined the effects of carnivore activities on body part distributions; Binford and Bertram (1977) and Lyman (1984) have examined the relationship between bone density and the survival of different body parts; and Payne (1972, 1975) and Maltby (1985) have studied the relationship between recovery methods and body part frequencies. From the perspective of 1989, it is difficult to imagine that this was not always the case. It should be noted, however, that Perkins and Daly were among the first Near Eastern zooarchaeologists to recognize that body part distributions could provide valuable information for archaeological interpretation.

Pedagogical contributions

One of the most important contributions that Perkins and Daly made to the field of archaeology was their recognition that faunal analysis could make a valuable contribution to archaeological interpretation. They rejected the "tendency to regard animal remains as being of rather second class status, ranking well below stone tools and potsherds in potential cultural significance" (Daly 1969:146). Perkins and Daly argued that animal bone remains could provide useful information on prehistoric lifeways and paleoeconomy. Daly (1969:151-152) suggested that,

> ...the main function of the analysis of faunal material is to aid in determining the economic basis of a culture, whether it be hunting, herding, trapping, or stealing. Its further function can be to suggest human behavior patterns, such as hunting techniques, butchering styles, and seasonal or regional dietary selection. How does a group of people go about killing a perfect random sample of a wild population of animals? Why do shore-line settlements contain fish in some areas, and none at all in others? Does the presence of domestic animals indicate trade, stealing, or animal husbandry? These, I submit, are not zoological questions, but anthropological ones, arising out of archaeological material.

In taking this position, Perkins and Daly were instrumental in removing faunal reports from the appendices of site reports. They argued that the analysis of faunal materials was an archaeological rather than a zoological enterprise, and that archaeologists could be trained to identify and analyze faunal materials (Daly 1969:152).

The view that archaeologists should analyze their own faunal collections is widely accepted today, but it was certainly a minority viewpoint in the late 1960s. At the first meeting of the International Council for Archaeozoology (Matolcsi 1973), most of the papers were presented by zoologists rather than archaeologists.

In order to enable archaeologists to analyze their own faunal materials, Perkins and Daly taught a number of graduate courses in faunal analysis at Columbia University and the University of Pennsylvania in the 1970s. They also trained a number of other faunal analysts, principally at Harvard University. At Penn and Columbia they trained an entire generation of Old World archaeologists in the principles and procedures of faunal analysis. Many of their former students have made valuable contributions to the study of early animal domestication in the Near East and Europe, and to our understanding of the ways in which domestic animals were used by complex societies in the Old World.

In recognition to their contributions to the field of archaeology, we have dedicated this book to the memory of Patricia Daly and Dexter Perkins, Jr. The book is entitled *Early Animal Domestication and Its Cultural Context*, since Pat and Dexter recognized that the process of animal domestication was as much a cultural as a zoological process. The papers, most of which are contributed by scholars who were once their students, focus on a range of topics that were of particular interest to Pat and Dexter.

Notes

1. A total of 80 cattle bones recovered from a pit could represent the remains of 80 different cattle, or they could simply be 80 bones from a single animal skeleton.

2. Suppose that we recover a sheep radius and a sheep femur in pit 1 and a sheep tibia and a horse femur in pit 2. We therefore have a minimum of one sheep in pit 1 and one sheep plus one horse in pit 2. If we combine the two pits into a single Phase A, we would now have one sheep and one horse overall (not the two sheep and one horse that we would get if we simply added the MNIs from pit 1 to those from pit 2).

3. It is tempting to suggest that criticism by Binford is a good indication of the importance of one's scholarship in archaeology.

References

Binford, L.R. 1981. *Bones: Ancient Men and Modern Myths*. Academic Press, New York.

Binford, L.R., and J.B. Bertram. 1977. Bone Frequencies—and Attritional Processes. In *For Theory Building in Archaeology*, ed. L.R. Binford, pp. 77-153. Academic Press, New York.

Bogucki, P. 1984. Ceramic Sieves of the Linear Pottery Culture and Their Economic Implications. *Oxford Journal of Archaeology* 3(1):15-30.

———— 1986. The Antiquity of Dairying in Temperate Europe. *Expedition* 28(3):51-58.

Bökönyi, S. 1969. Archaeological Problems and Methods of Recognizing Animal Domestication. In *The Domestication and Exploitation of Plants and Animals*, ed. P. Ucko and G. Dimbleby, pp. 219-229. Duckworth, London.

Brain, C.K. 1967. Hottentot Food Remains and Their Bearing on the Interpretation of Fossil Bone Assemblages. *Papers of the Namib Desert Research Station* 32:1-11.

_____ 1981. *The Hunters or the Hunted: An Introduction to African Cave Taphonomy.* University of Chicago Press, Chicago.

Chaplin, R.E. 1971. *The Study of Animal Bones from Archaeological Sites.* Seminar Press, London.

Collier, S., and J.P. White. 1976. Get Them Young? Age and Sex Inferences on Animal Domestication in Archaeology. *American Antiquity* 41(1):96-102.

Daly, P. 1969. Approaches to Faunal Analysis in Archaeology. *American Antiquity* 34(2):146-153.

Daly, P., D. Perkins, Jr., and I. Drew. 1973. The Effects of Domestication on the Structure of Animal Bones. In *Domestikationsforschung und Geschichte der Haustiere,* ed. J. Matolcsi, pp. 157-161. Akadémiai Kiadó, Budapest.

Davis, S. 1983. The Age Profiles of Gazelles Predated by Ancient Man in Israel: Possible Evidence for a Shift from Seasonality to Sedentism in the Natufian. *Paleorient* 9(1):55-62.

_____ 1987. *The Archaeology of Animals.* Batsford, London.

Drew, I.M., D. Perkins, Jr., and P. Daly. 1971. Prehistoric Domestication of Animals: Effects on Bone Structure. *Science* 171:280-282.

Ducos, P. 1969. Methodology and Results of the Earliest Domesticated Animals in the Near East (Palestine). In *The Domestication and Exploitation of Plants and Animals,* ed. P. Ucko and G. Dimbleby, pp. 265-275. Duckworth, London.

_____ 1984. La contribution de l'archeozoologie a l'estimation des quantites de nourriture: evaluation du nombre initial d'individus. In *Animals and Archaeology. 3: Early Herders and Their Flocks,* ed. C. Grigson and J. Clutton-Brock, pp. 13-23. BAR International Series No. 202, Oxford.

Dyson, R.H. 1953. Archaeology and the Domestication of Animals in the Old World. *American Anthropologist* 55:661-673.

Elder, W.H. 1965. Primeval Deer Hunting Pressures Revealed by Remains from American Indian Middens. *Journal of Wildlife Management* 29(2):366-370.

Fagan, B.M. 1986. *People of the Earth: An Introduction to World Prehistory,* 5th ed. Little, Brown, and Co., Boston.

Flannery, K. 1969. The Animal Bones. In *Prehistory and Human Ecology of the Deh Luran Plain,* by F. Hole, K.V. Flannery, and J.A. Neely, pp. 262-330. Memoirs No. 1. Museum of Anthropology, University of Michigan, Ann Arbor.

Gautier, A. 1984. How Do I Count You, Let Me Count the Ways? Problems of Archaeozoological Quantification. In *Animals and Archaeology. 4: Husbandry In Europe,* ed. C. Grigson and J. Clutton Brock, pp. 237-251. BAR International Series No. 227, Oxford.

Gilbert, A.S., and B.H. Singer. 1982. Reassessing Zooarchaeological Quantification. *World Archaeology* 14:21-40.

Gilbert, A.S., B.H. Singer, and D. Perkins, Jr. 1981. Quantification Experiments on Computer-simulated Faunal Collections. *OSSA* 8:79-94.

Grayson, D.K. 1979. On the Quantification of Vertebrate Archaeofaunas. In *Advances in Archaeological Method and Theory,* vol. 2, ed. M.B. Schiffer, pp. 199-237. Academic Press, New York.

_____ 1984. *Quantitative Zooarchaeology.* Academic Press, Orlando, FL.

Guilday, J.E. 1970. Animal Remains from Archaeological Excavations at Fort Ligonier. *Annals of the Carnegie Museum* 42:177-186.

_____ 1971. *Biological and Archaeological Analysis of Bones from a 17th Century Indian Village (46 PU 31), Putnam County, West Virginia.* Report of the Investigations No. 4. West Virginia Geological and Economic Survey, Morgantown, WV.

Hecker, H.M. 1982. Domestication Revisited: Its Implications for Faunal Analysis. *Journal of Field Archaeology* 9:217-236.

Hesse, B. 1978. *Evidence for Husbandry from the Early Neolithic Site of Ganj Dareh in Western Iran.* Ph.D. dissertation, Columbia University. University Microfilms, Ann Arbor, MI.

_____ 1982. Slaughter Patterns and Domestication: The Beginnings of Domestication in Western Iran. *Man* 17:403-417.

_____ 1984. These Are Our Goats: The Origins of Herding in West Central Iran. In *Animals and Archaeology. 3: Early Herders and Their Flocks,* ed. C. Grigson and J. Clutton-Brock, pp. 243-264. BAR International Series No. 202, Oxford.

Hesse, B., and D. Perkins, Jr. 1974. Faunal Remains from Karatas-Semayuk in Southwest Anatolia: An Interim Report. *Journal of Field Archaeology* 1:149-160.

Higgs, E.S., and M.R. Jarman. 1969. The Origins of Agriculture: A Reconsideration. *Antiquity* 43:31-41.

Hopkins, J. 1967. Identification of the Domestication of Animals without Morphological Change. Ms. on file, Department of Anthropology, University of Chicago, Chicago.

Jarman, M.R., and P.W. Wilkinson. 1972. Criteria of Animal Domestication. In *Papers in Economic Prehistory,* ed. E.S. Higgs, pp. 83-96. Cambridge University Press, Cambridge.

Klein, R.G., and K. Cruz-Uribe. 1984. *The Analysis of Animal Bones from Archaeological Sites.* University of Chicago Press, Chicago.

Legge, R.J. 1981. The Agricultural Economy. In *Grimes Graves Norfolk Excavations 1971-72,* vol. 1, ed. R.J. Mercer, pp. 79-103. Department of the Environment Archaeological Reports No. 11. London.

Lie, R.W. 1980. Minimum Number of Individuals from Osteological Samples. *Norwegian Archaeological Review* 13:24-30.

Lyman, R.L. 1984. Bone Density and Differential Survivorship of Fossil Classes. *Journal of Anthropological Archaeology* 3:259-299.

Maltby, M. 1981. Iron Age, Romano-British, and Anglo-Saxon Animal Husbandry—A Review of the Faunal Evidence. In *The Environment of Man: The Iron Age to the Anglo-Saxon Period,* ed. M. Jones and G. Dimbleby, pp. 155-203. BAR British Series No. 87, Oxford.

_____ 1985. Patterns in Faunal Assemblage Variability. In *Beyond Domestication in Prehistoric Europe,* ed. G. Barker and C. Gamble, pp. 33-73. Academic Press, London.

Matolcsi, J. (editor). 1973. *Domestikationsforshung und Geschichte der Haustiere.* Akadémiai Kiadó, Budapest.

Meadow, R.H. 1975. Mammal Remains from Hajji Firuz: A Study in Methodology. In *Archaeozoological Studies,* ed. A.T. Clason, pp. 265-283. American Elsevier, New York.

_____ 1978. Effects of Context on the Interpretation of Faunal Remains: A Case Study. In *Approaches to Faunal Analysis in the Middle East,* ed. R.H. Meadow and M.A. Zeder, pp. 15-21. Peabody Museum Bulletin No. 2. Harvard University, Cambridge, MA.

Payne, S. 1972. Partial Recovery and Sample Bias: The Results of Some Sieving Experiments. In *Papers in Economic Prehistory,* ed. E.S. Higgs, pp. 49-64. Cambridge University Press, Cambridge.

_____ 1975. Partial Recovery and Sample Bias. In *Archaeozoological Studies,* ed. A.T. Clason, pp. 7-17. American Elsevier, New York.

Payne, S., and P.J. Munson. 1985. Ruby and How Many Squirrels? The Destruction of Bones by Dogs. In *Paleobiological Investigations: Research Design, Methods and Data Analysis,* ed. N.R.J. Fieller, D.D. Gilbertson, and N.G.A. Ralph, pp. 31-39. BAR International Series No. 266, Oxford.

Perkins, D., Jr. 1964. Prehistoric Fauna from Shanidar, Iraq. *Science* 144:1565-1566.

_____ 1973a. The Beginnings of Animal Domestication in the Near East. *American Journal of Archaeology* 77(3):279-282.

_____ 1973b. A Critique on the Methods of Quantifying Faunal Remains. In *Domestikationsforschung und Geschichte der Haustiere,* ed. J. Matolcsi, pp. 367-369. Akadémiai Kiadó, Budapest.

Perkins, D., Jr., and P. Daly. 1968. A Hunters' Village in Neolithic Turkey. *Scientific American* 219(5):96-106.

_____ 1974. The Beginning of Food Production in the Near East. In *The Old World: Early Man to the Development of Agriculture,* ed. R. Stigler, pp. 71-97. St. Martins, London.

Prummel, W. 1982. The Archaeozoological Study of Urban Medieval Sites in the Netherlands. In *Environmental Archaeology in the Urban Context,* ed. A.R. Hall and H.K. Kenward, pp. 117-122. Research Report No. 43. London.Council for British Archaeology.

Reed, C.A., and D. Perkins, Jr. 1984. Prehistoric Domestication of Animals in Southwestern Asia. In *Der Beginn der Haustierhaltung in der "Alten Welt,"* ed. G. Nobis, pp. 5-23. Bohlau Verlag, Koln and Wien.

Schiffer, M.B. 1972. Archaeological Context and Systemic Context. *American Antiquity* 37:156-165.

_____ 1976. *Behavioral Archaeology.* Academic Press, New York.

Simmons, A.H., and G. Ilany. 1975-77. What Mean These Bones? Behavioral Implications of Gazelles' Remains from Archaeological Sites. *Paleorient* 3:269-274.

Sherratt, A. 1981. Plough and Pastoralism: Aspects of the Secondary Products Revolution. In *Pattern of the Past,* ed. I. Hodder, G. Isaac, and N. Hammond, pp. 261-305. Cambridge University Press, Cambridge.

Solecki, R.L. 1981. *An Early Village Site at Zawi Chemi Shanidar.* Biblioteca Mesopotamica No. 13. Undena, Malibu.

Uerpmann, H.-P. 1979. *Probleme der Neolithisierung des Mittelmeerraums.* Reichert, Weisbaden.

Watson, J.P.N. 1975. Domestication and Bone Structure in Sheep and Goats. *Journal of Archaeological Science* 2:375-383.

White, T.E. 1953. A Method for Calculating the Dietary Percentage of Various Food Animals Utilized by Aboriginal Peoples. *American Antiquity* 18:396-398.

Zeder, M. 1978. Differentiation Between the Bones of Caprines from Different Ecosystems in Iran by the Analysis of Osteological Microstructure and Chemical Composition. In *Approaches to Faunal Analysis in the Middle East,* ed. R.H. Meadow and M. Zeder, pp. 69-84. Peabody Museum Bulletin No. 2. Harvard University, Cambridge, MA.

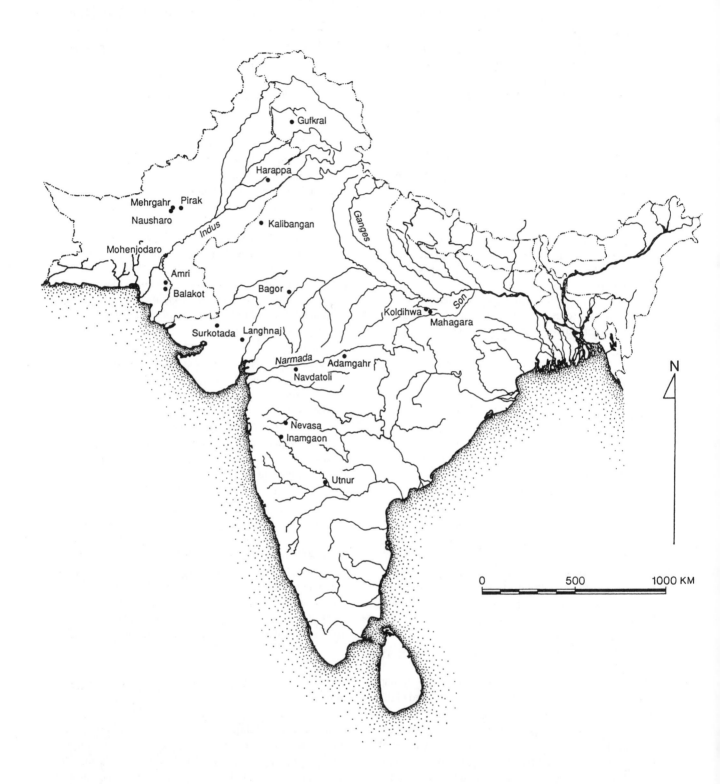

Fig. 1:
Map of Pakistan and India showing location of sites discussed in text.
Drawing by Carl P. Beetz with modifications.

THE STATUS OF RESEARCH ON ANIMAL DOMESTICATION IN INDIA AND ITS CULTURAL CONTEXT

Paul Rissman

29 Bedford Rd., Summit, NJ 07901

Introduction

The region defined by the borders of modern India contains a number of domesticable wild animal species, as well as a long record of human habitation. These factors have led some scholars to distinguish India as a hearth of domestication where, at various points in time, local taming and/or breeding of cattle, buffalo, elephant, horse, camel, sheep, goat, pig, dog, and fowl took place (see Allchin 1969 for summary). These pronouncements have, until very recently, remained pure speculation. Indeed, our data for animal domestication within India are so poor that for a more complete presentation I must refer the reader to another chapter of this volume. Richard Meadow's pathbreaking work on domestication in the Indo-Iranian borderlands (modern Pakistan) makes a good case for local domestication of zebu cattle and sheep by 6000 B.C. In contrast, India proper has not yielded any site of that antiquity for which solid evidence of herding is available. By 5000 B.C. there are hints of herding scattered through the archaeological record, but widespread indications of controlled husbandry cannot be found until the late fourth millennium B.C. This is long after most economically useful species assumed their modern forms and behaviors in neighboring regions of Asia.

There are several reasons for this dearth of knowledge. The most obvious is that until recently there simply was not much interest in the study of faunal remains from Indian caves and mounds. In pre-partition days Sewell and Guha (1931) and Prashad (1936) wrote reports of the fauna recovered from the third millennium cities of Mohenjodaro and Harappa; reports of subsequent excavations of fourth and third millennium sites offered only brief summaries of species recovered, and occasionally included bone counts (Fairservis 1956; Clutton-Brock 1961, 1965; Khan 1965; Mackay 1943; Nath 1963; Poulain-Josien 1964). The flurry of interest in animal domestication and early husbandry fostered by the Economic Prehistorians and New Archaeologists of the 1960s nearly passed India

by. Certain scholars showed great interest in Indian fauna at that time, including Juliet Clutton-Brock, Caroline Grigson, and the Allchins; Sir Mortimer Wheeler on the other hand devoted only a paragraph to the subject in his classic guide to the Indus Civilization (1968).

Faunal research was conducted in a casual way. Comparative collections were compiled only rarely, specialists were drawn from the ranks of zoologists and veterinarians with no formal archaeological training, and standards of recording and publication were low. Thus, much of what has been said about animal domestication in India either cannot be substantiated or is unreliable.

This state of affairs began to change in the early 1970s at the instigation of H.D. Sankalia and V.N. Misra of Deccan College, Pune. Through their efforts A.T. Clason in 1972 established the most complete zooarchaeology laboratory in India. Her former student, P.K. Thomas, continues to train zooarchaeologists with his colleague, paleontologist G.L. Badam. It is necessary to examine these academic genealogies because the quality of data on Indian domestication varies enormously with the identity of the analyst. This article summarizes the reliable research regarding domestication in India, and raises questions about its cultural context and consequences that ought to be addressed in the future.

A critical review of the evidence for early domestication

To set the baseline for this summary, Meadow's results from the site of Mehrgarh, Pakistan, must be briefly mentioned. Mehrgarh is an overlapping series of mounds spread out along the Bolan River as it flows through the Kachi Plain (Fig. 1). This is a transitional zone between Baluchistan, which is geologically a part of the Iranian Plateau, and the Indo-Gangetic alluvium. The occupations commence with an Aceramic Neolithic village and end at approximately 2500 B.C. (Jarrige 1984; Jarrige and Lechevallier 1979; Jarrige and Meadow 1980). Dating of the Mehrgarh sequence is problematic, but the Aceramic levels apparently begin before 6000 B.C. and last into the mid- to-late sixth millennium. Meadow demonstrated an increase in the frequency of cattle, sheep, and goats throughout the Aceramic Neolithic. Totalling less than 50% of bone fragments at the start of this period, potential domesticates predominated over wild species at its close. In addition, marked diminution in the size of individual zebu cattle and sheep indicates the possibility of on-going local domestication within the Neolithic.

There is nothing from India to compare in age or quality with the carefully documented Mehrgarh assemblage. No reliable sequence of faunal collections exists that exhibits a transition from hunting to herding, whether through morphological change, alteration of slaughter patterns, or the appearance of animals far from their natural ranges. The possible candidates for early animal domestication in India are reviewed below.

The Gangetic plain and the Son and Belan river valleys of Central India constitute one area from which claims of early domestication have been made (e.g. Sharma 1985). The types of sites range from rock shelters in the Vindhyan hillsides to settlements on alluvial ridges and lakeshore occupations on the flood plain. An integrated program of regional survey and excavation, conducted by Allahabad University and the University of California at Berkeley, has exposed a cultural sequence that stretches from the Lower Paleolithic to the second millennium B.C. Interest is directed to the Upper Paleolithic, Mesolithic, and Neolithic occupations, from which the evidence for domestication is cited.[1] Upper Paleolithic faunal remains were recovered from the site of Mahagara in the Belan Valley (Sharma et al. 1980). Beneath a Neolithic period mound, a layer of cemented river gravels (III) contained evidence of a blade and burin industry that has been radiocarbon dated to *ca.* 24,000 to 17,000 B.C. (Possehl and Rissman in press). Stratified above this was another layer of cemented gravels (IV), dated 12,000 to 8000 B.C., from which a transitional microlithic assemblage was recovered. Accompanying both of these stone industries were faunal remains identified as sheep and goat (Alur 1980). These species were hundreds of miles from their natural ranges in the foothills and peaks of Baluchistan and the Himalayas (Possehl and Rissman in press). If removal of a species from its natural habitat is accepted as evidence for domestication (Bökönyi 1969), then sheep and goats were arguably domesticated by the Upper Paleolithic in India.

At this point the certainty of identification and the standards of publication become factors in accepting these results. For example, central India is included in the natural ranges of blackbuck (*Antilope cervicapra*) and several species of deer. An examination of late Pleistocene and early Holocene fauna from the neighboring Son Valley by Blumenschine and Chattopadhya (Clark and Williams

1986:36) identified these wild species, but not sheep or goat. In the absence of a good comparative collection, it would be difficult to separate post-cranial remains of blackbuck and even small deer from those of sheep and goat. In addition, standard measurements and detailed illustrations that would allow substantiation of this very important claim were not included in Alur's preliminary report. Thus, it seems prudent to discount the report of domestic sheep and goats in the Upper Paleolithic until corroborating evidence is forthcoming.

The Neolithic horizon which follows the microlithic facies in Central India is characterized by cord-marked pottery, rice agriculture, and the utilization of domestic cattle, sheep, and goats (Sharma et al. 1980). Evidence for stockraising includes a cattle pen at Mahagara, comprising a perimeter marked by post-holes and hoof impressions within (Sharma et al. 1980:146). The early date claimed for this horizon is derived from three radiocarbon determinations from the site of Koldihwa. These range from the eighth to the sixth millennia B.C. (Possehl and Rissman in press), which would make the Central Indian Neolithic the earliest known example of an economy based on rice agriculture, as well as a hearth of animal domestication.[2]

A final assertion for early animal domestication involves the rock shelters at Adamgarh, also located in Central India in the valley of the Narmada River (Joshi 1978:83). Excavation of several shelters revealed a stratigraphic sequence characterized, from the top down, by a mixed layer of microliths, pottery, glass, and iron fragments; then a series of layers containing microliths and potsherds; next, levels with microliths but no pottery; and finally, Middle and Lower Paleolithic deposits. Bones of domestic cattle, buffaloes, goats, sheep, and pigs were associated with an uncalibrated radiocarbon date in the mid-sixth millennium (TF-120; see Nath 1967 for faunal report). As at Koldihwa, this date is questionable. The sample was shell taken from a trench that contained a mixed microlithic and ceramic deposit (Joshi 1978:44). The only other radiocarbon determination from the site, from uncharred bone in a Middle Paleolithic level, is dated to the first millennium B.C. Although it is plausible that this suite of domesticates was utilized in Central India by 5000 B.C., Adamgarh should not be taken as the proof.

If the Adamgarh date is to be allowed any credence, it is due to the parallel findings from Bagor in Rajasthan (Misra 1973) where the only solid evidence for early domestication within India is found. The site is situated upon a sand dune above the Kothari River, east of the Aravalli Range. The lowermost phase at Bagor, comprising an assemblage of microliths as well as a rich faunal collection, has been dated to the fifth and fourth millennia by four stratigraphically consistent, calibrated radiocarbon samples (Possehl and Rissman in press). The fauna have been analyzed by P.K. Thomas (1977) whose research constitutes one of the most complete zooarchaeological investigations to date involving an Indian site.

Fauna from Bagor included cattle, sheep, goat, blackbuck/gazelle, pig, deer, hare, fox, and mongoose—of which sheep/goat comprised 65% of total fragments (Thomas 1975:325). Sheep seem to have outnumbered goats, judging from measurements on distal metapodia (Thomas 1977:172). The ovicaprines of Bagor are alleged to have been under human control on the basis of their age profile. Dental and epiphyseal evidence indicated that 75% of the sheep/goat were slaughtered between the ages of two and three. Pig remains were inferred to have come from both wild and herded groups. It could not be determined if the cattle remains were of domesticated stock.

Bagor may represent the early penetration of pastoralism into the Indian peninsula, but notwithstanding the tenuous support from Adamgarh, there is little else known until village habitations spring up from Kashmir to Cape Comorin at the end of the fourth millennium. By this time domesticated cattle, sheep, goats, and pigs appear to be well-integrated with assorted cultivars into local mixed economies.

Future directions for research

Given our limited data base for Indian domestication, little can be said about the cultural context in which the process evolved. A bit of speculation is not totally inappropriate, however; much of the modern Indian farm economy centers upon cattle, buffaloes, sheep, goats, and pigs, a suite of domesticates that (buffaloes excepted) goes back at least seven or eight thousand years in South Asia. Clearly, animal domestication was a profoundly successful adaptation. It would be useful to know how widespread was the practice of taming local wild animals and exerting control over breeding. More important, perhaps, are the cultural conditions under which the adoption of the pastoral economy, indigenous or introduced, actually took place. In this regard India is a fascinating case because of its longstanding socio-economic diversity. In the ethnographic present, the caste system, the traditional foundation of Indian society, can in part be characterized as a proliferation of social units that are operationalized through their transactions. This rule applies to agriculturalists as well as herders and forest foragers, whose positions are defined by the goods and services they provide to others. Hence hunter-gathers were never mowed down by encroaching village cultivation; they were much too useful. Foragers in South Asia are economic specialists who provide honey, wild fruits, fibers, and meat to those with less access to the forests (see, for example, Fox 1969).

This jumble of specialists seems to have a long history. In the archaeological record, there is no layer-cake succession of hunting and gathering, village agro-pastoralism, and civilization on the subcontinent; simpler forms of

subsistence economy were never overwhelmed by the more complex, merely encapsulated and made specialized. Prehistoric India can instead be characterized as an interactive mosaic of technological and economic traditions—Mesolithic, Neolithic, Chalcolithic, and Urban—that in other parts of the world have missed each other by thousands of years. Such interdependence may have fostered stability that we do not normally expect to find in situations of culture contact and technology transfer; it may even be useful to postulate an active resistance to the adoption of agriculture in this context. Thus, rather than an artifact of the research effort, the late spread of animal domestication in India may be actual, the result of its peculiar prehistoric economy.

This point can be taken further by analyzing the archaeology of domestication as a function of settlement patterns and their associated ecofacts. I will heuristically divide settlement into the rough categories of permanent or semi-permanent farming villages, campsites (either of foragers or pastoralists), and towns. The potential contributions of the farming villages will be examined first.

As mentioned previously, Meadow's work at Mehrgarh has made an interesting case for local domestication of zebu cattle (*Bos indicus*) and sheep (*Ovis* sp.) in the Indo-Iranian borderlands, based on increasing frequency in the assemblage and reduction in individual size. The identification of zebu, as opposed to taurine cattle, was based on skull fragments and the occasional find of a bifid thoracic vertebra (Meadow 1984c:324). The early date of the sequence (Meadow suggests the eighth millennium) supports Zeuner's hypothesis, developed more fully by Grigson, of the autochthonous domestication of wild *Bos namadicus* (Grigson 1985). Meadow could not specify that the Mehrgarh sheep were ancestral to *Ovis aries*, citing evidence that the local wild urial (*Ovis vignei*) cannot have given rise to the modern domesticate (1984c:324). He did propose, however, that local breeds may have been domesticated at Mehrgarh, to be replaced by *Ovis aries* later in the history of the region.

The setting for this ongoing process of domestication was that of a village-based agricultural society. The earliest levels of Mehrgarh were characterized by mud-brick architecture and the presence of morphologically domestic barley and wheat (Costantini 1984). The developed character of the cultivars, in comparison with the rudimentary morphological changes in the fauna, prompted Meadow to comment that "just as in the western part of the Middle East, cereal cultivation on the eastern margins seems to have preceded the keeping of domestic ruminants by many hundreds of years" (1984c:324).

Though much later in time, sites within the borders of India also shed some light on village-based domestication. In Kashmir, for example, the beginning of the third millennium witnessed the formation of food-producing settlements consisting of pit-houses dug into loess. One such settlement, Gufkral (Sharma 1982), commences with an Aceramic occupation within which domestic wheat, barley, and lentil have been identified. Sheep and goats are claimed to be both wild and domestic, while cattle have been identified as entirely wild. In the next period, dating to the late third millennium (Possehl and Rissman in press), domestic cattle are introduced while goats exhibit a reduction in size. Although measurements and detailed illustrations have not been published, here again is an instance of ongoing domestication in a village context in the far north of the subcontinent. Neolithic Kashmir has also been cited as a possible "laboratory" for canine domestication (Gollan 1985).

In contrast to this pattern, several places associated with early domestication are presumed to have been the campsites of specialized pastoralists. These assumptions are not very certain, in light of the difficulty of identifying pastoralists in the archaeological record, but can be included in the speculations of this section. Nomadic occupation in India is often attributed to rock shelters and sand dunes devoid of permanent structures, the settings for Adamgarh and Bagor respectively. No permanent architecture was found at Adamgarh, while shelters at Bagor were floored with stone slabs and possessed perishable superstructures. If the Adamgarh date (mid-sixth millennium) is believable, and if one accepts the argument for nomadic occupation at these two sites, it follows that stockraising in India preceded the first village settlements by more than a thousand years.

This statement is contrary to the assertion that nomads must interact with settled agriculturalists to remain economically viable (Spooner 1971:198-210). Nevertheless, this nomadic movement has been credited with fostering culture change throughout the length of the subcontinent. Deep within South India, at the onset of the third millennium, the regions of Karnataka, eastern Andhra Pradesh, and northern Tamil Nadu were characterized by a horizon termed the Southern Neolithic. Material culture consisted of ground stone axes, a rather plain blade industry, other ground stone utensils, and rudimentary ceramics. Settlements were of two types: hillside villages of stone-floored houses existed simultaneously with, and were preceded by, sites termed "ashmounds," artificial hills of burnt cow dung. The most thoroughly excavated ashmound, Utnur, has revealed a double stockade of palm trunks. The inner stockade was filled with hoof prints while human habitational debris filled the outer stockade. The natural conclusion of the excavator was that the ashmounds were prehistoric cattle pens (Allchin 1963).

Cattle bones at Utnur were of varying size, leading the excavator and faunal analyst to propose that both wild and domestic forms were represented. By analogy with the method used to capture and tame elephants in South India,

it has been suggested that these sites were actually places where wild cattle were tamed and domesticated with the help of their more docile cousins (Allchin and Allchin 1974). Again, measurements have not been presented to substantiate these claims, an unfortunate omission in light of the sexual dimorphism inherent in cattle (Higham 1969). Since ashmounds seem to have been established earlier than village communities, the Southern Neolithic is consistent with the evidence of Bagor, implying that specialized pastoralists were domesticating herd animals in some parts of India before settled agriculture was ever practiced. If we propose that pastoralists obtained plant resources through interaction with foragers rather than cultivators, the above implication loses its objectionable qualities. I will return to this idea later.

Urbanism appeared in India and Pakistan in the form of the Harappan Civilization by the mid-third millennium B.C. Harappan economy presumably depended upon intensified agriculture and inter-regional exchange, prompting a shift in demand for domesticated animals. For example, modern Indian buffaloes give more milk of higher quality than their bovine relatives, a quality that would enhance their value to an economy growing rapidly in scale. Camels and horses would have been very useful to carry the increasing volume of trade. Unfortunately, we again lack the data base that would convincingly verify such proposed effects of urbanism upon the spread of domestication.

It is questionable whether buffaloes were domesticated during Harappan times despite their appearance as models on engraved stamp seals. Certain seals show buffaloes attacking humans, hardly the subject of a pastoral scene. In any case it is very difficult to distinguish the remains of wild and domestic species other than by size, and, as is common in Indian faunal reports, measurements are scarce. Domestic buffalo has not been claimed for Southeast Asia before 1600 B.C. (Higham and Kijngam 1985), and measurements on buffalo from the western Indian site of Inamgaon, dating to the late second millennium, are consistent with wild dimensions (Badam 1985:414). For now the assumption that buffaloes were hunted rather than herded in Harappan times seems reasonable.

It is more certain that domestic camels were used in the Harappan period. This animal has received attention in theoretical discussion because of Shaffer's suggestion that the expansion of Harappan material culture, over an area larger than that of contemporary Egypt or Akkad, was largely facilitated by a newly-introduced caravan trade (Shaffer 1987). According to Shaffer, camels were imported from Central Asia, explaining the existence of the Harappan outpost of Shortugai in northern Afghanistan (Francfort and Pottier 1978). Camel remains are reported from Mohenjodaro, Harappa, and the Indian site of Kalibangan, and Meadow suggests that they derive from Bactrian stock (see Meadow 1984b for summary). The absence of camel depictions on seals led some investigators to conclude that camels were unknown to the Harappans, but these scattered finds suggest that another explanation must be sought.

Finally, it has been asserted that the domestic horse was a Harappan import into India, but further scrutiny has never borne out this hypothesis. Horses are reported from the Harappan site of Surkotada (Sharma 1974), as well as from Mohenjodaro (Sewell and Guha 1931) and Harappa itself (Nath 1962). Third millennium horse remains also have been identified at the Central Indian site of Kayatha (Alur 1975) and at the South Indian site of Kodekal (Shah 1973); however, Clason re-examined these remains and did not corroborate the presence of horse bones (Clason 1977). Similarly, Meadow has emphasized the difficulty of distinguishing *Equus caballus* from *E. asinus* and *E. hemionus*, and underscored the importance of proper illustrations and measurements which are lacking in the above faunal reports (Meadow 1986). Until more reliable evidence is presented, the earliest remains of horse in South Asia should be those identified from the second millennium sites of Pirak in Pakistan (Meadow 1986) and Navdatoli, Nevasa, and Inamgaon in Western India (Clason 1977).

While Harappan Civilization did not have a great impact in terms of new domesticates, its economic impact on surrounding populations may have been profound. All along the borders of the Harappan culture area lived groups of foragers and pastoralists engaged in various degrees of economic and social symbiosis with the urban milieu. For example, the third millennium levels at Bagor yielded a find of arrowheads typologically similar to those manufactured in the Indus Valley (Misra 1970), while in Gujarat, a campsite of foragers called Langhnaj was found to contain third millennium beads and a copper knife that were Harappan in style (Sankallia 1964). In addition there are suggestions of gene flow between urban and forest populations (Possehl and Kennedy 1979; Kennedy et al. 1984). Harappan towns such as Balakot, Amri, Naushuro, and Harappa exhibit higher frequencies of wild fauna than do the agricultural villages that precede them (Richard Meadow, pers. comm.).

Vast areas of Western and Central India lack any firm traces of permanent settlement until the late third/early second millennium B.C. It is assumed that pastoralists and foragers occupied these areas until the abrupt and widespread appearance of village farming communities. In certain of these border zones, such as southeastern Rajasthan (the Banas Culture) and western Madhya Pradesh (the Kayatha Culture), farming commenced contemporaneously with Harappan Civilization (see Possehl and Rissman in press). Other regions, the Ganga-Jamuna Doab and

Maharashtra among them, seem to lack village settlement until the latest phases of Harappan urbanism, or even after the Harappan cities lost population and their inter-regional focus about 2000 B.C. Chakrabarti (1987) has suggested that the rise of village life was related to processes of culture contact between Harappan townspeople and the foragers and pastoralists to their east and south, but has left the precise mechanism unstated.

Here, I propose a model for the spread of domestication in Western India during the late third/early second millennia B.C., one that is grounded in the context of specialized, interacting groups of foragers, pastoralists, and later, city folk. The initial conditions of this model are derived from the scant evidence of the fifth millennium B.C. in eastern Rajasthan, when the herders of Bagor are found within an agricultural vacuum. This circumstance is echoed in South India in the early third millennium as well. Bagor and the ashmounds were probably not the sole sites of their periods, however. Dozens of microlithic settlements are known from Rajasthan and South India, and many have been excavated (Misra 1985; Allchin 1985). Bone preservation is often poor, but it is not unreasonable to suggest that some sites represent the camps of foragers, exemplified by the entirely wild faunal assemblage from the third millennium settlement of Langhnaj (Clutton-Brock 1965). Dating the microlithic settlements is another problem; while absolute dates are rare and unreliable, it has long been assumed that microlithic sites span nearly the entire Holocene. Given our bias against pastoralist self-sufficiency, and the ethnographic evidence of hunter-gatherers as interactive specialists, it would not be extraordinary to postulate a regional subsistence system linking herders and foragers in symbiotic bonds of exchange. And with a successful, functioning economy of this sort, it is not clear what the incentives to sedentarize would be.

A system which depends upon transactions in the products of forest and meadow grows less viable as it becomes more homogeneous. A system of this type selects for specialization, and may help to explain the resistance to the spread of farming that our spotty archaeological record implies. Foragers continued to exploit their niche even as pastoralists expanded their ranges and improved their breeds from the fifth to the third millennia.

It seems that not even the encroachment of civilization, in the mid-third millennium, prompted sedentism by pastoral and hunter/gatherer populations. Evidence was cited above, for example, that Harappan towns actually display heightened frequencies of wild fauna, perhaps through interaction with populations such as that of Langhnaj. As for pastoralists, both Possehl (1979) and Shaffer (n.d.) have evoked their presence in discussing inter-regional exchange. It is also instructive to refer to Fairservis' (1967) calculations of cultivated acreage, cattle population, and fodder requirements in the ancient Indus Valley. Fairservis postulated a severe shortfall in fodder production, which necessitated such abusive grazing in surrounding forests and grasslands that serious environmental degradation followed. There is an alternative to purely local management of burdensome herds, however, which involves contracting out animals to migrating pastoralists (e.g. Horowitz 1975:397-400). Thus there is reason to suppose that both pastoralists and foragers had roles to play in Harappan Civilization, and that they were able to maintain and strengthen their economic specializations by re-orienting them towards a much greater source of demand for their products and services.

Pastoral and foraging groups may have become ever more specialized in response to urban demand throughout the late third millennium. At this point, however, demand began to slacken as Harappan towns lost population, certain sites were abandoned altogether, and the inter-regional character of resource utilization started to fade. By the early second millennium the Harappan Civilization had degenerated into a collection of regionally circumscribed village cultures, within which town life was much less pronounced than before. One can forecast what might have happened to encapsulated specialists in the face of this recession. They crossed the threshold from specialized to over-specialized. With a continuously shrinking demand for their products, it is fair to suspect that they were confronted with the loss of their economic viability. It was time for the specialists to become generalists.

Conclusions

Indian village subsistence systems are a mixed strategy that has proven its resilience over time. The combination of dry and irrigated farming, cattle and small stock pastoralism, and the keeping of swine in a small-scale, relatively self-sufficient settlement possesses favorable risk-reducing characteristics (Rissman 1985, 1986) that a more specialized subsistence system lacks. Generalized settlements precipitated out of a specialized matrix all across India in the late third and early second millennia. I have related this shift to overproduction by pastoralists and foragers oriented to Harappan demand, who found their viability threatened as the level of demand decreased toward 2000 B.C. Obviously, at the moment this "just-so story" requires extensive testing ultimately to decide its validity. It does help to account for the peculiarities of the archaeological record as it is now known.

India may yet attain the status of a hearth of domestication, as the region to its immediate west has so recently. Further field work may very well reveal early and widespread processes of intensified animal husbandry. Whatever the outcome of future research it is important to believe, as did Dexter Perkins and Patricia Daly, that the study of animal domestication is meaningless when removed from its cultural context. In India, cultural context makes the study of animal domestication very meaningful indeed.

Notes

1. Mesolithic and Neolithic are terms that adopt unusual glosses for India. The microlithic technology which defines the Mesolithic elsewhere has, in India, extremely diffuse chronological and economic associations. There is good evidence, for example, that microlithic technology continued to be used into historic times. In the sense used here, the Mesolithic simply refers to all occupations dating to the early Holocene. Neolithic occupations are those that exhibit indications of village-based food production but have little association with metal. In India the term has referred to sites that date from the fourth to the second millennium B.C.

2. Unfortunately, the Koldihwa dates are stratigraphically inconsistent; the earliest comes from an Iron Age pit (Agrawal et al. 1977:231). Dates of typologically similar sites range from 3500 to 1300 B.C. when calibrated (Possehl and Rissman in press).

References

Agrawal, D.P., R.V. Krishnamurthy, S. Kusumgar, and R.K. Pant. 1977. Physical Research Laboratory Radiocarbon Date List II. *Radiocarbon* 19:229-236.

Allchin, B. 1972. Hunters or Pastoral Nomads? Late Stone Age Settlements in Western and Central India. In *Man, Settlement, and Urbanism*, ed. P.J. Ucko, R. Tringham, and G.W. Dimbleby, pp. 115-120. Duckworth, London.

_____ 1977. Hunters, Pastoralists, and Early Agriculturalists in South Asia. In *Hunters, Gatherers, and First Farmers Beyond Europe*, ed. J.V.S. Megaw, pp. 127-144. Leicester University Press, Leicester.

_____ 1985. Some Observations on the Stone Industries of the Early Holocene in Pakistan and Western India. In *Recent Advances in Indo-Pacific Prehistory*, ed. V.N. Misra and P. Bellwood, pp. 129-136. E.J. Brill, Leiden.

Allchin, F.R. 1963. Cattle and Economy in Neolithic South India. In *Man and Cattle*, ed. A.E. Mourant and F.E. Zeuner. RAI Occasional Papers No. 18.

_____ 1969. Early Domesticated Animals in India and Pakistan. In *The Domestication and Exploitation of Plants and Animals*, ed. P.J. Ucko and G.W. Dimbleby, pp. 318-321. Duckworth, London.

Allchin, F.R., and B. Allchin. 1974. Some New Thoughts on Indian Cattle. In *South Asian Archaeology 1973*, ed. J.E. Van Lohuizen-De Leeuw and J.M.M. Ubaghs, pp. 71-77. E.J. Brill, Leiden.

Alur, K.R. 1975. Report on the Animal Remains from

Kayatha. In *Excavations at Kayatha*, ed. Z.D. Ansari and M.K. Dhavalikar, pp. 157-163. Deccan College Postgraduate and Research Institute, Pune.

_____ 1980. Faunal Remains from the Vindhyas and the Ganga Valley. In *Beginnings of Agriculture*, ed. G.R. Sharma, V.D. Misra, D. Mandal, B.B. Misra, and J.N. Pal, pp. 201-227. Abinash Prakashan, Allahabad.

Badam, G.L. 1984. Holocene Faunal Material from India with Special Reference to Domesticated Animals. In *Animals and Archaeology. 3: Early Herders and Their Flocks*, ed. J. Clutton-Brock and C. Grigson, pp. 339-354. BAR International Series No. 202, Oxford.

_____ 1985. The Late Quaternary Fauna of Inamgaon. In *Recent Advances in Indo-Pacific Prehistory*, ed. V.N. Misra and P. Bellwood, pp. 413-416. E.J. Brill, Leiden.

Bökönyi, S. 1969. Archaeological Problems and Methods of Recognizing Animal Domestication. In *The Domestication and Exploitation of Plants and Animals*, ed. P.J. Ucko and G.W. Dimbleby, pp. 219-229. Duckworth, London.

Chakrabarti, D.K. 1987. De-urbanization in the Northern Plains: Some Aspects of the Indian Archaeological Data of the Second Millennium B.C. Abstract of paper presented at the symposium Urban Form and Meaning in South Asia. National Gallery of Art, Center for Advanced Study in the Visual Arts, December 3-5.

Clark, J.D., and M.J. Williams. 1986. Paleoenvironments and Prehistory in North Central India: A Preliminary Report. In *Studies in the Archaeology of India and Pakistan*, ed. J. Jacobson, pp. 19-42. Oxford and IBH, New Delhi.

Clason, A. 1977. Wild and Domestic Animals in Prehistoric and Early Historic India. *Eastern Anthropologist* 30(3):241-289.

Clutton-Brock, J. 1961. The Mongoose Skeleton Found at the Microlithic Site, Langhnaj, Gujarat. In *Technical Reports on Archaeological Remains*, ed. J. Clutton-Brock, Vishnu-Mittre, and A.N. Gulati, pp. 1-10. Deccan College, Pune.

_____ 1965. *Excavations at Langhnaj 1944-63. Part 2: The Fauna*. Deccan College Postgraduate and Research Institute, Pune.

Costantini, L. 1984. The Beginning of Agriculture in the Kachi Plain: The Evidence of Mehrgarh. In *South Asian Archaeology 1981*, ed. B. Allchin, pp. 29-33. Cambridge University Press, Cambridge.

Fairservis, W.A., Jr. 1956. Excavations in the Quetta Valley, West Pakistan. *Anthropological Papers of the American Museum of Natural History* 45(2):169-402.

_____ 1967. The Origin, Character, and Decline of an Early Civilization. *Novitates* 2302.

Fox, R. 1969. Professional Primitives. *Man in India* 43:139-152.

Francfort, H.-P., and M.H. Pottier. 1978. Sondage préliminaire sur l'établissement protohistorique harappéen et post-harappéen de Shortugai (Afghanistan du N.E.). *Arts Asiatiques* 34:29-69.

Gollan, K. 1985. Prehistoric Dogs in Australia: An Indian Origin? In *Recent Advances in Indo-Pacific Prehistory*, ed. V.N. Misra and P. Bellwood, pp. 439-446. E.J. Brill, Leiden.

Grigson, C. 1985. *Bos indicus* and *Bos namadicus* and the Problem of Autochthonous Domestication in India. In *Recent Advances in Indo-Pacific Prehistory*, ed. V.N. Misra and P. Bellwood, pp. 425-428. E.J. Brill, Leiden.

Higham, C.F.W. 1969. The Metrical Attributes of Two Samples of Modern Bovine Bones. *Journal of Zoology* (London) 157:63-74.

Higham, C.F.W., and A. Kijngam. 1985. New Evidence for Agriculture and Stockraising in Monsoonal Southeast Asia. In *Recent Advances in Indo-Pacific Prehistory*, ed. V.N. Misra and P. Bellwood, pp. 419-424. E.J. Brill, Leiden.

Horowitz, M.M. 1975. Herdsman and Husbandman in Niger: Values and Strategies. In *Pastoralism in Tropical Africa*, ed. T. Monod, pp. 387-405. Oxford Press, Ibadan.

Jarrige, J-F. 1984. Chronology of the Earlier Periods of the Greater Indus as seen from Mehrgarh, Pakistan. In *South Asian Archaeology 1981*, ed. B. Allchin, pp. 21-28. Cambridge University Press, Cambridge.

Jarrige, J-F., and M. Lechevallier. 1979. Excavations at Mehrgarh, Baluchistan: Their Significance in the Prehistorical Context of the Indo-Pakistan Borderlands. In *South Asian Archaeology 1977*, ed. M. Taddei, pp. 463-536. Instituto Universitario Orientale, Seminario di Studi Asiatici, Series Minor VI, Naples.

Jarrige, J-F., and R.H. Meadow. 1980. The Antecedents of Civilization in the Indus Valley. *Scientific American* 243(2):122-133.

Joshi, R.V. 1978. *Stone Age Cultures of Central India*. Deccan College Postgraduate Research Institute, Pune.

Kennedy, K.A.R., J. Chimet, T. Disotell, and D. Meyers. 1984. Principal-components Analysis of Prehistoric South Asian Crania. *American Journal of Physical Anthropology* 64(2):105-118.

Khan, F.A. 1965. Excavations at Kot Diji. *Pakistan Archaeology* 2:13-85.

Mackay, E.J.H. 1943. *Chanhu-daro Excavations 1935-36*. American Oriental Series. Museum of Fine Arts, Boston.

Meadow, R.H. 1981. Early Animal Domestication in South Asia: A First Report of the Faunal Remains from Mehrgarh, Pakistan. In *South Asian Archaeology 1979*, ed. H. Hartel, pp. 143-179. Dietrich Reimer Verlag, Berlin.

_____ 1984a. Notes on the Faunal Remains from Mehrgarh, with a Focus on Cattle (*Bos*). In *South Asian Archaeology 1981*, ed. B. Allchin, pp. 34-40. Cambridge University Press, Cambridge.

_____ 1984b. A Camel Skeleton from Mohenjodaro. In *Frontiers of the Indus Civilization*, ed. B.B. Lal and S.P. Gupta, pp. 133-139. Books and Books, Delhi.

_____ 1984c. Animal Domestication in the Middle East: A View from the Eastern Margin. In *Animals and Archaeology. 3: Early Herders and Their Flocks*, ed. J. Clutton-Brock and C. Grigson, pp. 309-337. BAR International Series No. 202, Oxford.

_____ 1986. Faunal Exploitation in the Greater Indus Valley: A Review of Recent Work to 1980. In *Studies in the Archaeology of India and Pakistan*, ed. J. Jacobson, pp. 43-64. Oxford and IBH, New Dehli.

Misra, V.N. 1970. Cultural Significance of Three Copper Arrowheads from Rajasthan, India. *Journal of Near Eastern Studies* 29:221-232.

_____ 1973. Bagor: A Late Mesolithic Settlement in NW India. *World Archaeology* 5(1):92-110.

_____ 1985. Microlithic Industries in India. In *Recent Advances in Indo-Pacific Prehistory*, ed. V.N. Misra and P. Bellwood, pp. 111-122. E.J. Brill, Leiden.

Nath, B. 1962. Remains of Horse and Indian Elephant from Prehistoric Site of Harappa. *Proceedings, First All-India Congress of Zoology*, Part 2:1-14.

_____ 1963. Animal Remains from Rangpur. *Ancient India* 18-19:153-160.

_____ 1967. Animal Remains from Adamgarh Rockshelter. *Indian Museum Bulletin* 2(1):28-37.

Possehl, G.L. 1979. Pastoral Nomadism in the Indus Civilization: An Hypothesis. In *South Asian Archaeology 1977*, ed. M. Taddei, pp. 537-551. Instituto Universitario Orientale, Seminario di Studi Asiatici, Series Minor VI, Naples.

Possehl, G.L., and K.A.R. Kennedy. 1979. Hunter-gatherer/Agriculturalist Exchange in Prehistory: An Indian Example. *Current Anthropology* 20:592-593.

Possehl, G.L., and P.C. Rissman. In press. The Chronology of Prehistoric India. In *Chronologies in Old World Archaeology*, 2nd ed., ed. R.W. Ehrich. University of Chicago Press, Chicago.

Poulain-Josien, T. 1964. Étude de la faune. In *Fouilles D'Amri*, ed. J-M Casal, pp. 164-169. Fayard, Paris.

Prashad, B. 1936. Animal Remains from Harappa. *Memoirs of the Archaeological Survey of India* 51.

Rissman, P.C. 1985. The Oriyo Test Excavation and the End of the Harappan Tradition in Gujarat. In *South Asian Archaeology 1983*, ed. J. Schotsmans and M. Taddei, pp. 345-356. Instituto Universitario Orientale, Dipartimento di Studi Asiatici, Series Minor XXIII, Naples.

_____ 1986. Seasonal Aspects of Man/Cattle Interaction in Bronze Age Western India. *Journal of Ethnobiology* 6(2):257-277.

Sankallia, H.D. 1964. *Excavations at Langhnaj. Vol. 1: Archaeology*. Deccan College, Pune.

Sewell, R.B., and B.S. Guha. 1931. Zoological Remains. In *Mohenjo-daro and the Indus Civilization*, ed. Sir John Marshall, pp. 649-672. A. Probsthain, London.

Shaffer, J.G. 1987. One Hump or Two: The Impact of the Camel on Harappan Society. In *Orientalia Josephi Tucci Memoriae Dicata*, ed. E. Curaverunt, G. Gnoli, and L. Lanciotti, pp. 1315-1328. Instituto Italiano per il Medo ed Estremo Oriente, Serie Orientale Roma 56(2), Vol. 3, Rome.

Shah, D. 1973. Animal Remains from Kodekal Excavation. In *Investigations on the Neolithic Culture of the Shorapur Doab, South India*, ed. K. Paddayya. E.J. Brill, Leiden.

Sharma, A.K. 1974. Evidence of Horse from the Harappan Settlement at Surkotada. *Puratattva* 7:75-76.

_____ 1982. Excavations at Gufkral—1981. *Puratattva* 11:19-25.

Sharma, G.R. 1985. From Hunting and Food Gathering to Domestication of Plants and Animals in the Belan and Ganga Valleys. In *Recent Advances in Indo-Pacific Prehistory*, ed. V.N. Misra and P. Bellwood, pp. 369-372. E.J. Brill, Leiden.

Sharma, G.R., V.D. Misra, D. Mandal, B.B. Misra, and J.N. Pal. 1980. *Beginnings of Agriculture*. Abinash Prakashan, Allahabad.

Spooner, B. 1971. Towards a Generative Model of Nomadism. *Anthropological Quarterly* 44:198-210.

Thomas, P.K. 1975. Role of Animals in the Food Economy of the Mesolithic Culture of Western and Central India. In *Archaeozoological Studies*, ed. A.T. Clason, pp. 322-328. North-Holland, Amsterdam.

_____ 1977. *Archaeozoological Aspects of the Prehistoric Cultures of Western India*. Ph.D. dissertation, Deccan College Postgraduate and Research Institute, Pune.

Wheeler, R.E.M. 1968. *The Indus Civilization*, 3rd ed. Supplement to the Cambridge History of India. Cambridge University Press, Cambridge.

Stamp seal, Harappan bull. From the site of Mohenjodaro, ca. 2300 B.C.
(Photograph: Courtesy of James Blair, National Geographic Society.)

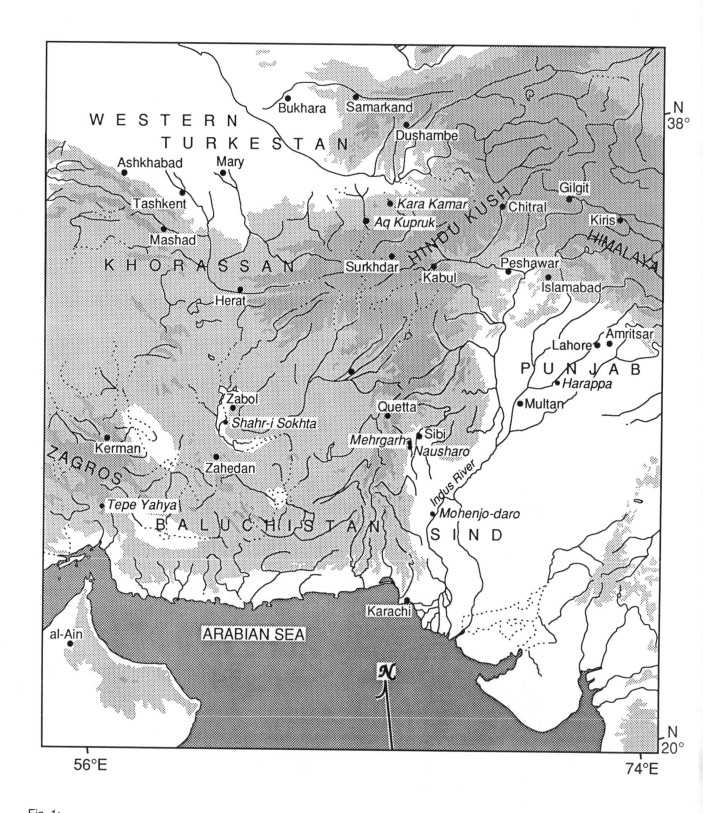

Fig. 1:
The eastern Middle East centered on the areas of modern Pakistan and Afghanistan. Contours at 500 and 2000 m. Names of archaeological sites in italics.

PREHISTORIC WILD SHEEP AND SHEEP DOMESTICATION

ON THE EASTERN MARGIN OF THE MIDDLE EAST

Richard H. Meadow

Zooarchaeology Laboratory, Peabody Museum, Harvard University, 11 Divinity Avenue, Cambridge, MA 02138

Dedication

This essay, dedicated to the memories of Dexter Perkins, Jr. (1927-1983) and Louis Dupree (1925-1989), testifies to the importance of their joint work in northern Afghanistan, and provides a contribution to our understanding of Holocene zoogeography and the question of the domestication of wild goat and especially wild sheep (Ovis sp.). Perkins was always particularly interested in the "ovicaprines"—he wrote his doctoral dissertation on postcranial osteological differences between sheep and goats (Perkins 1959). Not long after finishing that work, he was given the opportunity by Louis Dupree to examine the faunal remains from cave deposits excavated in 1962 at Ghar-i-Mar (also known as Snake Cave or Aq Kupruk I [AK-I]) near the village of Aq Kupruk in the northern foothills of the Hindu Kush (36°05′N, 66°51′E: Dupree 1964). Whether Perkins actually travelled to Afghanistan before 1965 is unclear, but he was present that year to visit the continuing excavations at Aq Kupruk I as attested by a published photograph (Dupree 1972:fig. 5a). Also in 1965, Dupree excavated at Ghar-i-Asp (Horse Cave or Aq Kupruk II), at an open air site called Aq Kupruk III, and at Skull Cave (Aq Kupruk IV) (Fig. 1). Only the first of these yielded "identifiable" faunal remains. These were examined together with those from AK-I by Perkins who wrote "The fauna of the Aq Kupruk Caves: a brief note" for Dupree's preliminary report to the American Philosophical Society (Dupree 1972). Unfortunately, a final report on the Aq Kupruk work was never published, and with the passing of the two investigators, we are left with intriguing questions concerning the nature of the prehistoric occupation that must now be answered by others.

Aq Kupruk and the indigenous development of agriculture

The significance of Dupree's work in northern Afghanistan has been evaluated by Davis (1974, 1978), Shaffer (1978), Kohl (1984), and Vinogradov and Ranov (1985). Together with Coon's work at Kara Kamar (Coon and Ralph 1955; Coon 1957) and Soviet work to the north (reviewed in Ranov and Davis 1979; Kohl 1984; Vinogradov and Ranov 1985), it forms the basis for our understanding of the Paleolithic through Neolithic of the southern part of Western Turkestan. Taken at face value, the radiocarbon ages from the "Upper Paleolithic" and "Non-Ceramic Neolithic" levels of Aq Kupruk (Table 1) appear to indicate the early development, respectively, of a non-geometric microblade lithic tradition and of an economy based at least in part on cereal-crop agriculture and domestic animals. Vinogradov and Ranov (1985, 1988), however, argue on typological grounds (based upon their work farther north) that the Kuprukian cannot be considered Upper Paleolithic but "Epi-Paleolithic," and that the radiocarbon age obtained is too early. Davis (1978), on the other hand, is willing to accept the radiocarbon age, and the possibility that an epi-paleolithic tradition of microblades might have developed early and persisted for thousands of years in Northern Afghanistan just as it did in the Levant. Also on typological grounds—and in spite of the presence of sickle blades—Vinogradov and Ranov maintain that the neolithic Aq Kuprukrian economy was based on hunting and gathering and not on locally developed agriculture as suggested by Dupree (1972) and supported by Shaffer (1978).

Table 1. Radiocarbon dates from Aq Kupruk.

Lab no.	Site	Culture	Years B.P.
Hv-425	Aq Kupruk I	Non-Cer. Neo.	8,650±100
Hv-1355	Aq Kupruk II	Non-Cer. Neo.	10,210±235
Hv-1358	Aq Kupruk II	Kuprukian B	16,615±215

Table 2. Aq Kupruk fauna (compiled from Perkins 1972).

Site*	AK-II	AK-I	AK-II	AK-I	AK-II	AK-I	AK-II	AK-I	AK-I	AK-II	AK-II
Period**	Kupruk. A	Kuprukian B		Non-Ceramic Neo.		Ceramic Neo.		Chalco lithic	Iron Age	Islamic	
Taxon†											
Ovis orientalis cycloceros (wild)	4	X††	4	-	-	-	-	-	X	-	-
Ovis sp. (probably domestic)	-	-	-	-	-	-	1	-	-	-	-
Ovis sp. (presumably domestic)	-	-	-	-	-	-	-	-	-	2	-
Ovis sp. (domestic)	-	-	-	X	X	X	-	X	X	-	-
Capra hircus aegagrus (wild)	8	-	1	-	-	-	-	-	-	-	-
Capra hircus ssp. (wild/domestic)	-	-	-	-	-	-	2	-	-	-	-
Capra sp. (presumably domestic)	-	-	-	-	-	-	-	-	-	2	-
Capra hircus hircus (domestic)	-	-	-	X	X	X	1	X	X	-	-
Ovis/Capra	51	-	12	-	X	-	20	-	-	15	4
Gazella subgutturosa ssp.	-	-	-	X	-	-	1	-	-	-	-
Bos sp.	-	-	-	-	-	-	4	-	-	4	-
Bos (probably domestic)	-	-	-	X	-	-	-	-	-	-	-
Bos (domestic)	-	-	-	-	-	-	-	-	X	-	-
Cervus elaphus	1	-	0	X	-	-	5	-	-	-	-
Bos/Cervus	5	-	0	-	-	-	-	-	-	-	-
Equus caballus	-	-	-	X	-	-	1	-	X	-	-
Equus sp.	0	-	1	-	-	-	3	-	-	-	-
Equus (?) *hemionus*	-	-	-	-	-	-	-	1	-	-	-
Canis aureus	1	-	1	-	-	-	-	-	-	-	-
Canid	-	-	-	-	-	-	-	-	-	1	-
Vulpes sp.	0	-	1	-	-	-	-	-	-	-	-
Hystrix sp.	-	-	-	-	-	-	-	-	X	-	-
Total	70	n.a.	20	n.a.	n.a.	n.a.	38	n.a.	n.a.	24	4

*   AK-I = Aq Kupruk I (Ghar-i-Mar or Snake Cave); AK-II = Aq Kupruk II (Ghar-i-Asp or Horse Cave).
** For periods, see Dupree 1972:75-77.
†   See text for discussion of nomenclature; that used here is that of Perkins (1972).
†† X = present.

The principal difficulty in accepting Dupree's arguments for the indigenous development of agriculture and animal husbandry in northern Afghanistan is the lack of published paleobiological evidence. For example, no studies of the macro-botanical remains have been reported and Perkins's "brief note" on the fauna (Perkins 1972) tabulates identifications for only 156 specimens from the later paleolithic through the early historic periods at Aq Kupruk II. These faunal data together with information on the presence of certain taxa in Aq Kupruk I are presented here in Table 2.[1] Perkins notes that the "Chalcolithic and both the Ceramic and Non-Ceramic Neolithic [of AK-I] have definite domesticated sheep and goat," but how he determined this is not stated, just as his bases for similar identifications of AK-II material are not given. The assemblages appear too small to have permitted evaluation of kill-off patterns from dental and epiphyseal data; therefore, Perkins must have used horncore morphology (following Zeuner 1955, 1963; Reed 1960; Flannery 1969) or skeletal part size as the basis for his "domesticated" characterization.

Although size diminution as an indicator of domestication in ovicaprines (e.g. Uerpmann 1979) was not used in a comprehensive fashion by Perkins in any of his studies, that he was concerned with animal size is clearly indicated by his discussion of the distribution of wild forms of sheep and goat in northern Afghanistan (Perkins 1972:73):

According to Ellerman and Morrison-Scott (1951) and Kullmann (1965) the range of the Argali (*Ovis ammon*) and the Siberian Ibex (*Capra ibex siberica*) extended into the Hindu Kush, whereas the range of the smaller kindred species, the Urial (*Ovis orientalis*) and the Bezoar (*Capra hircus aegagrus*) extended no farther east than Herat. However, the small size of the sheep/goat material from the Kuprukian of Horse Cave (Aq Kupruk II) indicates that these latter two species were represented in prehistoric times. That they were present in the Hindu Kush until recently is indicated by the remains of sheep and goat sacrifices at Ajdahar-i-Sorkh Dar....The skulls found in a fissure near the shrine are *O. orientalis* and *C. h. aegagrus*.[2]

With these statements, Perkins broached the complex subject of ovicaprine (particularly, sheep) systematics, nomenclature, and zoogeography. Considering for the moment the situation only in northern Afghanistan, where overall size and weight differences between the argali and urial are marked (e.g. Roberts 1977; Shaller 1977), the presence of relatively small sheep bones in the Kuprukian period collection could be a valid indication of absence of the former species. Final judgment, however, must await metrical data from collections apparently still in Afghanistan and consideration of overlap in size between male urials and female argalis. Even so, it should be noted that modern studies do not indicate the presence of argali anywhere very near the Aq Kupruk area; instead, that region is considered within the range of the urial (Shaller 1977; Valdez 1982). These factors all lend support to Perkins's wild sheep identifications.

The situation is different with the goats. The two species of wild goat—ibex and bezoar—differ little in weight, although the ibex is said to be higher at the shoulder than the bezoar (Roberts 1977; Shaller 1977). Considerable study would be necessary to distinguish the fragmented post-cranial bones of the two, if such distinctions can be made at all.[3] Casting more doubt on Perkins's identification of the bezoar is the presence of a *Capra ibex* horncore in Iron Age levels of Aq Kupruk I (Fig. 2c),

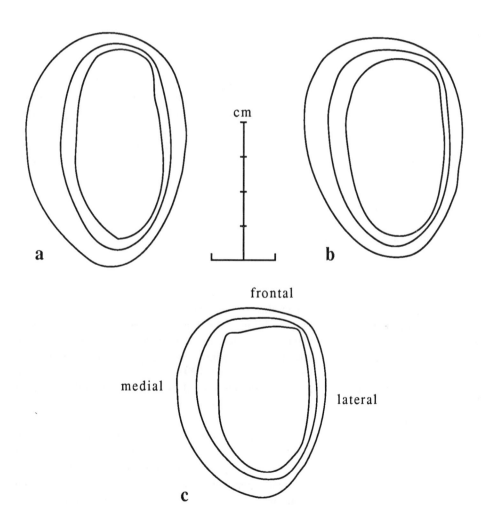

cm

a

b

frontal

medial

lateral

c

Fig. 2:
Cross-sections of *Capra ibex* horncores taken ca. 1 cm above the base and one-third and two-thirds up the preserved core (see Table 4 for dimensions):
a. *Capra ibex*, MCZ-34620, from Kashmir near the village of Kiris on the north side of the River Indus (ca. 76°E 35°20'N), killed in June/July and received 6 January 1937 by the Museum of Comparative Zoology, Harvard University, from Miss Mary Ogden Abbott; catalogued as *Capra sibirica pedri* Lorenz; subspecific identification as *Capra ibex siberica* appropriate on zoogeographic grounds;
b. *Capra ibex*, MCZ-34619, as with **a** above;
c. cf. *Capra ibex*, archaeological specimen from the site of Aq Kupruk I (Ghar-i-Mar or Snake Cave), northern Afghanistan (excavation unit TR1, Cuts 3+4, above Gravels 1); probably Iron Age (1st millennium B.C./A.D.); collection of the Peabody Museum of Archaeology and Ethnology, Harvard University.

Table 3a. Aspects of the taxonomy and nomenclature of *Ovis*.

Common name	Subspecies after Valdez (1982)	2n =*	Corbet (1978)	Corbet (1984)	Uerpmann (1987)
European mouflon	*Ovis orientalis musimon*	54	*O. ammon musimon*	*O. aries* (feral)	*O. aries* (feral)
Cyprian mouflon	*Ovis orientalis ophion*	54 (?)	*O. ammon musimon*	*O. aries* (feral)	*O. aries* (feral)
Armenian mouflon	*Ovis orientalis gmelini*	54	*O. ammon orientalis*	*O. orientalis*	*O. orientalis*
Esfahan mouflon	*Ovis orientalis isphahanica*	54	*O. ammon orientalis*	*O. orientalis*	*O. orientalis*
Laristan mouflon	*Ovis orientalis laristanica*	54	*O. ammon orientalis*	*O. orientalis*	*O. orientalis*
Transcaspian urial	*Ovis orientalis arkal*	58	*O. ammon vignei*	*O. vignei*	*O. vignei*
Afghan urial	*Ovis orientalis cycloceros*	58	*O. ammon vignei*	*O. vignei*	*O. vignei*
Punjab urial	*Ovis orientalis punjabiensis*	58	*O. ammon vignei*	*O. vignei*	*O. vignei*
Ladak urial	*Ovis orientalis vignei*	58	*O. ammon vignei*	*O. vignei*	*O. vignei*
Severtzov's urial	*Ovis orientalis severtzovi*	58 (?)	n.a.**	*O. vignei*	*O. vignei*
Altai argali	*Ovis ammon ammon*	56	*O. ammon ammon*	*O. ammon*	n.a.
Gobi argali	*Ovis ammon darwini*	56	*O. ammon hodgsoni*	*O. ammon*	n.a.
Tian Shan argali	*Ovis ammon karelini*	56	*O. ammon poloi (=polii)*	*O. ammon*	n.a.
Marco Polo's argali	*Ovis ammon polii*	56	*O. ammon poloi (=polii)*	*O. ammon*	n.a.
Tibetan argali	*Ovis ammon hodgsoni*	56	*O. ammon hodgsoni*	*O. ammon*	n.a.
Kara Tau argali	*Ovis ammon nigrimontana*	56	*O. ammon poloi (=polii)*	*O. ammon*	n.a.

*   Karyotypes from Nadler et al. (1973), Valdez (1982).
**   n.a. = not noted in that reference.

indicating that, at least by the first millennium B.C., the ibex was found near Aq Kupruk.[4]

In sum, based upon current understandings of ovicaprine zoogeography, the ibex (*Capra ibex*) and the urial (*Ovis vignei*) but neither the bezoar (*Capra aegagrus*) nor the argali (*Ovis ammon*) would be present in the Aq Kupruk area. Perkins is correct, however, in pointing out that distributions change with time. Indeed, zooarchaeology adds a most important diachronic dimension to the otherwise synchronic exercise in distributional mapping of modern fauna. But like the paleontologist, the zooarchaeologist has a limited scope of remains suitable for identification to the species, especially to the subspecies level. One set of features that has been used for this purpose in the ovicaprines is horncore morphology. The significance of the ibex horncore from Aq Kupruk has been noted. The situation with sheep in the eastern regions of the Middle East is more complex than that with goats, however, and deserves further discussion in light of data gathered and studies made since the early 1970s.

Sheep

Between one and seventeen species and eight and thirty-eight subspecies of Old World *Ovis* have been recognized in the literature (summarized in Nadler et al. 1973; Valdez 1982). An attempt by Valdez (1982) to reconcile

cytogenetic and morphological data resulted in the recognition of sixteen subspecies in the central and southern Palearctic belonging to two species, *Ovis orientalis* (distribution west of the Himalaya) and *Ovis ammon* (distribution in and north of the Himalaya). Those same sixteen subspecies can also be classified in four species with the two European forms as feral domesticates (*O. aries*), the three Turkish and Zagros subspecies as mouflons (*O. orientalis*, karyotype: 2n = 54), the five eastern Middle East subspecies as urials (*O. vignei*, 2n = 58), and the remainder still classed as argalis (*O. ammon*, 2n = 56) (Table 3a and b).

Because urials and mouflons can and do interbreed in the wild, Valdez (Valdez et al. 1978; Valdez 1982) has preferred to view them as semispecies of a single species *orientalis* of the superspecies *ammon* which includes the argalis (species *ammon*) as well. Another possibility is that advocated by Corbet in his first edition (1978) where, following Pfeffer (1967) and Heptner et al. (1988; originally published in 1961), he recognized a single polytypic species, *Ovis ammon* and seven subspecies (Table 3, plus *O. a. kozlovi* not noted by Valdez 1982). This is a considerable modification of the position of Ellerman and Morrison-Scott (1951) who recognized four species, namely *Ovis ammon* (argalis), *Ovis laristanica* (southern Iranian sheep only), *Ovis musimon* (mouflons of Sardinia and

Table 3b. Aspects of the taxonomy and nomenclature of *Ovis* (continued).

Common name	Hassinger* & Roberts** Afghanistan and Pakistan
European mouflon	n.a.†
Cyprian mouflon	n.a.
Armenian mouflon	n.a.
Esfahan mouflon	n.a.
Laristan mouflon	n.a.
Transcaspian urial	n.a.
Afghan urial	*O. ammon cycloceros* **O. orientalis blanfordi*
Punjab urial	**O. orientalis punjabiensis*
Ladak urial	**O. orientalis vignei*
Severtzov's urial	n.a.
Altai argali	n.a.
Gobi argali	n.a.
Tian Shan argali	n.a.
Marco Polo's argali	*O. ammon poli (**polii)*
Tibetan argali	n.a.
Kara Tau argali	n.a.

* Hassinger (1973).
** Roberts (1977).
† n.a. = not noted in references.

Corsica), and *Ovis orientalis* (comprising eastern mouflons and urials). In his 1984 supplement, however, Corbet gave more weight to the cytogenetic and zooarchaeological evidence and recognized three species (*O. ammon, O. vignei*, and *O. orientalis*), noting that the Mediterranean island forms were probably feral domesticates (following Poplin 1979). Corbet's later position is essentially that followed by Uerpmann (1987) in his review of the Holocene zoogeography of ungulates in the Middle East.

Of importance to note in this matter of systematics are two "hybrid zones" in Iran where viable crosses between urials and mouflons, defined by karyotype, have been documented in the wild (Nadler et al. 1973; Valdez et al. 1978; Valdez 1982). One of these is in the region south of the Caspian Sea in the Elburz Mountains, and the other is in southeastern Iran (Fig. 1). This hybridization is thought to be the result of the joining of formerly distinct populations of sheep either through the removal of the isolating snow barriers of the last glacial maximum (e.g. Nadler et al. 1973) or through the more recent destruction of forests in the Elburz and southeastern Zagros (as forests are more

effective than snowfields as barriers to sheep dispersal according to Valdez et al. 1978 following Geist 1971). In other words, as Uerpmann (1987:126) notes, "Although forms with different chromosome numbers still intergrade, it seems possible to consider them as species in formation. Another Ice Age may be sufficient to separate these sheep completely." Clearly sheep have great genetic plasticity, amply attested by the hundreds of breeds that have been developed since the first animals were domesticated in the seventh or eighth millennium B.C. (Ryder 1983). Even in the wild animals, isolation of populations can lead to the development of distinctive phenotypes reflected in pelage characteristics and horn configurations (Valdez et al. 1978). This is of particular importance to zooarchaeologists who are currently dependent upon horncore morphology for distinguishing different species of wild sheep.

Sheep horncores

Although male wild sheep horns have been frequently described in publications of natural history or zoology, information on the shape and dimensions of the horn*cores* of modern animals from different areas is much harder to come by and, when presented, usually only concerns single specimens (e.g. Flannery 1969; Stampfli 1983). Uerpmann (1987; published first in Uerpmann and Frey 1981) has provided cross-sections of single cores of urial (*Ovis vignei*) and mouflon (*Ovis orientalis*) from northern Iran (which are reproduced here as Fig. 3a and d). He notes that "In contrast to the mouflon, the urial has a sharply angled horncore. The orbital angle is particularly pronounced and situated more frontally than in the mouflon horn" (Uerpmann 1987:127). Referring to the horn shapes of these western forms, Valdez (1982:83, 91) notes the following:

O. orientalis gmelini horns: "Supracervical. Fronto-orbital edge and frontal surface rounded, front(o)-nuchal edge sharp";
O. orientalis arkal (= *O. vignei arkal*) horns: "Homonymous horns growing in a tight circle or forming an open spiral; frontal surface flat with sharp angles and distinct ridges, triangular in cross-section."

These descriptions match the morphology of the horncore sections (Fig. 3d and a respectively). Cross-sections of specimens from the eastern zones of distribution of the two forms are also presented in Fig. 3 (**b, c** and **e, g, h**), and the morphologies are quite different. Valdez (1982:88, 96) describes the horn forms as follows:

O. orientalis laristanica horns: "Homonymous. Frontal surface flat with sharp angles";
O. orientalis vignei (= *O. vignei vignei*) horns: "Usually tending toward supracervical";
O. orientalis cycloceros (= *O. vignei cycloceros*) horns: "Homonymous."

While the descriptions for the urial forms are of little value for this discussion,[5] that for *O. o. laristanica* is similar to that for *O. v. arkal*. This is symptomatic of the difficulties in dealing with horn and horncore morphologies.

In sum, in order to use horncore morphology effectively at the species or subspecies level, it is necessary to document variation within individual populations as well as between populations. The importance of such an approach is shown by *Ovis orientalis laristanica* cores **e**, **g**, and **h** (Fig. 3). All come from animals said to have been captured in southern Iran (somewhere southeast of Shiraz) and transported to the al-Ain zoo where they subsequently died, although how soon after arrival is not clear. The larger core is from an animal aged between six and seven years judging from the horn sheath growth rings, while the two smaller cores are from animals aged between four and five years. All the cores are relatively broad in relation to depth at the base (Table 4), and the widest part is situated at or just in front of (fronto-medially to) an imaginary line bisecting the long axis of the cross-section at right angles. Furthermore, at the base, the nucho-medial profiles (right sides of profiles in Fig. 3) are convex or only slightly flattened (**h**) but much less convex than the fronto-lateral profiles (left sides of sections in Fig. 3). Otherwise, there is considerable variation in core morphology, with nucho-medial margins of profiles distal from the base being somewhat convex (**e**) to flat (**h**), and frontal and lateral margins being more (**e**) or less (**g**, **h**) flattened. To what degree some of this variation might be due to age is not clear.

If the illustrated *Ovis orientalis* cores (including **d**) appear relatively symmetrical fronto-medially/nucho-laterally (top half of the core compared with bottom half in Fig. 3), the illustrated *Ovis vignei* horncores (**a-c**) are markedly asymmetrical in that respect and much more symmetrical fronto-laterally/nucho-medially. In other words, if one draws a line through the long axis of the profile, the left and right sides are more nearly mirror images in the urial than in the Asiatic mouflon, reflecting a less markedly convex fronto-lateral profile. Also characteristic of the urial are a generally somewhat flatter fronto-medial margin (top in Fig. 3) and more pointed or "keeled" nucho-lateral margin (bottom in Fig. 3). As is evident in Fig. 3, however, there is considerable variation, and attribution of any single core, in the absence of other information, may prove difficult. This is certainly the situation with the archaeological specimens also illustrated in Fig. 3 (**f, i, j**).

Horncores that can be identified as belonging to wild sheep are quite rare in zooarchaeological collections from what are today southeastern Iran and Pakistan. Only small fragments of ovicaprine horncores have been recovered from the excavations at Mehrgarh (Kachi District, Baluchistan, Pakistan), where, judging from the size of the bones in the post-cranial skeleton, wild sheep were exploited throughout the Aceramic Neolithic (ca. 7000-5500

Fig. 3:
Cross-sections of *Ovis* sp. horncores taken ca. 1 cm above the base and one-third and two-thirds up the preserved core (note: all are depicted as left cores: see Table 4 for actual side and dimensions):
a. *Ovis vignei*, Field Museum of Natural History-58025, from Elburz Mountains north of Damghan, northern Iran, published as such by Uerpmann (1987:fig. 59; Uerpmann and Frey 1981:abb. 2), subspecies probably *O. v. arkal* based on zoogeography (following Valdez 1982);
b. *Ovis vignei*, MCZ-34621, from Kashmir near the village of Kiris on the north side of the River Indus (ca. 76°E 35°20'N), killed in June/July and received 6 January 1937 by the Museum of Comparative Zoology, Harvard University, from Miss Mary Ogden Abbott; catalogued as *Ovis vignei vignei*; subspecific identification appropriate on zoogeographic grounds;
c. *Ovis vignei*, MCZ-6030, from "NW India" and "bought of E. Gerrard by L. Agassiz"; received 28 September 1878 by the Museum of Comparative Zoology, Harvard University; catalogued as *Ovis vignei cycloceros*; subspecific identification possible as also are *O. v. punjabiensis* and *O. v. vignei* depending upon from where exactly in "NW India" the specimen came;
d. *Ovis orientalis*, Field Museum of Natural History-58046, from Koyun Island in Lake Rezaiyeh, northwestern Iran, published as such by Uerpmann (1987:fig. 59; Uerpmann and Frey 1981:abb. 2), subspecies probably *O. o. gmelini* based on zoogeography;
e. *Ovis orientalis*, CP-95, from the al-Ain (abu Dhabi) zoo said to come originally from southern Iran (southeast of Shiraz, south and west of Kerman), collection of the Archaeozoology Laboratory of the Institut für Urgeschichte, Universität Tübingen; catalogued as *O. laristanica*; identification as *O. o. laristanica* possible on zoogeographic grounds although could also be a cross between that subspecies and *O. v. cycloceros* (following Nadler et al. 1973; Valdez et al. 1978; Valdez 1982);
f. *Ovis* sp., 221663-84, archaeological specimen from the site of Naushari (excavation unit NS.P9D-63), west of Dadhar, Kachi District, Baluchistan, Pakistan; Harappan period (Naushari II/III - ca. 2300 B.C.); collection of the French Archaeological Mission in Pakistan;
g. *Ovis orientalis*, CP-78, same as **e** above; date in catalogue: 5/85;
h. *Ovis orientalis*, CP-85, same as **e** above; date in catalogue: 28/4/85;
i. *Ovis* sp., 113665, archaeological specimen from the site of Tepe Yahya (excavation unit A.75.1), 220 km south of Kerman, Iran; non-architectural deposits between Periods IV and III (?end 2nd millennium B.C.); collection of the Peabody Museum of Archaeology and Ethnology, Harvard University;
j. *Ovis* sp., 110903, archaeological specimen from the site of Tepe Yahya (excavation unit XB.70.5A.1), 220 km south of Kerman, Iran; Period IVA.2 (?first half 2nd millennium B.C.); collection of the Peabody Museum of Archaeology and Ethnology, Harvard University.

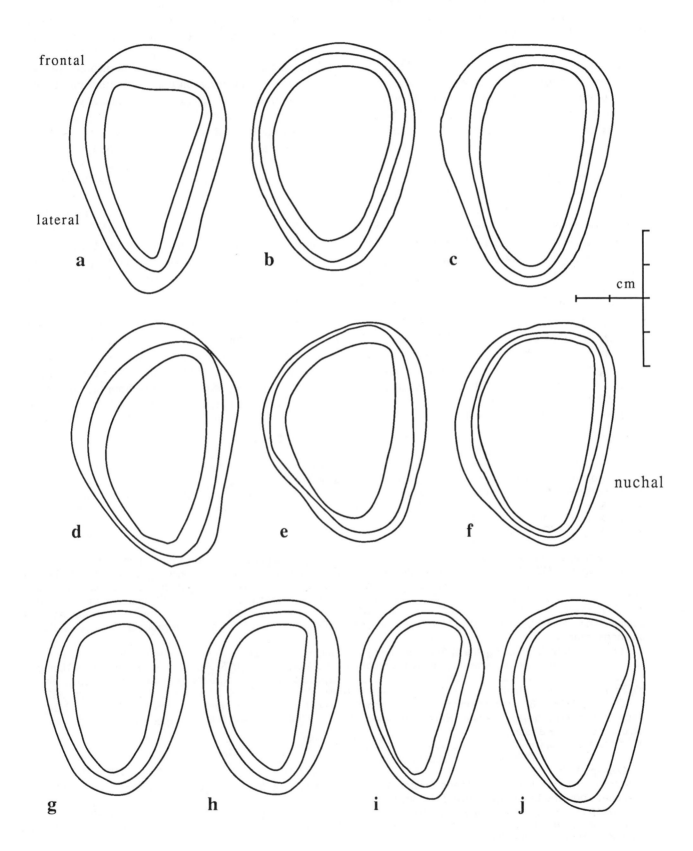

Table 4. Side, age stage, and dimensions of horncores in Figs. 2-4.

		Taxon	Specimen number	Side	Age grade based on maxillary tooth wear	GD (mm)	LD (mm)
Fig. 2:	a	*Capra ibex*	MCZ-34620	R	?	69.6	51.8
	b	*Capra ibex*	MCZ-34619	R	M3 fully in wear	65.6	51.8
	c	*Capra ibex*	A.K. I, TR1, Cuts 3+4 above Gravels 1	R	M3 fully in wear	60.0	50.6
Fig. 3:	a	*Ovis vignei*	FMNH-58025	R	?	[73]*	[46]*
and	b	*Ovis vignei*	MCZ-32621	L	M3 fully in wear	68.8	51.5
Fig. 4:	c	*Ovis vignei*	MCZ-6030	L	M3 fully in wear	71.9	52.8
	d	*Ovis orientalis*	FMNH-58046	R	?	[72]*	[49]*
	e	*Ovis orientalis*	Tübingen CP-95	R	M3 fully in wear	65.0	53.5
	f	*Ovis* sp.	Nausharo 221663-84	L	?	65.5	46.0
	g	*Ovis orientalis*	Tübingen CP-78	L	M3 fully in wear	56.3	43.0
	h	*Ovis orientalis*	Tübingen CP-85	L	M3 fully in wear	57.3	44.0
	i	*Ovis* sp.	Tepe Yahya 113665	R	?	56.5	40.0
	j	*Ovis* sp.	Tepe Yahya 110903	R	?	61.2	48.0
Fig. 4:	k	*Ovis* sp.	Tepe Yahya 111932-19	R	?	59.0	47.0
only	l	*Ovis* sp.**	FMNH 97983	L	adult	56.0	41.0
	m	*Ovis* sp.†	Shahr-i Sokhta 67	R	adult?	59.0	40.5
	n	*Ovis vignei*†	BMNH 1937.4.8.4	R	?	61.5	38.5
	o	*Ovis vignei*†	BMNH 1909.11.17.1	R	?	62.0	40.5

* Approximate dimensions obtained from drawings in Uerpmann (1987:fig. 59).
** Field Museum of Natural History specimen reported as "*Ovis orientalis cycloceros*" from Kerman by Stampfli (1983:tables 35-36).
† Reported in Compagnoni (1980); Shahr–i Sokhta specimen is from Locus XIG-4.20; British Museum (Natural History) specimens are from "Punjab" (1937.4.8.4) and "Khorassan" (1909.11.17.1) and are reported as *O.vignei* and *O. cycloceros*, respectively.

B.C.; e.g. Meadow 1981, 1984). At the nearby site of Nausharo, however, a horncore specimen in good condition from a late third millennium Harappan period deposit was recovered (see cross-sections in Fig. 3f). In the analyzed portion of the faunal remains from the early periods (ca. 5500-3000 B.C.) at Tepe Yahya (220 km south of Kerman, Iran), only a single badly damaged horncore base from a wild sheep was identified (Meadow 1986a:142 and plate Xc). The second millennium levels at Tepe Yahya, however, yielded two well-preserved horncores (see cross-sections in Fig. 3i-j). Finally, Compagnoni (1980) reports a largely complete braincase with horncores from third millennium Shahr–i Sokhta (Period II, phases 6-5, ca. 2500 B.C.).

All southeast Iranian *Ovis* horncores, whether ancient or modern, are relatively broad at the base (larger in least diameter) when compared to modern specimens identified as *Ovis vignei* or to the single *Ovis orientalis* specimen from northwest Iran (Table 4 and Fig. 4). The Shahr–i Sokhta (eastern Iran) core (Fig. 4m) falls between the two groups. Compagnoni (1980) has identified this specimen as *Ovis vignei* but Uerpmann (1987:130) has stated that it "is too small to be from a typical urial. However, it differs from the domestic sheep of the site, and may actually represent a young or female wild sheep or a hybrid form." To judge from the photographs published by Compagnoni (1980:fig. 3 and 4:5), the specimen is neither from a female nor from a particularly young animal. The second conclusion is based on the fact that all basal sutures are fused and there is some obscuring of the line between frontals and parietal. The published section of the right horncore (Compagnoni 1980:fig. 1) shows much more right-left than top-bottom symmetry, indicating closer morphological affinity to *O. vignei* than to *O. orientalis* based on the observations above. Conversely, it might belong to a hybrid like those documented by Valdez (1982); or the

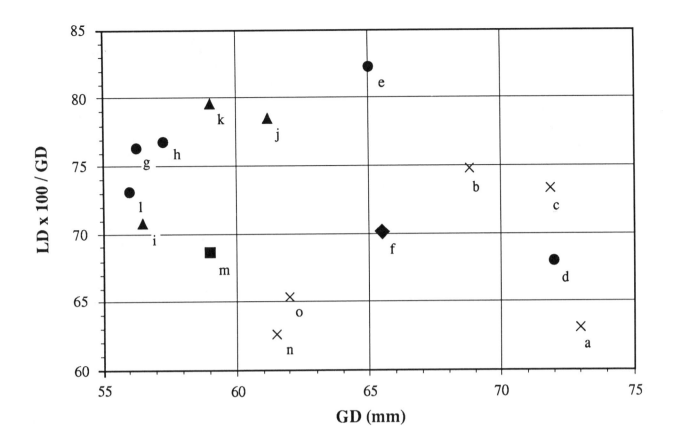

Fig. 4:
Least diameter (LD) at the base of horncores of sheep (*Ovis* sp.) as a proportion of greatest diameter (GD) plotted in relation to greatest diameter. Letters refer to sheep specimens listed in Table 4. Solid circles are modern horncores identified as mouflon (*O. orientalis*); crosses are modern specimens identified as urial (*O. vignei*); solid triangles are specimens from Tepe Yahya; the solid square is the horncore from Shahr–i Sokhta; and the solid diamond is the specimen from Nausharo.

animal may have been malnourished for a time as is suggested by what appears to be an almond-shaped depression near the base of the right core on the lateral side in the published photographs (especially, Compagnoni 1980:fig. 4:5; see Hatting 1975:346).

Like the Shahr–i Sokhta specimen, the Nausharo horncore raises difficulties. Following Valdez (1982), its origin in the North Kachi plain in eastern Baluchistan is considered the southeastern end of the modern range for the Afghan urial (*Ovis orientalis cycloceros* to Valdez or *Ovis vignei cycloceros* following Uerpmann). The basal dimensions of the Nausharo core place it squarely in the "vignei" group (Fig. 4f). Its cross-section (Fig. 3f), however, is markedly asymmetrical right-to-left and, although somewhat keeled nucho-laterally, it is relatively symmetrical top-to-bottom. These characteristics make the Nausharo specimen morphologically closer to the southeastern Iranian mouflon cores than to the urial specimens illustrated in Fig. 3.

Identifying the Nausharo horncore as belonging to an animal more closely related to the Zagros forms than to the Afghan/Central Asian forms of wild sheep has important implications for our understanding of both Holocene zoogeography and domestication. It could indicate a considerable restriction in the range of Zagros sheep during the last 4000 years coupled with an extension in range of the Central Asian forms. This possibility is extremely difficult to evaluate, however, without information on the horncore morphology and cytogenetics of modern wild sheep of Baluchistan and without greater numbers of horncores from archaeological sites.

As for domestication, cytogenetic studies indicate that all domestic sheep have karyotypes identical to those of West Asiatic wild sheep (2n = 54). Therefore, other forms such as the urial and the argali "should not be considered among the ancestors of domestic sheep" (Nadler et al. 1973:121). If the Indus region did lie outside of the range of distribution of the mouflon, then the size diminution over time evident in sheep remains from Mehrgarh (Meadow 1981, 1984) was due not to indigenous domestication, but instead to a decrease in the hunting of local urials coupled with an increase in imported, mouflon-related, domestic stock. As noted elsewhere (Meadow 1986b:60), a hole in this argument "lies in the assumption that all breeds of domestic sheep tested cytogenetically in fact include direct descendants of the early domestic sheep of the greater Indus Valley." Instead, locally domesticated animals could have been replaced at a later date by improved breeds brought from the West. The possible inclusion of Baluchistan within the ancient range of the West Asiatic mouflon, however, also would place it within the potential "main line" of sheep domestication.

In sum, the currently available horncore evidence does not permit a definitive outline of Holocene wild sheep zoogeography. Unequivocal identification of wild sheep species or subspecies based on horncore proportions or morphology or both is often not possible. This is clear from Figs. 3 and 4 and from the discussion above. For example, the "*vignei*" group in Fig. 4 includes both a definite "*orientalis*" horncore from Rezeiyeh and the Nausharo specimen, while the Shahr-i Sokhta core, morphologically urial-like, lies closer to the southeastern Iranian mouflons in its proportions. The difficulty is that a number of factors are operating: for example, change in population distributions and in horncore morphology through many generations, inter-individual variation, and intra-individual age- and nutrition-related morphological changes. Thus, there are problems of space, deep time, and shallow time, and any truly satisfactory resolution will involve defining trends in large numbers of horncores from narrowly defined regions covering extensive periods of time. It is encouraging that the seven specimens from southeastern Iran (ancient and modern) are relatively similar to each other, especially in proportions, but also in morphology. The keeled nature (latero-nuchally) of the two Yahya specimens (Figs. 3**i**, **j**) may indicate an additional complication, however—namely, the influence of captivity or incipient domestication on the wild *Ovis orientalis* phenotype (Uerpmann, pers. comm. 1989).

Conclusion

Returning to the Aq Kupruk material, the northern Afghanistan sites of Ghar-i-Asp (AK-II) and Ghar-i-Mar (AK-I) lie clearly outside of the modern range of the mouflon and well within that of the urial. Yet Perkins has defined the presence of domestic sheep (and goats) in those sites at a time as early as anywhere in the Middle East. Here we have the Mehrgarh problem again, only much more clearly defined. Are the early dates valid? Is the characterization as domestic valid? If the dates are early and the animals domestic, did sheep domestication take place locally using urial stock? Unfortunately, in the absence both of the faunal collections and of detailed morphological or metrical data, we cannot even try to answer these important questions. If the evidence from Mehrgarh does represent the foundation of the agro-pastoral complex that came to underlie the Harappan Civilization, the Aq Kupruk data might be interpreted similarly in relation to the Bronze Age civilizations of Central Asia (Kohl 1984; Ligabue and Salvatori 1989).

Because of the amount of work that has been done, particularly in the Levant, the literature on the domestication and exploitation of plants and animals in the Middle East is dominated by material from the "Fertile Crescent." In regions equally favored with "prodomesticates" (wild relatives of domestic plants and animals: Dyson 1953), there is very little understanding of the parallel processes of transformation of the economic base of human society, or indeed of human society itself. Increased attention needs to be paid to the early Holocene period in the vast area between the Euphrates and the Indus and into Central Asia from the point of view not only of artifacts and architecture, but more specifically of the recovery, analysis, and interpretation of paleobiological remains. Dexter Perkins, Jr. and Louis Dupree were pioneers in this respect. Once the political situation permits, their proposals concerning the indigenous development of agriculture in the eastern part of the Middle East deserve to be tested anew.

Acknowledgments

Special thanks are due to Hans-Peter Uerpmann for assistance with various aspects of this paper along with his personal and professional hospitality in Tübingen. Gratitude is also owed the editors of this volume for the patience they have exhibited during the preparation of this contribution. The support of the National Science Foundation (award number: BNS-8821712) is gratefully acknowledged.

Notes

1. In Shaffer's 1978 discussion of the evidence from the Aq Kupruk caves, two errors are apparent: 1) the date of "14,665 b.c." (Shaffer 1978:75) is for the *later* phase of the Upper Paleolithic (= Kuprukian B) and not the "earliest phase"; and 2) there is no discrepancy between the reporting of Perkins and Dupree (Shaffer 1978:75). The Non-Ceramic Neolithic B material listed by Dupree (1972:76) is from AK-I and is discussed by Perkins only in the text of his note (Perkins 1972:73). The Ceramic Neolithic material from AK-II listed by Perkins in his table 16 is also listed by Dupree (1972:77) in the appropriate location.

2. Note that *Ovis orientalis* and *Capra hircus aegagrus* would now be rendered as *Ovis vignei* and *Capra aegagrus*. *Capra hircus* is best reserved for the domestic species (following Clutton-Brock 1981:appendix I). The situation with *Ovis* will be discussed below.

3. See Hecker (1975) for difficulties in distinguishing bezoar and nubian ibex bones in the Levant.

4. The archaeological collections from Dupree's excavations in Afghanistan that were exported to the United States were moved

from the American Museum of Natural History, New York City, to the Peabody Museum of Archaeology and Ethnology, Harvard University, Cambridge, MA, in the spring of 1989 together with collections made by Walter A. Fairservis, Jr. in Pakistan and Afghanistan. Among the Aq Kupruk material there are a few animal bones, one of which can be identified as the right horncore of an ibex (Fig. 2c and Table 4; the basal two thirds of the core is preserved, although broken in half). The cross section and the radius of curvature of the core are similar to those for two specimens in the collections of the Museum of Comparative Zoology (Fig. 2a and b). The section of the Aq Kupruk specimen, however, is somewhat rounder, the frontal margin is flatter toward the tip, and the body of the core is hollow for only about a third of what must have been its original length. Because the core is convex medially and nearly flat laterally (the frontal suture is preserved, thus permitting definite orientation) and the radius

of curvature is large, it could not have come from a urial. The absence of an anterior keel and lens-shaped or quadrangular cross section eliminates bezoar (Zeuner 1955; Reed 1960; Flannery 1969). The short sinus cavity and relatively thick walls probably reflect an animal younger than the fully adult specimens used for comparison.

5. Even with the horncore attached to the frontal, it is difficult to determine from the core alone whether the horn was cervical (i.e. tips growing toward the neck), supracervical (tips curving above and behind the neck), or homonymous (right tip spiraling right, left tip spiraling left) because such morphologies are reflected usually only beyond the tip of the bony core. In archaeological specimens, which often occur detached from the frontal, the difficulties are much greater; indeed, it is probably impossible to make such a distinction.

References

Clutton-Brock, J. 1981. *Domesticated Animals from Early Times*. British Museum (Natural History), London.

Compagnoni, B. 1980. On the Probable Presence of the Urial (*Ovis vignei* Blyth) at the Protohistoric Site of Shahr–i Sokhta (Sistan, Iran). *East and West* (n.s.) 30(1-4):9-15.

Coon, C.S. 1957. *The Seven Caves*. Alfred Knopf, New York.

Coon, C.S., and E.K. Ralph. 1955. Radiocarbon Dates for Kara Kamar, Afghanistan, University of Pennsylvania II. *Science* 122:921-922.

Corbet, G.B. 1978. *The Mammals of the Palaearctic Region: A Taxonomic Review*. British Museum (Natural History) and Cornell University Press, London and Ithaca, NY.

_____ 1984. *The Mammals of the Palaearctic Region: A Taxonomic Review—Supplement*. British Museum (Natural History), London.

Davis, R.S. 1974. *The Late Paleolithic of Northern Afghanistan*. Unpublished Ph.D. dissertation, Department of Anthropology, Columbia University, New York.

_____ 1978. The Palaeolithic. In *The Archaeology of Afghanistan*, ed. F.R. Allchin and N. Hammond, pp. 37-70. Academic Press, London.

Dupree, L. 1964. Prehistoric Archeological Surveys and Excavations in Afghanistan: 1959-1960 and 1961-1963. *Science* 146:638-640.

Dupree, L. (editor). 1972. *Prehistoric Research in Afghanistan (1959-1966)*, pp. 1-84. Transactions of the American Philosophical Society (n.s.) 62(4). American Philosophical Society, Philadelphia.

Dyson, R.H., Jr. 1953. Archeology and the Domestication of Animals in the Old World. *American Anthropologist* 55:661-673.

Ellerman, J.R., and T.C.S. Morrison-Scott. 1951. *Checklist of Palaearctic and Indian Mammals 1758 to 1946*. British Museum (Natural History), London.

Flannery, K.V. 1969. The Animal Bones. In *Prehistory and Human Ecology of the Deh Luran Plain*, ed. F. Hole, K.V. Flannery, and J.A. Neely, pp. 262-330. Memoirs No. 1. Museum of Anthropology, University of Michigan, Ann Arbor.

Geist, V. 1971. *Mountain Sheep: A Study in Behavior and Evolution*. University of Chicago Press, Chicago.

Hassinger, J.D. 1973. *A Survey of the Mammals of Afghanistan Resulting from the 1965 Street Expedition (Excluding Bats)*. Fieldiana: Zoology Vol. 60. Field Museum of Natural History, Chicago.

Hatting, T. 1975. The Influence of Castration on Sheep Horns. In *Archaeozoological Studies*, ed. A.T. Clason, pp. 345-351. North-Holland/American Elsevier, Amsterdam, NY.

Hecker, H.M. 1975. *The Faunal Analysis of the Primary Food Animals from Pre-Pottery Neolithic Beidha (Jordan)*. Ph.D. dissertation, Columbia University. University Microfilms 76-12743, Ann Arbor, MI.

Heptner, V.G., A.A. Nasimovich, and A.G. Bannikov. 1988. *Mammals of the Soviet Union. Vol. I: Artiodactyla and Perissodactyla*. Amerind Publishing, New Delhi. Originally published 1961, Vysshaya Shkola Publishers, Moscow.

Kohl, P.L. 1984. *Central Asia: Palaeolithic Beginnings to the Iron Age*. Éditions Recherche sur les Civilisations, Paris.

Kullmann, E. 1965. Die Säugetiere Afghanistans (Teil I): Carnivora, Artiodactyla, Primates. *Science, Quarterly Journal of the Faculty of Science of Kabul University* (August):1-17.

Ligabue, G., and S. Salvatori. 1989. *Bactria: An Ancient Oasis Civilization from the Sands of Afghanistan*. Erizzo, Venice.

Meadow, R.H. 1981. Early Animal Domestication in South Asia: A First Report of the Faunal Remains from Mehrgarh, Pakistan. In *South Asian Archaeology 1979*, ed. H. Härtel, pp. 143-179. Dietrich Reimer Verlag, Berlin.

———— 1984. Animal Domestication in the Middle East: A View from the Eastern Margin. In *Animals and Archaeology. 3: Early Herders and Their Flocks*, ed. J. Clutton-Brock and C. Grigson, pp. 309-337. BAR International Series No. 202, Oxford.

———— 1986a. *Animal Exploitation in Prehistoric Southeastern Iran: Faunal Remains from Tepe Yahya and Tepe Gaz Tavila-R37, 5500-3000 BC*. Ph.D. dissertation. University Microfilms 87-04479, Ann Arbor, MI.

———— 1986b. Faunal Explorations in the Greater Indus Valley: A Review of Recent Work to 1980. In *Studies in the Archaeology of India and Pakistan*, ed. J. Jacobson, pp. 43-64. Oxford and IBH Publishing Co./American Institute of Indian Studies, New Delhi.

Nadler, C.F., K.V. Korobitsina, R.S. Hoffmann, and N.N. Vorontsov. 1973. Cytogenetic Differentiation, Geographic Distribution, and Domestication in Palearctic Sheep (*Ovis*). *Zeitschrift für Säugetierkunde* 38:109-125.

Perkins, D., Jr. 1959. *The Post-cranial Skeleton of the Caprinae: Comparative Anatomy and Changes under Domestication*. Unpublished Ph.D. dissertation, Department of Biology, Harvard University, Cambridge, MA.

———— 1972. The Fauna of the Aq Kupruk Caves: A Brief Note. In *Prehistoric Research in Afghanistan (1959-1966)*, ed. L. Dupree, p. 73. Transactions of the American Philosophical Society (n.s.) 62(4). American Philosophical Society, Philadelphia.

Pfeffer, P. 1967. Le mouflon de Corse (*Ovis musimon*): position systematique, écologie et éthologie comparées. *Mammalia* 31:1-262.

Poplin, F. 1979. Origine du Mouflon de Corse dans une nouvelle perspective paléontologique: par marronnage. *Annales de Génétique et de Sélection animale* 11(2):133-143.

Ranov, V.A., and R.S. Davis. 1979. Toward a New Outline of the Soviet Central Asian Paleolithic. *Current Anthropology* 20:249-270.

Reed, C.A. 1960. A Review of the Archeological Evidence on Animal Domestication in the Prehistoric Near East. In *Prehistoric Investigations in Iraqi Kurdistan*, ed. R.J. Braidwood and B. Howe, pp. 119-145. Studies in Ancient Oriental Civilization Vol. 31. University of Chicago Press, Chicago.

Roberts, T.J. 1977. *The Mammals of Pakistan*. Ernest Benn, London.

Ryder, M.L. 1983. *Sheep & Man*. Duckworth, London.

Schaller, G.B. 1977. *Mountain Monarchs: Wild Sheep and Goats of the Himalaya*. University of Chicago Press, Chicago.

Shaffer, J.G. 1978. The Later Prehistoric Periods. In *The Archaeology of Afghanistan*, ed. F.R. Allchin and N. Hammond, pp. 71-186. Academic Press, London.

Stampfli, H.R. 1983. The Fauna of Jarmo with Notes on Animal Bones from Matarrah, the 'Amuq and Karim Shahir. In *Prehistoric Archaeology along the Zagros Flanks*, ed. L.S. Braidwood, R.J. Braidwood, B. Howe, C.A. Reed, and P.J. Watson, pp. 431-483. Oriental Institute Publications Vol. 105. Oriental Institute of the University of Chicago, Chicago.

Uerpmann, H-P. 1979. *Probleme der Neolithisierung des Mittelmeerraums*. Beihefte zum Tübinger Atlas des Vorderen Orients, Reihe B (Geisteswissenschaften) Vol. 28. Dr. Ludwig Reichert Verlag, Wiesbaden.

———— 1987. *The Ancient Distribution of Ungulate Mammals in the Middle East*. Beihefte zum Tübinger Atlas des Vorderen Orients, Reihe A (Naturwissenschaften) Vol. 27. Dr. Ludwig Reichert Verlag, Wiesbaden.

Uerpmann, H.-P., and W. Frey. 1981. Die Umgebung von Gar-e Kamarband (Belt Cave) und Gar-e 'Ali Tappe (Beh-Sahr, Mazandaran, N-Iran) heute und im Spätpleistozän. In *Beiträge zur Umweltgeschichte des Vorderen Orients*, ed. W. Frey and H.-P. Uerpmann, pp. 134-190. Beihefte zum Tübinger Atlas des Vorderen Orients, Reihe A (Naturwissenschaften) Vol. 8. Dr. Ludwig Reichert, Wiesbaden.

Valdez, R. 1982. *The Wild Sheep of the World*. Wild Sheep and Goat International, Mesilla, NM.

Valdez, R., C.F. Nadler, and T.D. Bunch. 1978. Evolution of Wild Sheep in Iran. *Evolution* 32:56-72.

Vinogradov, A.V., and V.A. Ranov. 1985. Les cultures de la fin de l'Age de la Pierre entre l'Hindukush et le Pamir-Alaï. In *L'Archéologie de la Bactriane ancienne*, pp. 63-75. Éditions du Centre National de la Recherche Scientifique, Paris.

———— 1988. La périodisation de l'âge de la pierre en Bactriane ancienne. In *L'Asie centrale et ses Rapports avec les Civilisations orientales des Origines à l'Age du Fer*, pp. 49-51. Mémoires de la Mission Archéologique Française en Asie Centrale Vol. 1. Diffusion de Boccard, Paris.

Zeuner, F.E. 1955. The Goats of Early Jericho. *Palestine Exploration Quarterly* 87:70-86.

———— 1963. *A History of Domesticated Animals*. Hutchinson, London.

PALEOLITHIC FAUNAL REMAINS FROM GHAR-I-KHAR, WESTERN IRAN

Brian Hesse

The University of Alabama at Birmingham, Department of Anthropology, 338 Ullman, UAB, Birmingham, AL 35294

Dedication

Dexter Perkins, Jr. was certain that an animal bone specialist had to be in the field during the excavation of a site to make the best use of the osteological materials presented for analysis. This conviction was based on two principles: first, that archaeological contexts are best understood first-hand; second, that many important animal bone finds are not obvious to the inexperienced eye and require specialized conservation. Thus Perkins created the now familiar role of 'itinerant zooarchaeologist', one in which over a number of field seasons he visited Pleistocene and early Holocene sites from Anatolia to Afghanistan, from Iran to Nubia. This broad geographic perspective gave him unique regional insight into the question which most dominated his research—the origins of domestic animals. In the course of these travels, he made preliminary observations on faunal collections from a number of important sites. A number of these collections have been fully described, but some have not. The following brief report completes one of the projects he undertook, but was not able to finish before his untimely death.

Introduction

The consuming research interest of Dexter Perkins, Jr. and Patricia Daly, the origins of domestic animals, was perfectly timed, since the search for the origins of the Neolithic lifestyle was a central question for archaeologists in the 1950s, 1960s and 1970s. The general problem was to discover early evidence of a local sequence where pristine sedentism supported by domestic crops and flocks could be identified. This challenge generated multidisciplinary expeditions from the Sudan to Afghanistan, from Turkey to southern Iran, all searching for late Pleistocene and early Holocene sites that were part of this process. Then, even more than now, the number of specialists capable of contributing biological data and interpretations to these projects was limited. Nevertheless a rough culture history for late Pleistocene and early Holocene exploitation of plant and animal resources began to emerge. Pat and Dexter's enormous contribution to this work through their collaboration with the Soleckis in Iraq and Syria, Bordaz in Turkey, Kirkbride in Jordan, Smith in Iran, and Dupree in Afghanistan, as well as others, has already been chronicled in this volume.

Along the Zagros-Taurus-Lebanon mountain arc some form of nomadic hunting and gathering began to be replaced in the 8th or perhaps 9th millennium B.C. by village-based agriculture. Despite the fact that little was known of the subsistence strategies that characterized the ancestral, presumably foraging, cultures, a number of models quickly emerged to account for the new domestic development. For instance, Braidwood suggested that the resource richness of the 'hilly flanks' of this region provided the opportunity for experimentation with new subsistence styles (e.g. Braidwood and Howe 1962). Flannery and Hole proposed a 'Broad Spectrum Revolution' where a shift away from specialized hunting to more generalized collection set in process the development of new relationships between plants and animals and their human exploiters (Flannery 1965, 1969; Hole et al. 1969). Several authors emphasized the role of population growth on the process (Binford 1968; Cohen 1977; Smith and Young 1972), an approach that continues to be employed today (Redding 1988) despite some difficulties in showing how resource stress can be anticipated in societies of low complexity (Glassow 1978). In an earlier paper I also advocated stress, arguing that increased early Holocene environmental variability was a stimulus for innovation in subsistence technology (Hesse 1982). It is interesting to note that a difficulty with all the 'stress' approaches for the domestication revolution leads back to a re-evaluation of Braidwood's model. Cultural innovations in subsistence may be risky and have delayed payoffs. This is certainly true of the process of domesticating animals for meat. Thus, since they would have to wait for their first rewards, the innovation of pastoralism is less than an obvious choice for communities currently experiencing stress. Therefore animal husbandry is most likely to be adopted by stratified societies where either some people have the wealth to survive failure and so are tempted to invest in a new technology, or others see a ready market for the production of their new domestic ventures, commodities produced in an effort to raise their economic state (Stevenson and Hesse 1990). Ideas similar to this have been extensively elaborated in a model for food production proposed by Hayden (1990), one that emphasizes the opportunities of a rich environment.

All of these models predict changes in the early Holocene from an ancestral Pleistocene way of life. As a result, evaluation of each of them has suffered from a gap in the data base. Reports of animal bone remains from Paleolithic contexts along the Zagros mountain chain are rare despite the archaeological potential of the region (see, for example, the summary of Smith 1986). Thus we are not in a position to clarify the nature of the Pleistocene subsistence strategies which gave rise to food producing societies. Given the current political situation in Iran and Iraq and the real and potential damage to prehistoric sites in the region, even small samples, such as the one from Ghar-i-Khar in western Iran reported here, take on particular importance as we develop a picture of the area's culture history.

During a survey in 1965 conducted by P.E.L. Smith and T.C. Young, Jr. (Smith 1967; Young and Smith 1966), a sondage was excavated into Ghar-i-Khar. This cave is located in the Kuh-i-Parau, a major orographic feature that forms part of the northern margin of the Kermanshah Valley of west-cental Iran (Fig. 1). The site is close to the modern town of Bisitun and just above the deposit (Hunter's Cave) excavated by Coon (1951). The stratigraphic sequence includes the three basic Zagros Late Pleistocene techno-complexes—Mousterian, Baradostian, and Zarzian (Smith 1986:27, whose summary of Zagros prehistory structures the following discussion)—but the earliest of these levels was only touched in the trial excavations. This stratigraphic result nevertheless is important because it demonstrates a lack of a stratigraphic hiatus in the sequence. As Smith (1986:25) points out, combined with the evidence from Gar Arjeneh and Warwasi (see Fig. 1) it suggests that the Upper Paleolithic in the Zagros may trace its typological roots into the Middle Paleolithic though the alternative explanation, that similarities between the industries may be functional, linked to the technological

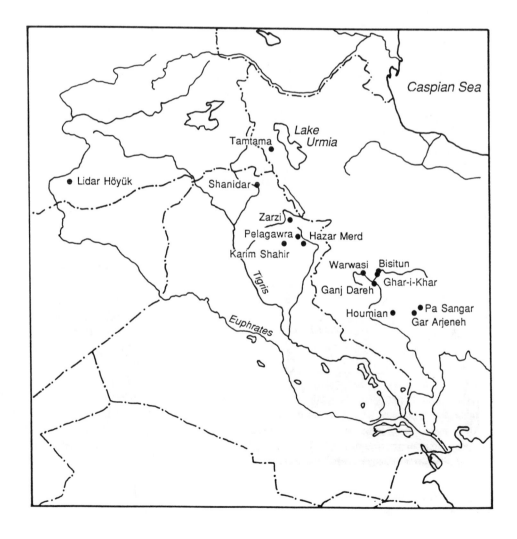

Fig. 1:
Map of archaeological sites mentioned in the text. Ghar-i-Khar is located above Hunter's Cave near the modern town of Bisitun in an escarpment of the Kuh-i-Parau, a mountain which forms part of the northern boundary of the Kermanshah Valley, one of the major east-west routes through the Zagros. Ganj Dareh is an early neolithic mound which characterizes the post Ghar-i-Khar occupation of the region. Lidar Höyük is a Bronze Age and later site from which a specimen useful for osteometric comparison is reported. The rest of the sites are late Pleistocene and early Holocene occupations of the Zagros.

necessities of adaptation to the region, cannot be excluded.

The term Baradostian was coined by R.S. Solecki on the basis of material found at Shanidar to refer to industries that may date as early as 38,000 B.C. based on a series of radiocarbon determinations. The end of the industry is less well dated though it seems to have persisted until approximately 20,000 B.C. Known from only six rockshelter and cave sites the Baradostian is a non-Levallois blade industry with numerous burins, scrapers, notched blades, and a distinctive Arjeneh point (Smith 1986:26). Hole and Flannery (1967) divide the industry into two phases, observing that implement size declines through time while microliths become more numerous. This typological process may reflect a shift toward different and broader resource selection, though there is no clear biological evidence to confirm this prediction. Hole and Flannery (1967) also suggest that the settlement system of the Baradostian included a base camp surrounded by a number of special purpose campsites.

The Zarzian is an Epipaleolithic microlithic industry that appeared in the Zagros somewhat before 13,000 B.C., perhaps after a break in the occupation of the mountain range, and persisted until about 11,000 or 10,000 B.C., based on radiocarbon dates from Palegawra and Shanidar (Smith 1986:28). Its relationship to the Baradostian is unclear because of the lack of overlap in radiocarbon determinations and the apparent stratigraphic gap, though Hole (1970) feels it is typologically descendant (Smith 1986:28). The broader distribution of sites in the Zarzian causes Smith (1986:29) to "wonder if seasonal movements were involved as the hunters followed the main game animals on their migratory cycles."

While the Baradostian and Zarzian are in very general terms comparable periods of animal exploitation, the scanty available evidence suggests that in the later period, i.e. Zarzian, the occupants of the various sites were exploiting different selections of large herbivores (see Table 4).

Specialization in the larger game species was accompanied by an intensification in the pursuit of small buffer species (Hesse 1978:chapter 3; Smith 1986:29). This subsistence system of simultaneous focus and diversity seems to have been ancestral to the first domesticating and food producing cultures in the region. It is against this pattern that the Ghar-i-Khar material is usefully evaluated.

The sample

Collection history

Dexter Perkins, Jr studied the faunal remains from this excavation in the field. After his initial examination, and in accordance with Iranian antiquities law, the collection was divided. Half remained in Iran, while the other was sent to The University of Montreal and thence to Birmingham, Alabama, where the bones are curated in the Archaeology Laboratories of the Department of Anthropology, University of Alabama at Birmingham. This division may be significant since the impression of the collection gained by Dr. Perkins during his preliminary examination of the material and mentioned to the author in the mid-1970s is not borne out by the material still available for study.[1] Specifically, and critically, the sample was said to contain abundant quantities of equid, a pattern congruent with other samples in the immediate region. For example, Coon's report (1951) of Hunter's Cave suggests that sheep or goat were absent in the Mousterian. Instead, his sample recorded a period when hunters focused equally on deer and equids. Coon's findings are paralleled in the material from the neighboring and contemporary site of Warwasi (Turnbull 1975), a rockshelter at the western end of the Kuh-i-Parau. There again equids were very common. Thus it is surprising that in the sample examined by the author and reported here only a single equid bone is present (Fig. 2). Even more remarkable, the one specimen does not appear to belong to the onager group, *Equus hemionus*, the

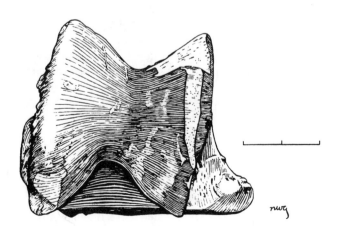

ANTERIOR ASPECT

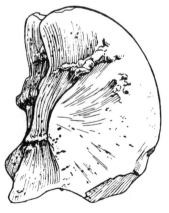

Fig. 2:
Equus ferus (Pleistocene horse) astragalus from a mixed Baradostian/ Mousterian stratum at Ghar-i-Khar. Illustration by Wade Gilbreath.

species identified by Coon and Turnbull, but, on the basis of its great size, seems to be a horse (*Equus ferus*). In addition, the Ghar-i-Khar sample contains almost no elements of the axial skeleton (ribs and vertebrae) of any species. Given the procedures that were standard in the zooarchaeology of two decades ago, this suggests strongly that the sample was presorted by Dr. Perkins. Thus, while the collection does not bear any other evidence of sampling bias affecting 'identifiable' specimens, as that term was understood twenty five years ago (it required the usual cleaning and numbering prior to study), the possibility that equid specimens were selectively culled must be considered.

Sample contexts

The collection is made up of material found in seven excavation lots sent to the author in May 1980. A total of 56 identifiable fragments are present in the surviving sample. (Table 1 outlines this distribution. Lot by lot descriptions are given in the Appendix.)

Analysis

Species present

These specimens can be assigned to the following species. Four shells of *Helix* sp. were recovered. This gastropod is a common find in Zagros archaeological sites. Two bird bones were recovered. One was a distal tibiotarsus of a large bird, perhaps heron sized, the other a humerus fragment from a small (pigeon or partridge sized) species. One mandible of a stone marten (*Martes foina*) was recovered. Of the large herd animals, three specimens of cattle (*Bos primigenius*), three of deer (almost certainly *Cervus elaphus*, see discussion of osteometry below), two of gazelle (*Gazella* sp.), five of goat (*Capra aegagrus*), and four of sheep (*Ovis orientalis*) were noted. One astragalus of an equid was recovered from the lowest layer of the deposit (see Fig. 2). While its condition does not permit measurement, it is larger than typically expected for an onager. It was offered for examination at the Equid Conference in Tübingen in 1982. There the assembled specialists concurred in its identification as *Equus ferus*. This find provides support to Uerpmann's (1987:17) assertion that the samples from Palegawra (Turnbull and Reed 1974) and Warwasi (Turnbull 1975) contain Pleistocene wild horses in addition to the reported *Equus hemionus*. The stratigraphic date of the Ghar-i-Khar specimen associates it with the period of greatest wild horse abundance following Uerpmann's (1987) re-evaluation of the data. Besides these specific identifications, 27 specimens could be assigned to either sheep or goats, one bone is assigned to the category large mammal (cattle or deer), one fragment was a medium mammal (sheep, goat, or gazelle), and the last a fragment of small mammal. These identifications can be arranged by period as in Table 2.

Table 1. Distribution of sample by excavated depth and associated archaeological materials.

Depth	Cultural Association	No. Specimens
2.80-3.00 m	Zarzian	19
3.00-3.30	Zarzian	15
3.30-3.50	Mixed Zarzian/Baradostian	7
3.50-3.70	Baradostian	7
3.70-4.00	Baradostian	6
4.00-4.30	probably Baradostian	1
4.20-4.45	probably mixed Baradostian/ Mousterian	1
	TOTAL	56

Table 2. The distribution of identified bone fragments by temporal period.

	Zarzian	Zar/Bar +	Baradostian and Earlier	= Total
Helix	2		2	2
Large Bird			1	1
Small Bird			1	1
Marten			1	1
Small Mammal			1	1
Cattle	3			
Deer	3			
Cattle/Deer	1			
Medium/Large	1			
Gazelle		1	1	2
Equid			1	1
Sheep	3	1		1
Goat	2	1	2	3
Sheep/Goat*	19 (18)	3 ◄(1)►	5	7
Medium Mammal		1		1
Total	34 (33)	7 (6.5)	15 (14.5)	21
GRAND TOTAL		56 (54)		

*Two sheep/goat specimens from the Zarzian, a naviculo-cuboid and a grand cuneiform, are clearly from the same animal. For the purposes of relative species abundance, these are considered as one fragment producing a total of 18 sheep/goat bones though there are in fact 19 bone specimens in the sample. Two fragments of the same sheep/goat distal metapodial were found in separate excavation units. The two units were assigned by the excavator to different temporal periods—mixed Zarzian/Baradostian and Baradostian, respectively. The bone join supports the linking of these two temporal/stratigraphic categories in the analysis. This decision requires a reduction in the count of sheep/goat finds by one.

Relative abundance

Considering only the larger and better identified food resources (the cattle, deer, sheep/goat, gazelle, and equid), and lumping the Zarzian/Baradostian material with the Baradostian/Mousterian assuming that taphonomic processes of redeposition and contamination are more likely to have worked earlier material into later deposits than the reverse, a pair of simple "Early" and "Late" species profiles is produced (using the number of specimens as estimator). These can be used to examine contrasts between the two main classifications of the final Iranian Pleistocene cultures. This temporal merging is well-founded because of the presence of a cross-lot join of two bone fragments linking the material in the 3.30-3.50 m sample to that found in the 3.50-3.70 m unit (Table 3).

If this tiny profile sample is a reliable measure of faunal availability, the emphasis on red deer and cattle coupled with the absence of gazelle and equids suggests the expansion of forested environment in Zarzian times.[2] However, the three bones which make up the deer sample are a fragment of proximal metatarsal, one of a distal metatarsal, and a piece of the distal end of a first phalanx. All could easily have come from the same animal though there is no way to be certain with the surviving specimens.

The most important taxa in the sample are sheep and goats. This finding may be compared to the small sample of other Zagros specimens which have been described

Table 3. Major resources profile. "Late" refers to the Zarzian sample, "Early" to the samples that contain mostly Baradostian or earlier associations. Values in percentages.

	Late	Early
Cattle	10	
Deer	10	
Cattle/Deer	3	
Total Cattle and Deer	23	
Sheep	10	7
Goat	7	21
Sheep/Goat	60	50
Total Sheep and Goat	77	79
Gazelle		14
Equid		7

(Table 4). The contrast with the immediately neighboring Bisitun (Hunter's) Cave is striking. It might be chronological, a comparison of largely Mousterian with largely upper Paleolithic materials. The Warwasi sample, however, lends no support to that suggestion. On the other hand, the Ghar-i-Khar material compares favorably to the Middle Paleolithic samples from Shanidar and Houmian, and Upper Paleolithic materials from Shanidar, Pa Sangar, and Karim Shahir.

Table 4. Proportions of resources at other Zagros Pleistocene sites, in percentages.

	S/G	Bos	Cervus	Gazelle	Equid	#	Site Reference
Middle Paleolithic							
Bisitun	0	2	43	10	45	124	Coon 1951
Tamtama	3	3	78	<1	15	179	Coon 1951
Shanidar	98	<1	<1	<1	0	1138	Evins 1982
Warwasi	23	2	8	0	67	114	Turnbull 1975
Gar Arjeneh	mostly aurochs, onager, and red deer						Hole and Flannery 1967
Hazar Merd	deer, gazelle, and goat (list order)						Bate 1930a
Houmian	mostly sheep/goat with a pig and deer and onager						Levine 1984
Upper Paleolithic							
Karim Shahir	76	5	12	7	0	163	Stampfli 1983
Palegawra	27	1	20	4	48	2312	Turnbull and Reed 1974
Warwasi							
Baradostian	5	7	0	0	88	44	Turnbull 1975
Zarzian	43	0	0	0	57	14	Turnbull 1975
Shanidar	98	0	2	0	0	???	Perkins 1964
Zarzi	gazelle and goat present						Bate 1930b
Zarzi	sheep/goat present as well as turtle, fish, and crab						Payne 1981
Gar Arjeneh	mostly aurochs, onager, and red deer						Hole and Flannery 1967
Pa Sangar	mostly goats						Hole and Flannery 1967

Table 5. Mortality based on tooth wear in sheep/goats (cf. Payne 1973).

0-3 mo.	3-6 mo.	6-12 mo.	1-2 yr.	2-3 yr.	3-4 yr.	4-6 yr.	6-8 yr.	8-10 yr.
		30%	10%	10%	10%	20%	10%	10%

Species mortality

Six mandibular tooth rows and molars from sheep and goats could be aged using the criteria of Payne (1973). Only one derives from the "Early" period and is a single lower molar from an animal that died between 6 months and 3 years. The five from the "Late" period provide slightly more information, yielding a distribution evenly spread over the various age categories save for the very young (Table 5). The thirteen long bone fragments where the state of epiphyseal fusion could be judged included no specimen from an animal less than 6-9 months of age. These data could support a late summer/fall occupation if further samples corroborate this tentative pattern. We lack sufficient information necessary to compare the Ghar-i-Khar material to Evins' (1982) proposition of Mousterian goat drives based on the Shanidar material.

Osteometry

A few specimens were measurable. One deer first phalanx has a distal breadth of 20.5 mm, while a distal metatarsal has a distal breadth of 48.7 mm and a distal depth of 32.6 mm (Table 6). In order to confirm their assignment to *Cervus elaphus*, these were compared to other finds from the region. The distal metatarsal is just smaller than the distribution of red deer metapodials from the contemporary site of Palegawra published by Turnbull and Reed (1974:124, figure 6). Since their scatterplot contains two clusters—the larger presumably metacarpals, the smaller metatarsals—the Ghar-i-Khar specimen would seem not out of bounds compared to that population.

Likewise, the first phalanx compares favorably to the range published by Kussinger (1988:143, table 52) from the Bronze Age and later site of Lidar Höyük in southeastern Turkey. Several sheep and goat specimens were measurable. Compared with criteria developed in the study of the Ganj Dareh fauna (Hesse 1978:283, figure 67), the sheep astragalus likely came from a ewe. Using Stampfli's (1983:467, table 36) criteria, the goat scapula came from a male. The sex of the others was not as determinable. The sheep/goat naviculo-cuboid is likely a male (Stampfli 1983:table 36). The gazelle first phalanx is somewhat larger than those found at Jarmo (Stampfli 1983:459, table 28).

Modifications

Five specimens, all from Zarzian contexts, were modified. Two, a sheep phalanx II and a sheep/goat mandible fragment, were burned. Also, two specimens, a sheep/goat calcaneus and a goat phalanx II, were gnawed, probably by a canid. The most interesting modified specimen is a goat left scapula. It has a notch in the center of the blade of the bone, rendering it wishbone-shaped. Since both the anterior and posterior margins of the bone are broken, it is impossible to determine how far the notch proceeds proximally into the blade of the bone. The base of the notch is approximately 54 mm from the most proximal point on the lateral margin of the glenoid fossa. The medial surfaces of both the anterior and posterior margins are highly polished. Comparable implements were found at Ganj Dareh in early Neolithic contexts.

Table 6. Measurements of Ghar-i-Khar bones. Measurement abbreviations follow von den Driesch (1976).

	Bd	Dd			
Cervus metatarsal	48.7	32.6			
Cervus phalanx I	20.5				
	GLl	GLm	DL	Bd	
Ovis astragalus	33.0	30.5		20.1	female
Ovis/Capra astragalus	24.4	23.0	12.8	15.5	young
	GLP	LG	BG	SLC	
Capra scapula	36.8	30.7	24.6	23.5	male
		GB			
Ovis/Capra naviculo-cuboid		29.1			male
	GLpe	SD			
Gazella phalanx I	(41.0)	9.5			large

Discussion and conclusions

Three significant observations can be made on the basis of this small sample. First is the unexpected recovery of the notched scapula in a pre-Neolithic context. Second is the recovery of the *Equus ferus* astragalus, a find that adds to the complexity of the Pleistocene distribution of equids in the Near East. Third is the pattern of exploitation implied by the relative frequency of the various species. The pattern of similarity to other middle and upper Paleolithic sites fits nicely into the model of game specialization based on site location hypothesized by Hole and Flannery (1967:162-165; see also Levine 1984:27). The sheep/goat focus (if the sample was not culled for equid specimens) would identify the site as a highland oriented hunting camp. Here, the inhabitants would specialize in stalking vertical migrators, species that also occupy much *smaller* home ranges than the horizontally migrating, plains dwelling herbivores such as onagers and gazelles. Even given the small size of the sample, the near absence of the 'buffer species', reported in other Zarzian contexts and so common in the early Neolithic at Ganj Dareh (chukar partridge and hare), is striking (Hesse 1978).

This sheep/goat subsistence orientation significantly affects the reconstruction of Paleolithic value and social systems. Successful long term exploitation of horizontal migrators is tied to scheduling, the tactics of making sure the hunters arrive at a strategic stand just in advance of the faster travelling herbivores. Since herds of these species may, on an annual basis, graze grasslands over a range *far larger* than any single base camp catchment, the link between hunter and hunting territory is both seasonal and geographically diffuse. There is little point in defending a hunting range from which the game has fled. On the other hand, successful long term exploitation of vertical migrators puts a premium on game management. Even given the fecundity of sheep and goats and the rapidity of their population rebound after an episode of heavy mortality (Murphy and Whitten 1976), overhunting is an ever-present danger since these species show strong attachment to their home range and there is a lag before migrants move into a depleted territory (based on the presumably comparable behavior of European and North American sheep and goats [Geist 1971; Murie 1944; Nievergelt 1966] as well as Asian species [Schaller 1977]). Since herds of the animals are resident year-round in the catchment of a base camp, even if exploitation was only carried out a few months of the year, the link between hunter and hunting territory would be non-seasonal and geographically precise—a link perhaps structured by bands of forest, a habitat sheep and goats are reluctant to exploit. One management technique might have been the restriction of competing predators, both non-human and human, in the home ranges hunted. How this would have been achieved in an increasingly seasonal environment given the need to move and exploit the ripening schedule of botanicals is not clear, although a possibility such as seasonal community fissioning could be considered. At a minimum, however, the need to be in two places at the same time would put a new strain on the social norms that structured the division and scheduling of labor in a Pleistocene migratory hunting and gathering community.

Acknowledgments

I would like to thank Prof. Philip E.L. Smith of the University of Montreal for making the Ghar-i-Khar collection available and encouraging its study. Mr. Wade Gilbreath prepared the illustration of the astragalus. I also appreciate the careful and useful anonymous review the manuscript received. Finally, the editors are to be congratulated for their friendly persistence in seeing this short note to publication.

Notes

1. This is paralleled in the experience of Stampfli (1983:451) in his restudy of the Karim Shahir material originally reported by Barth (cited by Stampfli as Braidwood 1952:26).

2. For the difficulties associated with these animal-plant correspondences, see Uerpmann (1987:71-72). Uerpmann's result is congruent with the botanical record (van Zeist and Bottema 1977; see the reconstruction in Smith 1986:figure 11).

Appendix I

Ghar-i-Khar Sample

Description of surviving sample. Measurement (in mm) abbreviations follow von den Driesch (1976). Coding of sheep/goat tooth wear follows Payne (1972).

2.80-3.00 m:

Zarzian # 2 (first bag)

   1 *Ovis/Capra* radial carpal; 1 *Helix*.

2.80-3.00 m:

Zarzian # 17 (second bag)

   1 *Bos primigenius* upper molar fragment; 1 *Bos primigenius* incisor; 1 *Cervus elaphus* distal metatarsal, mature, right, Bd=48.7, Dd=32.6; 1 *Cervus elaphus* phalanx 1, distal fragment, left, Bd=20.5; 1 *Cervus elaphus* proximal metatarsal fragment, left; 1 *Ovis orientalis* proximal radius, mature, right; 1 *Capra aegagrus* phalanx 2, mature, left, gnawed?; 1 *Capra aegagrus* scapula, mature, left, notched!, GLP=36.8, LG=30.7, BG=24.6, SLC=23.5; 1 *Ovis/Capra* naviculo-cuboid, GB=29.1, and grand cuneiform, left; 1 *Ovis/Capra* distal metacarpal, mature; 1 *Ovis/Capra* mandible fragment, right, burned black, including P4, M1, M2; 1 *Ovis/Capra* upper M1 or M2, right; 1 *Ovis/Capra* upper M1 or M2, left; 1 *Ovis/Capra* upper m1, right, worn; 1 *Ovis/Capra* incisor, right; 1 *Helix*.

3.00-3.30 m:
Zarzian # 15

1 *Bos primigenius* lower P3, unerupted; 1 *Ovis orientalis* phalanx 2, mature, left, burned; 1 *Ovis orientalis* phalanx 2, mature, right; 1 *Bos/Cervus* axis fragment; 1 *Ovis/Capra* calcaneus immature, right, gnawed; 1 *Ovis/Capra* lumbar spine; 1 *Ovis/Capra* thoracic spine; 1 *Ovis/Capra* astragalus (young), left, GLl=24.4, GLm=23.0, DL=12.8, Bd=15.5; 1 *Ovis/Capra* mandible, right, including m2, m3, M1; 1 *Ovis/Capra* mandible, left, including M1, M2; 1 *Ovis/Capra* mandible, left, including M2, M3; 1 *Ovis/Capra* lower M1 or M2 fragment; 1 *Ovis/capra* lower m2, right, very worn; 1 *Ovis/Capra* mandible fragment, dentary; 1 medium/large mammal proximal rib.

3.30-3.50 m:
Mixed Zarzian/Baradostian # 7
* joins specimen in next unit

1 *Capra aegagrus* phalanx 3, right; 1 *Ovis orientalis* astragalus, left, GLl=33.0, GLm=30.5, Bd=20.1; 1 *Gazella* sp. phalanx 1, mature, right, GLpe=(41.0), SD=9.5; 1* *Ovis/Capra* distal metapodial diaphysis, immature; 1 *Ovis/Capra* distal metacarpal, mature,

right; 1 *Ovis/Capra* mandible fragment, symphysis, left; 1 medium mammal vertebra fragment.

3.50-3.70 m:
Baradostian # 7
* joins specimen in previous unit

1 *Martes foina* right mandible; 1 *Gazella* sp. calcaneus, right, immature (both epiphysis and diaphysis present); 1 *Capra aegagrus* proximal femur epiphysis, immature; 1* *Ovis/Capra* distal metapodial diaphysis, immature; 1 *Ovis/Capra* tooth fragment; 1 small bird humerus; 1 *Helix.*

3.70-4.00 m:
Baradostian # 6

1 *Capra aegagrus* phalanx 1 epiphysis, immature; 1 *Ovis/Capra* distal tibia, mature, right; 1 *Ovis/Capra* phalanx 1, mature, left (very large); 1 *Ovis/Capra* lower M1 or M2, right; 1 small mammal long bone shaft (rabbit sized); 1 *Helix.*

4.00-4.30 m:
Probably Baradostian # 1

1 large bird distal tibiotarsus, Bd=16.9.

4.20-4.45 m:
Probably mixed Baradostian/Mousterian # 1

1 *Equus ferus* astragalus.

References

Bate, D.M.A. 1930a. *Animal Remains from the Dark Cave, Hazar Merd.* Bulletin of the American School of Prehistoric Research No. 6:38-41.

_____1930b. *Animal Remains from the Zarzi Cave.* Bulletin of the American School of Prehistoric Research No. 6:23.

Binford, L.R. 1968. Post-Pleistocene Adaptations. In *New Perspectives in Archaeology,* ed. S.R. Binford and L.R. Binford, pp. 313-341. Aldine Publishing Co., Chicago.

Braidwood, R.J. 1952. *The Near East and the Foundations for Civilization.* Condon Lectures, Oregon State System of Higher Education, Eugene, Oregon (cited by Stampfli 1983).

Braidwood, R.J. and B. Howe. 1962. Southwestern Asia Beyond the Lands of the Mediterranean Littoral. In *Courses Toward Urban Life,* ed. R.J. Braidwood and G.R. Willey, pp. 132-146. Aldine Publishing Co., Chicago.

Cohen, M.N. 1977. *The Food Crisis in Prehistory.* Yale University Press, New Haven.

Coon, C.S. 1951. *Cave Explorations in Iran, 1949.* Museum Monographs. The University Museum, University of Pennsylvania, Philadelphia.

Driesch, A. von den. 1976. *A Guide to the Measurement of Animal Bones from Archaeological Sites.* Peabody

Museum Bulletin No. 1. Harvard University, Cambridge, MA.

Evins, M.A. 1982. The Fauna fron Shanidar Cave: Mousterian Wild Goat Exploitation in Northeastern Iraq. *Paleorient* 8(1):37-58.

Flannery, K.V. 1965. The Ecology of Early Food Production in Mesopotamia. *Science* 147:1247-1256.

_____1969. Origins and Ecological Effects of Early Domestication in Iran and the Near East. In *The Domestication and Exploitation of Plants and Animals,* ed. P.J. Ucko and G.W. Dimbleby, pp. 73-100. Duckworth, London.

Geist, V. 1971. *Mountain Sheep: A Study in Behavior and Evolution.* University of Chicago Press, Chicago.

Glassow, M.A. 1978. The Concept of Carrying Capacity in the Study of Culture Process. *Advances in Archaeological Method and Theory* 1:32-48.

Hayden, B. 1990. Nimrods, Piscators, Pluckers, and Planters: The Emergence of Food Production. *Journal of Anthropological Archaeology* 9(1):31-69.

Hesse, B. 1978. *Evidence for Husbandry from the Early Neolithic Site of Ganj Dareh in Western Iran.* Ph.D. dissertation, Columbia University. University Microfilms, Ann Arbor, MI.

Hesse, B. 1982. Animal Domestication and Oscillating Climates. *Journal of Ethnobiology* 2(1):1-15.

Hole, F. 1970. The Paleolithic Culture Sequence in

Western Iran. In *Actes du VII Congrès International des Sciences Préhistoriques et Protohistoriques*, Vol. I, pp. 286-292. Prague (cited by Smith 1986).

Hole, F., and K.V. Flannery. 1967. The Prehistory of Southwestern Iran: A Preliminary Report. *Proceedings of the Prehistoric Society* (n.s.) 33:147-206.

Hole, F., K.V. Flannery, and J.A. Neely. 1969. *Prehistory and Human Ecology of the Deh Luran Plain*. Memoirs No. 1. Museum of Anthropology, University of Michigan, Ann Arbor.

Kussinger, S. 1988. *Tierknochenfunde vom Lidar Höyök in Sudostanatolien (Grabungen 1979-1986)*. Inaugural-Dissertation der Ludwig-Maximilians-Universitat, Munchen.

Levine, M. 1984. The Fauna from Houmain. In The Cambridge University Archaeological Expedition to Iran 1969, ed. R.H. Bewley, pp. 1-38. *Iran* 22.

Murie, A. 1944. *The Wolves of Mount KcKinley. Fauna of the National Parks of the United States*. Fauna Series No. 5. U.S. Government Printing Office, Washington, D.C.

Murphy, E.C., and K.R. Whitten. 1976. Dall Sheep Demography in McKinley Park and a Reevaluation of Murie's Data. *Journal of Wildlife Management* 40(4):597-609.

Nievergelt, B. 1966. *Der Alpensteinbock (*Capra ibex L.*) in Seinem Lebensraum. Mammalia Depicta*. Verlag Paul Parey, Hamburg.

Payne, S. 1973. Kill Off Patterns in Sheep and Goats: The Mandibles from Asvan Kale. *Anatolian Studies* 23:281-304.

_____ 1981. Appendix 3: The Animal Bones. In Ghanim Wahida, The Re-excavation of Zarzi, 1971. *Proceedings of the Prehistoric Society* 47:19-40.

Perkins, D., Jr. 1964. Prehistoric Fauna from Shanidar, Iraq. *Science* 144:1565-1566.

Redding, R.W. 1988. A General Explanation of Subsistence Change: From Hunting and Gathering to Food Production. *Journal of Anthropological Archaeology* 7(1):56-97.

Schaller, G. 1977. *Mountain Monarchs*. University of Chicago Press, Chicago.

Smith, P.E.L. 1967. Ghar-i-Khar and Ganj-i-Dareh. *Iran* 5:138-9.

_____ 1986. *Palaeolithic Archaeology in Iran*. American Institute of Iranian Studies Monograph No. 1. The University Museum, University of Pennsylvania, Philadephia.

Smith, P.E.L., and T.C. Young,Jr. 1972. The Evolution of Early Agriculture and Culture in Greater Mesopotamia: A Trial Model. In *Population Growth*, ed. B. Spooner, pp. 1-59. MIT Press, Cambridge, MA.

Stampfli, H.R. 1983. The Fauna of Jarmo with Notes on Animal Bones from Matarrah, the 'Amuq, and Karim Shahir. In *Prehistoric Archaeology along the Zagros Flanks*, ed. L.S. Braidwood, R.J. Braidwood, B. Howe, C.A. Reed, and P.J. Watson, pp. 431-483. Oriental Institute Publications Vol. 105, University of Chicago, Chicago.

Stevenson, T.B., and B. Hesse. 1990. 'Domestication' of Hyrax (*Procavia capensis*), in Yemen. *Journal of Ethnobiology*, in press.

Turnbull, P.F. 1975. The Mammalian Fauna of Warwasi Rock Shelter, West-central Iran. *Fieldiana Geology* 33(8):141-155.

Turnbull, P.F., and C.A. Reed. 1974. The Fauna from the Terminal Pleistocene of Palegawra Cave, a Zarzian Occupation Site in Northeastern Iraq. *Fieldiana Anthropology* 63(3):81-146.

Uerpmann, H.-P. 1987. *The Ancient Distribution of Ungulate Mammals in the Middle East*. Beihefte zum Tübinger Atlas des Vorderen Orients, Reihe A (Naturwissenschaften) Vol. 27. Dr. Ludwig Reichert Verlag, Weisbaden.

Van Zeist, W., and S. Bottema. 1977. Palynological Investigations in Western Iran. *Palaeohistoria* 19:19-85.

Young, T. C., Jr., and P.E.L. Smith. 1966. Research in the Prehistory of Central-western Iran. *Science* 153:386-391.

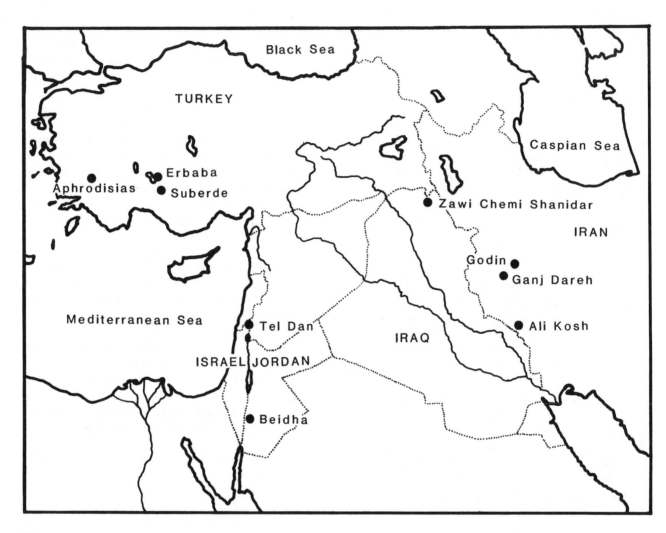

Fig. 1:
Map of the Near East showing sites mentioned in the text.

MICROSCOPIC BONE STRUCTURE IN WILD AND DOMESTIC ANIMALS:

A REAPPRAISAL

Allan S. Gilbert

Department of Sociology and Anthropology, Fordham University, Bronx, NY 10458

Introduction

In the late 1960s, Dexter Perkins, Jr. and Patricia Daly began a research collaboration with Isabella Drew at Columbia University. Their efforts culminated in the discovery of microstructural differences in the bones of wild and domestic ungulates from the late Pleistocene and early Holocene of the Near East, but preliminary publication of their findings generated controversy over the meaning of the observed phenomena. Due to the technically specialized nature of the investigation and the fact that it dealt with matters of bone growth that are still poorly understood, many cautiously pondered the methods and accepted the conclusions as intriguing possibilities. Others, however, questioned the results after attempting unsuccessfully to test them.

This paper readdresses the issue raised by Drew, Perkins, and Daly two decades ago. First, the history of their research is recounted. Second, relevant aspects of bone microstructure and the techniques (optical microscopy and X-ray diffraction) used to investigate them are explained in terms more accessible to non-specialists. Third, the evidence is reinterpreted to correct a number of inaccuracies in the original presentation. The paper concludes with discussions of the various challenges made by individuals whose experiments did not reproduce the results initially published or who posed objections on methodological grounds. Based upon current data, the summary condenses pertinent details about the extent of our knowledge of skeletal microstructure in the archaeological remains of wild and early domestic animals.

History of the research

At the time of her collaboration with Dexter Perkins and Pat Daly, Isabella M. Drew was conducting scientific analyses of ancient objects and materials at the Sackler Fund Laboratory for Archaeological Research, an installation supported by (the now late) Arthur M. Sackler and located in the basement of Low Memorial Library at Columbia University. Originally a chemist, Isabella joined the Sackler Lab in 1961 as a technical assistant to its director, William Samolin. While employed by the lab, she studied metallurgy, geology, and mineralogy at Columbia to prepare for her wide-ranging investigations into the thousands of archaeological artifacts and sediments that entered the lab for testing. Coursework evolved quickly into a degree program that culminated in a Ph.D. in geology. Her doctoral thesis (Drew 1966), produced under the guidance of Columbia mineralogist Paul F. Kerr, concerned the clays underlying Anchorage, Alaska, which, because of their instability and failure under shock, intensified the damage done by the severe earthquake of 1964. Working with surface and core samples of Anchorage area clays, Isabella established their chemical, mineralogical, and lithologic properties through optical, X-ray, granulometric, spectrographic, and other techniques, which led to an understanding of their load bearing capacity.

When William Samolin left for the University of Hartford in the fall of 1966, Isabella took over managerial functions in the Sackler Lab with the title of research associate.

After receiving his Ph.D. in zoology from Harvard University on the anatomy of sheep and goat skeletons (Perkins 1959), Dexter began his life-long commitment to the study of archaeological fauna by joining Ralph S. Solecki of Columbia and his field team in excavations at Shanidar, northern Iraq. Several years later, Solecki encouraged Dexter and Pat Daly, then a Columbia graduate student, to work with Isabella on the chemical and mineralogical examination of faunal remains and site earth from a number of Near Eastern deposits.

The problem was to find a means of distinguishing the bones of wild animals from those of the earliest domesticates, a task that was, and still can be, quite difficult (cf. Reed 1960:124; Zeuner 1963:68f.; Bökönyi 1969). Chemical analyses were prompted by Dexter and Pat's hypothesis that plants growing in different places might absorb different trace elements and thus pass diagnostic spectra into the skeletons of foraging herbivores (Daly et al. 1973). Compositional variability in fauna from different sites or burial contexts might then provide a dietary clue to the nature of the human-animal relationship.

Compositional analysis led nowhere, however. Isabella analyzed some forty samples of bone and site soil using an old spectrograph from the Manhattan Project's research of the 1940s. The machine's excellent optics allowed the quantification of nearly 60 elements. Duplicate samples were run as precision checks, but despite the careful controls, the data showed no correlations by species or site of burial. Only some groupings by skeletal part emerged that may have resulted from adsorbed impurities. The unsatisfactory results led to the abandonment of the chemical approach in favor of a structural one.

Bone sectioning

Treating the bones as fine-grained rocks, Isabella had petrographic thin sections ground from a number of samples under a grant to Ralph Solecki from the Wenner-Gren Foundation. Fred Roberts of Monterey Park, California, prepared most of the sections after vacuum impregnation with Lakeside cement to keep the fragile cancellous regions near articular ends intact during the grinding. Other sections were produced by G.S. Rév at Columbia, probably also with Lakeside consolidant. The sections were cut either sagittally or transversely through epiphyses or cross-sectionally through shafts so that crystalline and trabecular structure could be examined in coordinate planes while the shape of the specimen on the microscope slide would readily enable recognition of bone type and orientation of the section.

Samples were chosen from bones that could be identified on independent grounds as the remains of wild and domestic animals. The earliest known domesticated food animals in the Near East—sheep (*Ovis*) and goats (*Capra*)—possess skeletons that are difficult to distinguish from one another, so Dexter and Pat sampled only the most diagnostic elements from among the archaeological specimens: scapulae, distal humeri, astragali, distal metapodia, proximal first phalanges, and third phalanges. For comparability, the same bones were sectioned on cattle (*Bos*), which were domesticated at a later date.

The first bones to be sectioned came from the south central Anatolian sites of Suberde (ca. 6500 B.C.) and Erbaba (ca. 5600 B.C.). Both sites are located within the valley system of the Beyşehir-Suğla lake basins, just west of the Konya plain (see Fig. 1 for locations of sites mentioned) and were excavated by Jacques Bordaz (Bordaz 1968, 1969, 1973), then of New York University. Both faunal assemblages comprised largely sheep, goat, and cattle remains, which had been identified as wild at Suberde and domesticated at Erbaba. The comparison seemed an ideal one with which to begin.

Analysis of the Erbaba fauna was to have formed part of Pat's doctoral research. She planned to compare the Erbaba material to that already studied from Suberde (Perkins and Daly 1968), thus juxtaposing different animal exploitation strategies. Pat's death in 1977 left the work unfinished, however. The Erbaba fauna remain unpublished. Also, contention has followed the wild identification Dexter and Pat proposed for the Suberde fauna.

In addition to the Anatolian specimens—which initially included 17 sections from Suberde, 19 from Erbaba, and two from Aphrodisias in western Turkey—three bones were also sectioned from Zawi Chemi Shanidar (ca. 8900 B.C.), a Proto-Neolithic site in northeast Iraq excavated by Rose L. Solecki (1981). Dexter had analyzed some of the Zawi Chemi fauna (Perkins 1964) and had identified the sheep as domesticated but the goats as wild.

The collection of sections represented not only archaeological specimens but also slivers cut from modern skeletons kept by the Department of Mammalogy at the American Museum of Natural History in New York. The AMNH sections included mostly wild kills and zoo carcasses of ungulates, but sections were also made from the bones of five primate species. Fossil material from a mammoth and from Shanidar Cave Neanderthal III was also added eventually.

By 1972, the specimen total had expanded with the addition of camelid samples from Chilean sites of the Rio Loa (ca. 500 B.C. to A.D. 400) that had been the subject of doctoral work at Columbia by Gordon C. Pollard (1970). Bones from Neolithic Ganj Dareh Tepe (8th mill. B.C.) in western Iran (Smith 1976, 1990) and Epipaleolithic to Neolithic Beidha (10th-7th mill. B.C.) in western Jordan (Kirkbride 1966, 1968) were also sectioned. The Beidha and Ganj Dareh fauna were concurrently under study at Columbia by Howard M. Hecker and Brian C. Hesse, initial results appearing in their dissertations (Hecker 1975; Hesse 1978).

Late in 1972, a master file of punch cards was created by Brian Hesse to keep track of the collection, which by then numbered 236 slides taken from 187 discrete specimens. Lost for many years, this file turned up in 1985 in a basement storeroom of the Geology Department at Columbia and subsequently became an indispensable aid in accounting for the original slides.

Observations. As described in their publications (MASCA 1970, 1973; Drew et al. 1971a, 1971b; Daly et al. 1973; see also reports in Hicks 1971 and Anonymous 1971), the investigations revealed three main differences between archaeological specimens that had previously been identified as wild and domestic. Only the general findings are presented here. More detailed description and reinterpretation are left until the technical aspects of bone mineral crystallography have been reviewed.

1. *Articular surface.* Sections through weight-bearing epiphyses of archaeologically recovered specimens showed a birefringent layer at the articular surface in animals identified as domestic. Little or no birefringence occurred along this articular rim in specimens taken from animals identified as wild. Birefringence—about which more will be explained—is a general color effect produced under the microscope by polarizing filters.

Drew, Perkins, and Daly identified the birefringent material as hydroxyapatite, the mineral making up the inorganic part of bone tissue. Bone mineral crystallites are cryptocrystalline, however, and cannot be resolved using light microscopy. Reasoning from her geological training, Isabella assumed that tens of thousands of crystallite widths would fit within a petrographic section ground to the standard thickness of $30\,\mu$ (microns, or 10^{-4} mm). With all crystallites contiguous and aligned in the same direction, the entire $30\,\mu$ thick section would behave effectively as a single crystal, and only small self-correcting refractions would occur along the light path at consecutive crystal boundaries. If crystallites were not uniformly aligned, they could not then act as a single crystal and would not produce a uniform birefringence.

Some archaeological sections, especially from wild animals, displayed a dark, mottled, or felted coloration within the subchondral area. This condition was thought to indicate the capacity of randomly oriented crystallites to block the passage of transmitted light, producing various degrees of opacity dependent upon the blockage at any given point.

According to Drew, Perkins, and Daly, the articular surface of domestic animal epiphyses displayed birefringent rims because aligned crystallites acted as a single continuous crystal. By contrast, wild specimens exhibited either no birefringence or a darkened or "muddied" cast due to increasing randomization in crystallite orientation.

2. *Spongy bone.* At low magnification, the gross structure of spongy bone can be viewed. Cancellous texture differed appreciably in the domestic and wild specimens. First, trabecular thickness was greater in wild than in domestic animals, with average ranges reported as 0.2 to 0.4 mm in the former and 0.1 to 0.2 mm in the latter (Daly et al. 1973). Second, the intertrabecular voids appeared small and rounded in wild specimens but large and nearly rectangular in domestic ones. Third, the thicker trabeculae of the wild animals tended to form a zone of transition near the articular surface, blending gradually into the subchondral plate, which was also generally thick. In domestic specimens, a line of demarcation existed at which the thin trabeculae joined more abruptly onto an often thin subchondral plate.

3. *Shaft bone.* Cross-sections through long bone shafts showed birefringence in the circumferential layers, or lamellae, separated by thin cement-filled interlamellar spaces. Again, the color effects were attributed to the alignment of hydroxyapatite crystallites. In domestic specimens, the birefringence alternated from layer to layer. Some alternation was also observed in the shaft bone cross-sections of wild animals, but the evidence appeared to suggest that crystallites were more often vertical, i.e. parallel to the long axis of the bone.

The oriented textures apparent under the microscope were checked with X-ray diffraction. Powder samples from both wild and domestic specimens yielded essentially identical patterns, suggesting that the bone mineral remained chemically unchanged by the domestication process. Slices of bone sawed from articular surfaces and shafts were then mounted and the diffractions repeated to see if intact bone would yield exaggerated X-ray reflections as a result of an already preferred crystallite orientation. The results suggested that crystallites did have a greater tendency to align themselves in the articular surfaces of bones from domestic animals, but that shaft bone showed greater alignment in wild animals (Drew et al. 1971a:281).

Preliminary explanations. Only in 1973 was any functional explanation offered for the observed structural differences. It was hypothesized that the bone of domestic animals was

> more complexly organized than bone from wild animals, possibly as a sort of engineering response to a shortage of bone material in these animals. Since it is known that osteoporosous [sic] can occur quite quickly in an animal which is confined or disabled, the relative porosity of domestic animal bones will certainly appear at the very earliest stages of human control, perhaps linked in some way to confinement and a poorer diet than that of the wild animals (Daly et al. 1973:161).

They suggested again subsequently

> that the orientation of crystallites noted at the articular surfaces and in the shafts of the long bones developed as a response to stress in the weight-bearing bones of the bodies of domestic animals which, through lack of exercise, poor nutrition, or genetic deterioration, lacked sufficient material in their bones to form the sturdy bones characteristic of the wild animals studied (MASCA 1973:1).

Dexter and Pat anticipated from the start that behavior might be an important factor affecting skeletal structure. An already vast literature in mineralized tissue research, biomechanics, and orthopedics had linked bone shape and internal architecture with the compressional and tensional stresses of weight-bearing and habitual locomotion (e.g.

Kummer 1959; Enlow 1963; Frost 1964; and recently, Currey 1984). In addition, a piezoelectric mechanism guiding bone remodeling in the presence of strain had just been proposed by orthopedists at Columbia's own College of Physicians and Surgeons (e.g. Bassett and Becker 1962; Bassett et al. 1963). By the late 1960s, attempts had already been made to distinguish the remains of wild and domestic animals on the basis of their presumed response to weight-bearing stresses (Bökönyi et al. 1965), and anatomical structures were being used to infer secondary products exploitation of ancient cattle (Mateescu 1975).

Dexter and Pat summarized their discussion of causes by listing five factors that seemed to affect the microstructural characteristics of bone as it is viewed under polarized light (MASCA 1973):

1. The wild or domestic state of the animal;
2. The species in question (pigs appeared to differ from caprines in the way bones reacted to the domestication process, whatever it was);
3. Maturity of the specimen (unfused bones often mimicked the domestic pattern regardless of origin);
4. Anatomical locus and biomechanical stress (weight-bearing articular surfaces of lower limbs showed the effects most clearly);
5. Conditions of burial and diagenesis (soil characteristics possibly affecting a bone's organic content).

The end of research. Financial support for the Sackler Lab ceased in 1972, and although Isabella later completed a study (Pollard and Drew 1975) of the Chilean camelids with Gordon Pollard, then of SUNY-Plattsburgh, her departure from Columbia effectively ended the prospects for continued research on the matter with Dexter and Pat. Illness and Pat's death slowed Dexter down considerably in the late 1970s. He continued to think about faunal quantification, and one of his last papers on the subject was a collaboration with the writer (Gilbert et al. 1981). His death in the spring of 1983 came as he was beginning new research on the animals in Egyptian art. Though attributed to no specific cause, Dexter's symptoms were similar to those reported for RVF, or Rift Valley Fever, outbreaks of which had occurred in parts of Africa prior to his visit to the Nile valley in 1982.

There were nevertheless additions to the collection after 1972. For a short time in 1973-74, Sydne B. Marshall and Joan H. Geismar, as graduate students in anthropology at Columbia, began a study of Ica Nazca camelids from the excavated collections of William Duncan Strong. A few sections were prepared, but no conclusions were drawn due to lack of technical support. In 1975, Brian Hesse and Paula C. Wapnish sectioned ungulate bones from Tel Dan in Israel, and in 1982, the writer and Brian Hesse sectioned equid remains from the Iranian sites of Ali Kosh and Godin

Tepe. At present, 237 slides remain in the collection from the total 299 sections made.

I began graduate studies in archaeology at Columbia in 1970, just as the skeletal microstructure research was appearing in print. Contact with the Sackler Lab aroused an interest in materials analysis and, by the fall of 1972, led to coursework in mineralogy under geologist Ralph J. Holmes, who had succeeded Paul Kerr upon his retirement in 1965. Throughout the 1970s, the influence of the domestication process on bone microstructure remained a topic of interest to me, and discussions with Ralph Holmes prior to his death in 1977 helped to focus technical aspects of the issue, ultimately preparing the way for the present reappraisal.

Readers with basic knowledge of bone histology and the analytic techniques of optical mineralogy and X-ray diffractometry may skip the following section on methodology and proceed directly to my reinterpretation.

Methodology

As Drew, Perkins, and Daly described them, microstructural differences in the wild and domestic bone specimens they analyzed involved changes in the patterns of (1) birefringence at articular and diaphyseal locations and (2) trabecular morphology in weight-bearing epiphyseal areas. Comprehensive technical knowledge is not required to see this, but an understanding of bone crystallography and the relevant analytic methods is necessary before one can begin to explain the phenomena. Other issues concerning how bones acquire their internal structures lie near—or beyond—the frontier of our present knowledge of ossification, remodeling, and bone chemistry. Some of the effects seem to be post-depositional in origin and are thus probably unrelated to bone growth or functional adaptation. Although enough is known at this time to propose hypotheses about how ancient activity levels affect bones biomechanically, specific prehistoric behaviors cannot yet be offered to account for the evidence.

Owing to the complexity of the problem and its interpretation, it is unfortunate that previous papers dealing with the microstructural issue have tended to omit essential background documentation. In some articles, such details would have been out of place, but their complete absence has been to the great disadvantage of those unfamiliar with the methods of petrography and diffractometry. Use of terms has also varied from paper to paper, obscuring meaning in some cases. The present contribution introduces more of the technical detail in order to include nonspecialists in the exploratory process. With no discussion of the principles, methods, and findings using commonly accepted terminology, most archaeologists are left with no means to follow the arguments.

Relevant background information is provided in two parts: (1) bone crystallography and (2) mineral optics and diffractometry. Complicated aspects have been simplified, and only the essential concepts and relationships are discussed.

Bone crystallography

Bone is a composite substance with three main components: organic fibrous bundles, inorganic crystals, and cement (Pritchard 1972a). The cement is largely a mucopolysaccharide and represents only a very small percentage of the dry weight of mature bone, but it is intimately associated with the first two components, which it binds together.

The organic matrix. The organic bundles are groups of fibrils representing parallel molecules of the protein collagen. Making up about one-third of the bone by dry weight, the organic matrix contains the greatest part of a bone's constituent water, which is usually about 20% of fresh weight (Eastoe 1956:82-83). The strands are resolvable under the electron microscope, appearing as very long bundles ranging up to 1500 nm (nanometers, or 10^{-7} mm) in diameter that vary in their thickness, grouping, and orientation depending on the species, age of the individual, and tissue location. Eleven types of collagen (I-XI) are presently recognized (Miller 1985); types II and IX are major constituents of cartilage (Mayne and Irwin 1986; Shimokomaki et al. 1990).

Collagen formation follows a sequence: construction of procollagen molecules within cells, and assembly of collagen molecules from the procollagen, thought to be an extracellular process. The collagen macromolecules (tropocollagen) consist of three helically twisted polypeptide chains wrapped around the tropocollagen axis and held together by chemical bonds. The tropocollagen macromolecules, ca. 2800 Å long and 14 Å wide (Ångstroms, or 10^{-8} mm), then aggregate into fibrils (Trelstad et al. 1976) showing a characteristic banding every 640 Å along the fibril axis (Hodge 1967; Herring 1972).

The inorganic hydroxyapatite phase. The inorganic material makes up most of the remaining two-thirds of the dry weight of bone. X-ray examinations first suggested that these submicroscopic crystallites were acicular, i.e. long and narrow in the shape of a needle (reviewed in Carlström and Engström 1956), but early application of thin section techniques under the electron microscope, as well as radiography of fragmented and blended samples, showed them to be largely tabular or book-like, ca. 350-400 Å on a side and 50-75 Å thick (Robinson and Watson 1952; Robinson 1952). More recent investigations have made it clear that the crystallites are elongated and flattened (Bocciarelli 1970; Posner 1987:88).

Investigations by W.J. Schmidt in 1923 suggested that crystallite growth is guided by collagen fibers. Although the mechanisms by which collagen bundles are calcified are still poorly known, preferential alignment of the crystallites' long dimension parallel to the direction of the bundles was demonstrated by Robinson (1952).

The chemical composition of the crystals is complex, resembling most closely the calcium phosphate mineral apatite. Outside of biological systems, apatite is a frequent accessory mineral appearing well-crystallized in most igneous and many metamorphic rocks, as well as limestones (Berry and Mason 1959: 453ff.; Deer et al. 1962:323-338). It is commonly mined for fertilizer from larger sedimentary deposits, in which it occurs as a massive aggregate of tiny crystals formed from the diagenesis of phosphate-rich organic materials, such as those containing marine organisms or guano. Because apatite chemistry allows an appreciable degree of element substitution, the formula is generalized: $Ca_{10}(PO_4)_6(F,OH,Cl)_2$. A complete solid solution exists in which differing mixtures of F, OH, and Cl are possible. Endmembers representing nearly pure fluor-, hydroxy-, and chlor-isomorphs are also known. Because it is the least soluble and most stable isomorph, fluorapatite is the most familiar.

The inorganic component of biological exoskeletons is usually composed of carbonates or silicates, but endoskeletons are apatitic. The structure of bone mineral comes closest to that of the hydroxyapatite isomorph (De Jong 1926; Beevers and McIntyre 1946), but the ossification process creates an inexact version that has long been recognized as internally variable (cf. Dallemagne 1964; Eanes and Posner 1970).

Some apatites incorporate 1-5% carbonate. The minerals francolite and dahllite are naturally-occurring carbonate varieties. Francolite, named after the type locality at Wheal Franco in Devonshire, is usually designated as a carbonate-bearing fluorapatite, and dahllite, named after the Norwegian geologists T. and J. Dahll, is properly a carbonate-bearing hydroxyapatite (Deer et al. 1962:326). Carbonates can be present in apatites not only as substitutions within the crystal, but also as adsorbed ions or secondarily precipitated calcite or aragonite (both $CaCO_3$). A structural determination is usually necessary before a mineral can be accepted as a true carbonate-apatite.

Carbonates (CO_3^{2-}) are an important constituent of bone mineral as well but vary in both quantity and site of attachment to the hydroxyapatite structure (LeGeros et al. 1968; Vignoles et al. 1988). At low concentrations, carbonates tend to replace hydroxyls. With increasing weight percent of carbonate, there is increased structural strain as carbonate radicals begin to fill sites normally occupied by phosphates (Posner 1987:72). Bone mineral usually contains between 3-4 weight % of carbonate, most of which exists at the expense of phosphate. Electrostatic charge imbalance resulting from the substitution of CO_3^{2-} for PO_4^{3-} is balanced by some loss of OH^- and addition of hydrogen (H^+) bond linkages between some of the phosphate oxygens (Posner 1987:91). Most recent research suggests that, in comparison to pure hydroxyapatite, bone mineral is

> a calcium- and hydroxyl-deficient, hydrogen- and carbonate-containing analogue of hydroxyapatite characterized by structural imperfection and a high surface area (Posner 1987:91).

It is the atomic misalignment caused in part by ionic substitution, acting together with the very small size and large surface area of the crystallites, that accounts for the highly reactive properties of bone mineral. Chemical bonds can easily be forged and broken during bone formation and resorption as well as during the release of calcium and phosphate ions to other metabolic processes (Posner 1987:93). In addition, the principle of fluorine dating rests upon that inherent instability of hydroxyapatite. In burial contexts, bone mineral has a greater affinity over time for the F^- ion, which creates less distortion in the crystal than does the larger OH^- radical.

Because bone mineral crystals are very small, their crystal forms have been difficult to study. In rocks, individual growths of apatite are usually larger, and as a result, their general development, or *habit,* is more readily observed. Apatite usually exhibits a crystal habit of regular hexagonal prisms capped at both ends either by six-sided pyramids (dipyramids) or by flat surfaces (pinacoids). Fig. 2a shows the most common forms with their principal faces and crystallographic axes. Minerals of the *6m*, or hexagonal dipyramidal, class in which apatites crystallize have a single axis (designated the c axis) perpendicular to three other axes (designated a_1, a_2, and a_3) that lie in a single plane. The origin for all four axes lies within the crystal. The three a axes diverge from each other at angles of 120°, and each possesses both a positive and negative direction with reference to the origin.

The significance of the crystal faces and axes is the information they reveal about the crystal lattice—the planes of atomic alignment within the mineral. Ultimately, it is the behavior of light and X rays that are refracted and reflected by these planes of varying atomic density that makes petrography and diffractometry useful.

Crystal faces are numbered according to where they intercept the different axes. The numbers themselves (normally termed Miller indices, but in the case of hexagonal minerals with four coordinate axes, more appropriately called Bravais indices) are integers proportional to the distance along each crystallographic axis from the origin to the point of intersection with a crystal face. The indices for a crystal face (Fig. 2b) are given as a list of intercepts for each axis, in order, within parentheses: (a_1, a_2, a_3, c). Prismatic faces designated *m* may thus be assigned the indices $(10\bar{1}0)$, $(\bar{1}010)$, $(1\bar{1}00)$, $(\bar{1}100)$, $(01\bar{1}0)$, and $(0\bar{1}10)$, with intercepts in the negative direction of an axis indicated by a bar. All *m* faces are essentially the same in an apatite prism, and because orientation of the axes is relative, they are usually referred to simply as $(10\bar{1}0)$. The pinacoid c is always (0001), and the dipyramidal face *x* is usually $(10\bar{1}1)$. Crystal face indices, in effect, represent a set of parallel lattice planes running through the mineral and are frequently used to refer to any such plane, regardless of crystal thickness.

In contrast to the usually prismatic forms of apatite in rocks, hydroxyapatite crystallites in bone can be platey (Posner 1985) with flattening on opposing prism faces (Fig. 2c). Although its internal structure remains reasonably similar to geological dahllite, the different habit of bone mineral may relate to the chemical milieu in which the crystallites grow (Aaron S. Posner, pers. comm.).

Mineral optics and diffractometry

The behavior of light and X rays when they pass through a material provides the basis for petrography and diffractometry. A thorough treatment appears in one of many standard texts in optical mineralogy (e.g. Phillips 1971; Kerr 1977; Shelley 1985) or X-ray diffraction (e.g. Azároff and Buerger 1958; Carpenter 1966; Azároff 1968), but the main ideas, as they apply to common crystalline materials, are summarized here.

Light and polarization. Light is the visible part of the electromagnetic spectrum, having wavelengths (λ) between about .4 μ (at its violet end) and .7 μ (at its red end). Light waves possess both a direction of propagation and a plane within which the waves vibrate in sinusoidal fashion. White light usually represents a mixture of many wavelengths, and monochromatic light technically contains only one wavelength.

Normally, light vibrates in many different planes radial to the direction of propagation (Fig. 3a). Mineral microscopy employs plane polarized light, that is, light vibrating in one plane only (Fig. 3b). A polarizing filter below the stage of a petrographic microscope allows only one vibration direction (usually parallel to the north-south cross-hairs of the ocular) to pass through. The velocity and polarization of this plane polarized light are then variously affected by the crystal lattice of a non-opaque mineral placed in its path on the microscope stage. A mineral to be examined is either cut and ground to 30 μ thickness and mounted on a glass slide as a thin section, or it is crushed into particles of about 100-120 mesh and immersed in optical liquids under a cover glass. When the incident ray of polarized light enters the crystal, the light is slowed in inverse proportion to the *index of refraction* (n) of the mineral, and its polarization direction is either modified or left unchanged. When the ray emerges from the mineral, it resumes its velocity in air, but a second polarizing filter

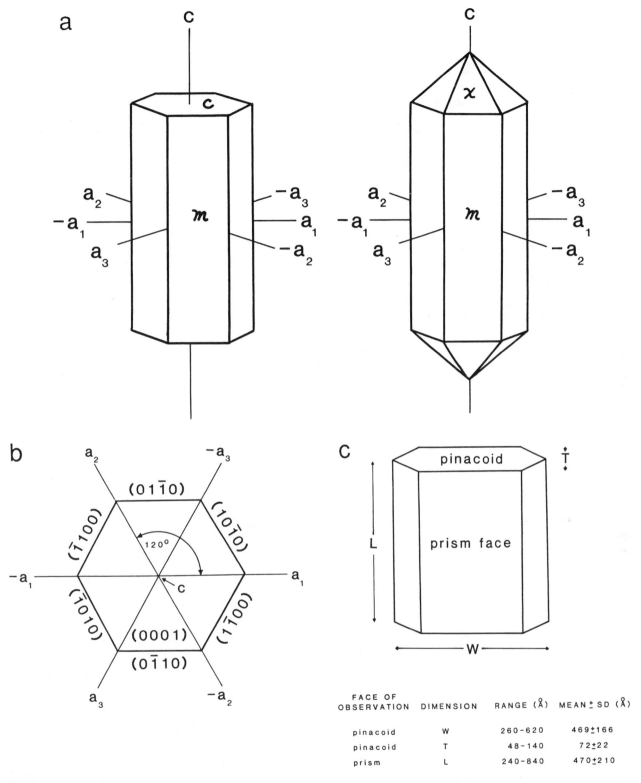

FACE OF OBSERVATION	DIMENSION	RANGE (Å)	MEAN ± SD (Å)
pinacoid	W	260-620	469±166
pinacoid	T	48-140	72±22
prism	L	240-840	470±210

Fig. 2:
a. Common habits of apatite crystals showing hexagonal prism surfaces, *m,* terminated with both pinacoidal, *c,* and dipyramidal, *x,* faces; three a axes and one c axis pass through the crystal's origin; redrawn with modifications from Berry and Mason (1959:figure 142). *b.* View along the c axis of an apatite crystal cross-section showing divergence of the a axes and Bravais indices for prismatic and pinacoidal faces. *c.* Schematic rendering of a bone crystallite showing presumed platey habit and crystal dimensions of length (L), width (W), and thickness (T); redrawn from Cuisinier et al. (1987:figure 2 and table 2).

53

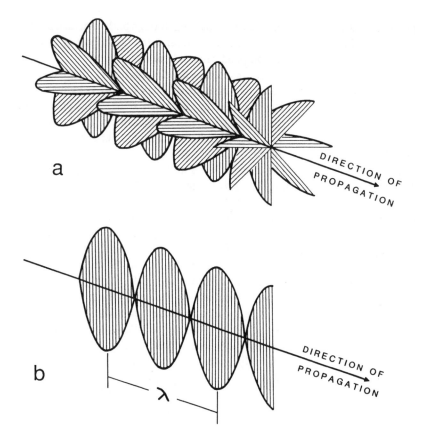

a

b

Fig. 3:
a. Ordinary monochromatic light of wavelength λ vibrating within many planes radial to the direction of propagation. *b*. Monochromatic light of wavelength λ plane polarized by a polarizing filter resulting in light vibrating within only one plane.

called the analyzer—oriented at right angles to the lower polarizer—eliminates all rays vibrating in a north-south direction. Thus, minerals between crossed polarizers (often called crossed nicols) appear dark if they do not somehow twist the polarization of the incident light out of its north-south orientation into some other plane that can pass through the analyzer.

Anisotropy. Apatites are anisotropic minerals, which means that transmitted light will be affected differently depending upon the angle it makes with the internal atomic planes of a crystal. A ray of polarized light traveling through the crystal along its c axis will be slowed by the density of the mineral but will not otherwise be affected by the crystal lattice. A mineral thin section cut perpendicular to the c axis would therefore appear completely black between crossed nicols because all north-south vibrating light emerging from the polarizer would pass through it undisturbed only to be canceled by the analyzer.

The c axis of a hexagonal mineral is termed the *optic axis*, and all anisotropic minerals with an optic axis at right angles to all other crystallographic axes are referred to as *uniaxial*. A ray of polarized light transmitted along the c axis is called an *ordinary* ray (abbreviated ω), and its retardation in velocity is related to n_ω, which is the index of refraction of the c axis direction.

A ray of polarized light transmitted through the crystal

in a direction other than along the c axis will not only be slowed but also refracted into two rays each polarized in mutually perpendicular planes of vibration. The phenomenon is termed double refraction. One ray behaves as an ordinary ray, moving through the crystal at the ordinary ray velocity (inversely proportional to n_ω), but with its plane of polarization normal to the optic axis. The other ray behaves extraordinarily, and thus it is termed the *extraordinary* ray (abbreviated ε). The extraordinary ray is polarized normal to the ordinary ray (i.e. parallel to the optic axis), but it moves either faster or slower, depending upon the mineral.

In dahllite, for example, n_ε (= ca. 1.622) is lower than n_ω (= ca. 1.629), and as a result, ε moves faster than ω. Hexagonal crystals like apatite, in which the extraordinary ray ε travels faster than the ordinary ray ω, are called *uniaxial negative*—that is, their *optic sign* is negative. Hexagonal minerals like quartz, with their ray velocities reversed are described as *uniaxial positive*—that is, their *optic sign* is positive. These characteristics can be visualized by imagining a light source sending rays outward in all directions from the center of a uniaxial crystal. Two surfaces would emerge at the leading edge of the advancing light due to the double refraction. In a uniaxial negative mineral such as apatite (Fig. 4a), the ordinary rays (ω) would take the form of a sphere, but the extraordinary rays (ε) would outdistance the ordinary rays in the a axis directions, forming a more oblate spheroid. Vibration

54

planes for the two rays would be mutually perpendicular, with ω vibrating normal to the plane of the c axis and ε vibrating parallel to it. A uniaxial positive mineral such as quartz (Fig. 4b) would maintain the same vibration planes for the two rays but reverse the ray velocities, producing with ε a prolate spheroid nestled within the sphere generated by the faster ω.

As an ordinary ray moving along the optic axis of an apatite crystal is shifted so that its orientation to the crystal lattice changes, it splits into ω and ε rays. The velocity of ω remains constant, but as the direction of light transmission approaches 90° to the optic axis, the faster ε approaches its maximum velocity. Thus, the greatest difference in velocity between ω and ε is obtained when light is transmitted normal to the c axis (i.e. the c axis lies flat upon the microscope stage).

The refraction and differential retardation of the incident light occurs because the bonding forces between ions in the mineral are not uniform in all directions:

1. Light passes through apatite and quartz at ordinary ray velocities when transmitted parallel to the c axis; its north-south polarization remains unaltered by the crystal structure of both minerals.
2. As the angle of incident light diverges from 0° and approaches 90° to c, the planes of lattice atoms repo-

larize the light passing through both minerals, producing in each case two refracted rays vibrating in mutually perpendicular directions.
3. The refracted ray vibrating normal to the plane of the c axis moves at the ordinary (ω) ray velocity.
4. The refracted ray vibrating parallel to the plane of the c axis moves at the extraordinary (ε) ray velocity, which is faster than ω in apatite but slower than ω in quartz.

The changes in vibration direction undergone by light passing through an apatite crystal between crossed nicols are illustrated in Fig. 5.

If a uniaxial crystal in any non-vertical orientation is rotated 360° on a microscope stage between crossed nicols, it will go dark four times at 90° intervals. This *extinction* occurs because the incident light, which is north-south polarized, will coincide with the ordinary ray vibration direction (normal to c) or the extraordinary ray vibration direction (parallel to c) four times during every stage rotation. Such a coincidence allows the ray from the polarizer to pass through the crystal unrefracted so that it is ultimately canceled by the analyzer. The extinction intervals thus reiterate the internal organization of the crystal lattice, indicating when its ω and ε vibration directions are aligned with the polarizer.

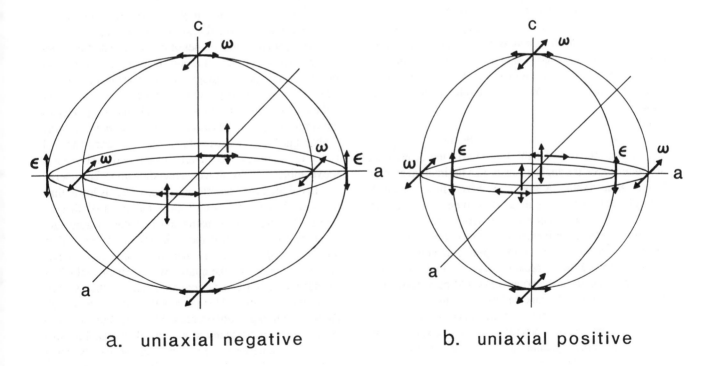

a. uniaxial negative   b. uniaxial positive

Fig. 4:
Uniaxial ray-velocity surfaces produced by light emerging from the center of a crystal, showing the different velocities of ordinary (ω) and extraordinary (ε) rays and their planes of vibration relative to crystallographic axes c and a; redrawn from Phillips (1971:figure 53). *a.* Uniaxial negative mineral (apatite). *b.* Uniaxial positive mineral (quartz).

Birefringence. The difference between n_ω and n_ε is termed birefringence (δ), a measure that relates specifically to the amount of retardation (Δ) between the ordinary and extraordinary rays. The degree to which one ray lags behind the other is an important quantity in mineral optics, for it is the characteristic that accounts for most of the color shown by transparent minerals under the polarizing microscope.

Light waves traveling in the same direction and polarized in the same plane interfere. The microscope creates this interference with the analyzer by canceling all north-south vibrating rays and passing only the east-west component of all others through its east-west vibration plane. The ordinary ray lags behind the extraordinary ray in an optically negative mineral, so that when the two rays are finally "squeezed" back into the same vibration plane by the analyzer, they are superimposed. Waves of each ray will add (intensify) in amplitude if two peaks coincide but will subtract (cancel out) if a peak coincides with a trough.

The degree to which ω lags behind ε will determine to what extent the two rays are out of phase. The retardation (Δ), or lag spacing, is measured directly in millimicrons ($m\mu$) representing fractions of a wavelength. Low birefringence results if indices of refraction for ω and ε are numerically close, which is a consequence of all internal lattice planes within the mineral being fairly similar in optical density. Apatites possess low birefringence (δ = .003-.009; Δ = 150-250 $m\mu$), but the carbonate-containing varieties exhibit the highest levels within that range. High birefringence results if indices of refraction for ω and ε are numerically far apart, an indication that substantially different optical densities characterize the various lattice planes. Calcite has one of the highest birefringences for a common mineral:

$$\delta = n_\omega - n_\varepsilon = 1.658 - 1.486 = .172$$

The color effect produced by birefringence is a series of rainbow hues, illustrated in most optical mineralogy texts as the Chart of Interference Colors. The amount of birefringence determines the range of colors a mineral will show between crossed nicols. With all light stopped by the analyzer, the field of view is black, and birefringence is zero. If a mineral with a low birefringence of .001 is ground to the standard 30 μ thickness, it becomes grayish white. "Low order white" is characteristic of minerals possessing birefringences between .003 and .009 (= retardations of 150-250 $m\mu$), after which the interference colors pass through straw yellow and orange, and, by about .017 (or 550 $m\mu$), red, to complete the first order. Second order colors are violet, blue, green, yellow, orange, and red, ranging from about .018 to .040 in birefringence. Third and fourth order colors are mostly pinks and greens (δ = .040 - .100), and beyond this, most minerals show extreme birefringence, displaying a glittery "high order white" that is not easily confused with the lower order colors.

When light is transmitted along the c optic axis of an apatite crystal, the analyzer cancels all rays that pass through the mineral. The eye sees total black within the crystal borders. As such a crystal is rotated away from the vertical so that light is transmitted at some angle to c, the blackness begins to lighten until it reaches maximum interference color when the light is transmitted normal to c (i.e. at the orientation in which maximum retardation occurs between the slow ordinary ray and the fast extraordinary ray). Maximum interference color for apatites is only first order white, so that between crossed nicols, the mineral displays a very limited palette of black, gray, and white. Quartz also possesses low birefringence (δ = .009), yielding a maximum interference color of first order white near the transition to straw yellow.

When detailed mineralogical work is done with low birefringent crystals, the color effect is often modified with the use of accessory plates of gypsum, mica, or quartz. Each plate serves a specific purpose, but they each act to vary the birefringence by introducing additional retardation into the light path. The gypsum plate alone is of concern here. This piece of clear, optical gypsum (or quartz) is often used to determine c axis orientation of a crystal. It is inserted into the light path with its c axis horizontal and oriented northeast-southwest, usually just below the analyzer. The birefringence of the gypsum (δ = .009) is low, but the piece is cut to approximately double thickness, thus creating twice the retardation and producing a full field interference color of first order red (Δ = 550 $m\mu$). The red is closer to magenta and is sometimes referred to as "sensitive violet." The gypsum plate is also known as a full wave or sensitive tint plate.

Gypsum is an optically positive mineral. Unlike apatite, its extraordinary ray (vibrating parallel to the c axis) is slower than its ordinary ray. With its c axis oriented northeast-southwest, its slow ray therefore must also vibrate northeast-southwest. When the birefringence of apatite, or any other crystal, is superimposed on the birefringence already produced by the gypsum, the effect varies depending upon how the apatite is oriented (Fig. 6a). If the slow ray of the apatite (= the ordinary ray vibrating normal to c) is aligned northeast-southwest in line with the slow ray of the gypsum, the interference colors add. If the apatite c axis is horizontal, the apatite's white (Δ = 150 $m\mu$) is added to the gypsum's magenta (Δ = 550 $m\mu$) producing the new color of second order blue (Δ = 700 $m\mu$). If the fast ray of the apatite (= the extraordinary ray vibrating parallel to c) is aligned northeast-southwest with the slow ray of the gypsum, the interference colors subtract. The apatite's white is subtracted from the gypsum's magenta, producing first order yellow (Δ = 400 $m\mu$).

An optically positive quartz crystal would show the opposite interference colors (Fig. 6b).

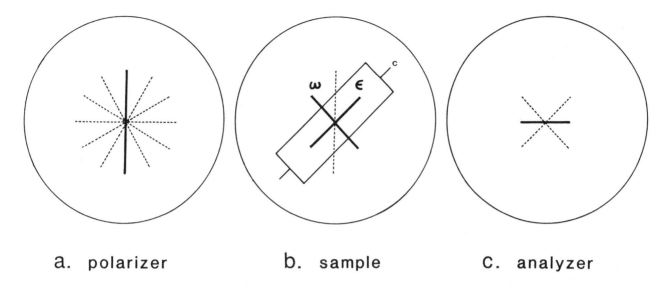

a. polarizer   b. sample   c. analyzer

Fig. 5:
Vibration direction changes in light passing through an apatite crystal between crossed nicols; apatite c axis is horizontal and oriented to produce maximum retardation; dotted lines indicate vibration directions entering filter or crystal, and solid lines indicate emergent vibration directions. *a.* Radially oriented vibration planes enter the polarizer; only the north-south plane passes through. *b.* Apatite crystal double refracts the north-south vibrating light into mutually perpendicular ordinary (ω) and extraordinary (ε) rays, with the former lagging behind the latter. *c.* Components of ω and ε are passed through the analyzer; both emerge in the east-west vibration plane and, as a result, produce optical interference.

Fig. 6:
Interference color change in oriented crystals of apatite and quartz (c axis horizontal in both) seen through a full-wave gypsum plate; gypsum produces a magenta (M) background. *a.* Length-fast, optically negative crystals of apatite are yellow (Y) when parallel to the slow ray of the gypsum and blue (B) when perpendicular. *b.* Length-slow, optically positive crystals of quartz are blue (B) when parallel to the slow ray of the gypsum and yellow (Y) when perpendicular.

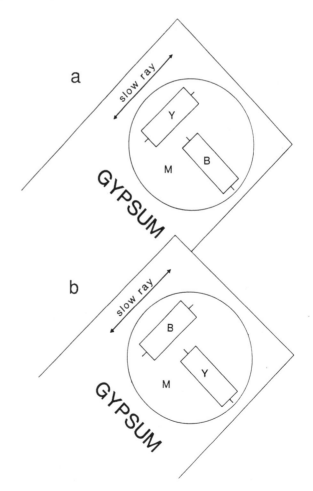

The gypsum plate also helps to establish a crystal's *sign of elongation.* Because apatite found in rocks usually occurs in a prismatic crystal habit, and because its faster extraordinary ray vibrates parallel to the c axis direction of crystal elongation, apatite crystals are said to be *length-fast*; this is the same as saying they show *negative elongation*. A prismatic uniaxial positive crystal of quartz would be termed *length-slow* or would show *positive elongation* because the extraordinary ray would be the slower ray (see again Fig. 6a, b). In this way, a length-fast prism of apatite would become yellow if its c axis of elongation was oriented northeast-southwest, or parallel to the gypsum's slow ray. Conversely, the apatite prism would become blue if its c axis was oriented northwest-southeast, or normal to the gypsum's slow ray.

X rays and diffraction. X rays are electromagnetic radiation with wavelengths in the range of .01 to 300 Å, much smaller than those of visible light. Because their wavelengths are comparable to the common interatomic distances in crystals, X rays can penetrate into solids, thereby providing a means of determining the internal structure of crystalline materials.

A crystal can be used as a diffraction grating to disperse incoming X rays into a pattern based on the planar spacing of the constituent atoms of that solid. The characteristic scattering of X rays can be recorded on photographic film and studied to reveal the internal atomic arrangement that produced the dispersion, but the single crystal method can be an exacting procedure.

Powder diffractometry is less difficult and better suited to simple chemical identification. It involves the recording of X-ray reflections off the planes of atoms in a crystal lattice. The principle is illustrated in Fig. 7.

A fraction of an X-ray beam penetrating a crystal reflects off the atomic planes in that crystal, the strength of the reflection being proportional to the density of atoms in the plane. Lattices consist of many stacked planes, and so reflections from the same incoming X-ray beam will be repeated with each successive plane (plane 1, plane 2, plane 3, ... plane n). If the reflections are out of phase with one another, i.e. if they do not move along with wave peaks and troughs in synchrony, then emergent reflections are canceled out by the ones that follow. A reflection survives only when Bragg's Law is satisfied:

$$n\lambda = 2d \sin\Theta,$$

where
- n = a whole integer
- λ = wavelength (in Å) of incident X-ray beam
- d = interplanar spacing (in Å)
- Θ = angle between incident X-ray beam and atomic plane

The equation says that a reflection will successfully leave the crystal only when an angle Θ of incidence is obtained that produces a whole number n of retarded wavelengths between it and the next planar reflection. As Fig. 7 shows, the d spacing must be such that the time taken for the continuing X-ray beam to travel the distance to the next atomic plane must result in a second reflection whose waves are in phase with the first reflection.

When a crystalline sample is ground to a fine powder, it is effectively turned into an aggregate of tiny particles whose atomic planes are randomly oriented with respect to the atomic planes of other particles. Such a powder sample can be mounted on a glass slide or compressed into a pellet for X-ray analysis. When X rays strike the powder, they encounter virtually all possible lattice orientations and therefore produce virtually all possible angles of incidence with atomic planes. As a detector is moved about the sample, it picks up X-ray reflections from different incident angles, and in so doing, it will sweep through certain Θs at which the d spacing between the most densely occupied atomic planes will allow X-ray reflections to emerge. The reflections are captured directly on photographic film, or they are converted to electrical impulses and transmitted to a pen plotter that records the peaks and troughs of reflection as a function of intensity and incident angle. The powder patterns can then be compared to standards in order to identify the sample's mineral constituents on the basis of (1) the number of strong reflections—i.e. the number of densely packed atomic planes, and (2) the characteristic Θs—i.e. the characteristic d spacings between densely occupied atomic planes.

Reinterpretation of the evidence

With relevant technical matters explained, the observations of Drew, Perkins, and Daly regarding skeletal microstructure may be reconsidered. Two kinds of evidence were used by them to discriminate between bone from wild and domestic animals: patterns of birefringence and trabecular morphology. The first step is to explain the phenomena that were observed.

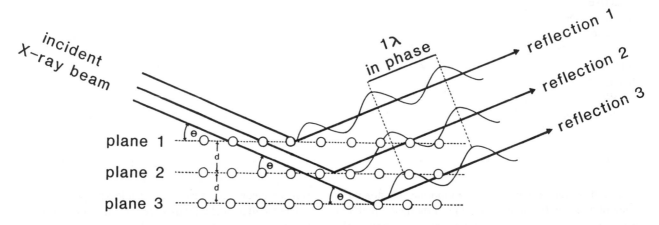

Fig. 7:
Diagram of the relationship between an incident X-ray beam and the atomic planes of a specimen particle when Bragg's Law is satisfied and an X-ray reflection is produced.

Birefringence and crystal structure

Drew, Perkins, and Daly characterized the bone of weight-bearing articular surfaces as showing (1) in wild animals either an absence of birefringence or a dark coloration that they took to be indicative of randomly oriented hydroxyapatite crystallites and (2) in domestic animals a bright birefringence emanating from what they suspected was a mass of aligned crystallites producing a "single-crystal" effect.

The optical effects were reported accurately, but their explanation incorporated several incorrect assumptions. Isabella described the wild pattern thus:

> The gypsum plate in the light path produces a magenta-red interference color. Random orientation of the submicroscopic crystallites of bone mineral does not alter this basic color. The bones from Suberde, which are from wild animals, produced little color change, which indicated that the crystallites are randomly oriented throughout most of the bone (Drew et al. 1971a:281).

The domestic pattern differed as follows:

> ...when the prismatic apatite crystals are aligned with their c optic axis (the vertical axis of the hexagonal prism) parallel to the slow ray of the gypsum plate, the background red is changed to blue. When the c axis is perpendicular to the slow ray, the red is changed to yellow. ... The bones from Erbaba ... showed strong blue interference colors on all articular surfaces, which indicated that in these areas the crystals are almost all aligned with their long axes perpendicular to the areas of bone-to-bone contact (Drew et al. 1971a:281).

Source of the birefringence. The first error involved the source of the birefringence. It matters little whether the crystallites are random or aligned. In fresh bone, they are too small and disconnected to display birefringence in the collective manner assumed and are thus not responsible for the interference colors observed. In biomedical sections, the scattered submicroscopic particles of essentially transparent bone mineral have little effect upon transmitted light, the wavelengths of which are 10 to 20 times larger than the dimensions of an average crystallite.

Without its collagen, a section of fresh bone shows nearly complete darkness between crossed nicols. Refraction effects can occur in protein-poor archaeological specimens, but they usually result from other organic residues, birefringent impurities, or diagenetic alterations. A gypsum plate inserted into the light path superimposes first order red overall and may reveal within the subchondral bone of some archaeological sections a mottled "muddiness," or felted quality, due most likely to deep staining by ferruginous and other opaque salts precipitated out of the ground water.

The interference colors in a fresh bone section are usually produced by collagen, which, like apatite, is an anisotropic crystalline material displaying low birefringence and having a c optic axis parallel to its length. Unlike apatite, collagen is optically positive and length-slow (Bear 1952:97f.). Collagen fibers also aggregate into large bundles that are visible with the light microscope.

The optical properties of collagen are not identical to those of solid crystals, however. Optically, collagen behaves as a colloid in which internal alignments are produced by fibrils embedded within a semi-solid gel (Frey-Wyssling 1953:83ff.). The birefringence of the fibrils themselves is due to their atomic structure and is thereby termed *intrinsic birefringence*. By contrast, the collagen bundles show *form birefringence*, a double refraction effect displayed because of the form or arrangement of their constituent fibers. Fresh bone sections containing collagen exhibit birefringence in the same range as apatite ($\delta < .009$) but with reversed optic sign. When cut to 30 μ, the same interference colors are obtained. Biomedical sections produced by microtome are routinely sliced as thin as 4-10 μ in order to obtain greater anatomical clarity. As a result, they show much lower interference colors and are less useful in identifying intrusive minerals precipitated within ancient specimens.

Anatomy of the articular rims. Drew, Perkins, and Daly correctly described the orientation of crystallites in the birefringent articular rims as having their "long axes perpendicular to the areas of bone-to-bone contact" (Drew et al. 1971a:281; 1971b:973). They presumed, however, that the rims were part of the subchondral plate. A closer look reveals a very different texture from that of the underlying bone. Between the rim and spongy bone, collagen bundles vary widely in orientation as a result of intensive remodeling; the "grain" of the bone is complex, ranging from curvilinear to twisted or woven (Fig. 8a, b:2). The overlying layer of uniform orientation at the articular surface is, in fact, not bone tissue at all but the innermost, mineralized layer of articular cartilage (Fig. 8a, b:1).

Synovial cartilage covers the articular surfaces to smooth, protect, and lubricate the joint (Freeman 1979; Ghadially 1983). Benninghoff (1925) divided the articular cartilage into four superposed zones, of which the innermost Zone IV is a layer of calcified cartilage that is mineralized by invasion of hydroxyapatite crystallites but not ossified. The apatite crystallites of the calcified zone are, as elsewhere, aligned with their c axes parallel to the collagen bundles, which, in Zone IV, run radially outward from the subchondral plate—more or less perpendicular to it. The bundles gradually diverge into "decussating arcs" that curve across the three overlying synovial cartilage zones, ending up parallel to the articular surface in the outermost Zone I (Ghadially 1983:43ff.; Schenk et al.

1986). None of the uncalcified synovial cartilage that once capped the calcified layer survived in any of the archaeological specimens.

Many sections cut by Drew, Perkins, and Daly reveal the dark remnants of cartilage-forming chondrocytes (Stockwell 1979) in the articular rims (Fig. 8a, b:4). Their large oval lacunae are deployed along the axes of the collagen bundles, while smaller, lentil-shaped osteocyte lacunae (Fig. 8a, b:5) appear only in the underlying subchondral bone. The material within these lacunae does not permit transmitted light to pass through and seems more likely to represent organic, cellular residue (whether well-preserved or not) than an opaque mineral precipitate.

The boundary between the calcified cartilage and subchondral plate (Fig. 8a, b:3) is highly irregular, with deep interdigitations serving to reinforce the bonding of cartilage to the bone surface. As a bone grows longer, it gradually replaces calcified cartilage along its inner sur-

face with fully ossified tissue containing osteocytes and blood vessels (Fig. 8a, b:6), a process known as endochondral ossification. To compensate, cartilage is continuously incremented in the direction of the joint, and calcification of its innermost zone advances along fronts termed tidemarks (Lane and Bullough 1980; Bullough and Jagannath 1983). Occasionally, multiple tidemarks can be seen at points where the calcification front leaves behind ghosts of its former location (Fig. 9). Chondrocytes engulfed by calcification in Zone IV may degenerate and disintegrate leaving empty lacunae, yet many remain viable, surrounded by an uncalcified envelope of cartilage termed the territorial, or pericellular, matrix (Green et al. 1970; Schenk et al. 1986).

Cartilage growth, calcification, and endochondral ossification appear to be in equilibrium throughout life (Green et al. 1970; Bullough and Jagannath 1983). The thickness of the articular cartilage varies, but usually both

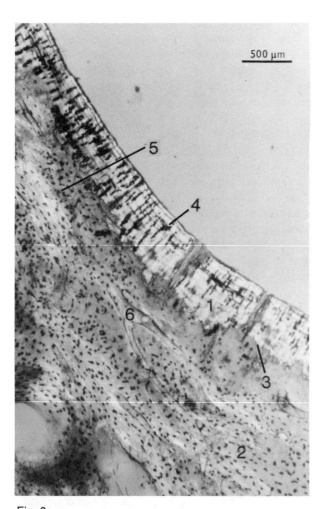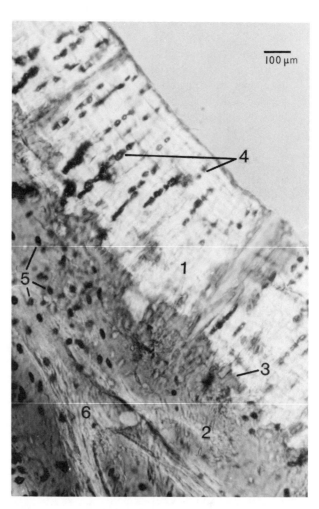

Fig. 8:
Photomicrograph of transverse section through the distal articular surface of a caprine metatarsal (*Capra hircus blythi*; AMNH 54612) showing textural differences between (1) articular rim layer (calcified cartilage) and (2) underlying subchondral bone; also visible are (3) uneven cartilage attachment boundary, and distribution patterns of (4) chondrocytes, (5) osteocytes, and (6) blood vessels; crossed nicols with gypsum plate. *a*. General view. *b*. Detail of cartilage/subchondral boundary.

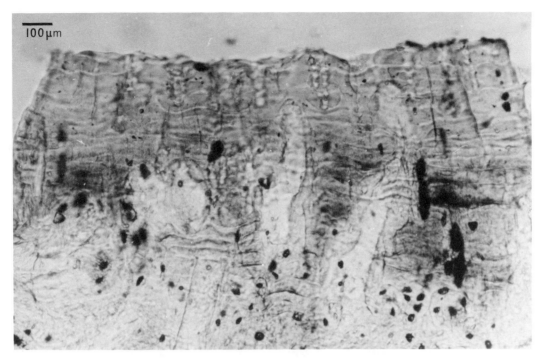

Fig. 9:
Photomicrograph of sagittal section through the distal articular surface of a caprine humerus (*Capra pyrenaica*; AMNH 19381); calcified cartilage layer showing abundant tidemarks; plane polarized light.

synovial and calcified layers are thickest at points receiving the greatest weight-bearing stress (Stougård 1974; Müller-Gerbl et al. 1987). The mechanisms controlling cartilage thickness and tidemark advance are still not completely understood.

The significance of optic sign. A third error emerged in the description of the domestic pattern. The interference colors that apatite would show in the specified orientations were reversed, and instead, the behavior of an optically positive mineral was illustrated—i.e. one in which the c optic axis was the vibration direction of a slow extraordinary ray. Apatite is optically negative. Its c optic axis is the vibration direction of a fast extraordinary ray.

Collagen is the major optically positive component of bone. In areas where trabecular lamellae are curved or circular, a positive optic sign can readily be confirmed (Fig. 10). A blue interference color appears in the northwest and southeast quadrants where the collagen bundles run parallel to the slow ray of the gypsum plate, a yellow interference color appears in the northeast and southwest quadrants where bundles run perpendicular, and a thin cross of magenta lines—which in Fig. 10 is quite irregular—frames the quadrants, marking the extinction positions created by the upper and lower nicols.

In specimens sectioned from the AMNH collections, the birefringence of the calcified cartilage and subchondral bone was always due to optically positive collagen. Many sections cut from archaeological specimens yielded the

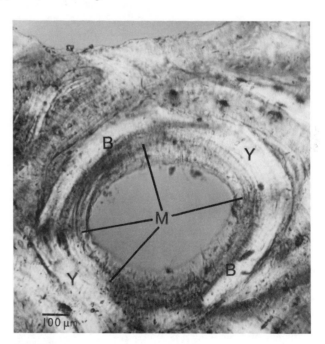

Fig. 10:
Photomicrograph of sagittal section through the distal epiphysis of an ovine humerus (*Ovis ammon orientalis*; AMNH 22829); circular lamellar structure in trabecular bone showing optically positive collagen birefringence; slow ray of the gypsum plate (NE-SW diagonal) produces a blue (B) interference color in the NW and SE quadrants, a yellow (Y) interference color in the NE and SW quadrants, and a thin cross pattern of magenta (M) lines marking the extinction positions; crossed nicols with gypsum plate.

same optic sign, but some displayed an opposite, negative, sign. Figures 11a and b show the same location on two distal metapodials similarly oriented under a gypsum plate. The chondrocyte traces indicating the direction of the collagen bundles run parallel to the slow ray of the gypsum in both photomicrographs. In Fig. 11a, the calcified cartilage layer of an Erbaba goat specimen yields a blue interference color, but in Fig. 11b, the same locus on a Zawi Chemi Shanidar goat specimen yields a yellow interference color. The opposite optic sign of the Zawi Chemi section is impossible in fresh bone. Isabella made this puzzling observation early in her studies. She ventured to explain the condition by hypothesizing different crystallite habits or contrasting crystallite orientations (MASCA 1970), but it is now well established that the crystallite c axis always coincides with that of the collagen fibers. The reversed birefringence (i.e. reversed with respect to positive collagen birefringence) is better explained as the result of post-depositional destruction of collagen with subsequent massive growth of secondary apatite.

Burial conditions affect the organic and inorganic phases of bone differently. Collagen will either be preserved or denatured and dissolved. It will not regenerate once it is lost. The first stages of decay involve the hydrolysis of peptide bonds that join the individual amino acids together into a protein chain (Hare 1980). The bonds between amino acids vary in their degree of stability (Hare et al. 1975), but once dissociated, the protein becomes more soluble and the amino acids may racemize. The presence of additional water can leach out organic components as well. Chemical changes apparently accompany the breakdown. In collagenous extracts from buried ancient animal bone, DeNiro (1985) has noted C^{13}/C^{12} and N^{15}/N^{14} ratios that differ from those of fresh bones from the same species, indicating diagenetic modification of the isotopes used in paleodiet research.

Collagen is curious, however, in its ability to show negative birefringence. In normal collagen, both form and intrinsic birefringence are positive, but earlier in this century, tanning agents were observed to exert peculiar influences on its optic sign (Frey-Wyssling 1953:346ff.). Mineral tanning agents such as chromic salts left the sign unchanged, but the use of pyrogallic agents (sumac, tannin), phenols, and higher aldehydes reversed the sign. Frey-Wyssling felt this change resulted from the attachment to collagen molecules of side chains possessing greater refracting power than the bundles themselves. Thus, under special conditions, collagen can exhibit form birefringence that is not positive.

But the optic sign inversion of "tanned" collagen does not explain the reversed birefringence phenomenon in the bones under investigation. Protein radioimmunoassays performed upon equid bones from Godin Tepe and Ali Kosh Tepe—the former showing normal collagen birefrin-gence and the latter showing reversed birefringence—revealed that almost no collagen remained in the Ali Kosh material (Gilbert et al. 1990). An earlier study by Saloman and Haas (1967) also established the variability of collagen content in ancient bones but did not connect the pattern with birefringence because staining techniques, not mineral optics, were used to investigate tissue structure.

The post-depositional impact on bone mineral is different. In contrast to collagen, bone mineral can remain unchanged, undergo partial ionic substitution within its crystal lattice, suffer various degrees of dissolution and crystallite loss, or experience conditions in which calcium, phosphate, and carbonate ions in the surrounding soil crystallize to produce new and larger apatite structures (White and Hannus 1983; Sillen 1981, 1989). Because fresh bone contains up to 50% collagen by volume, disappearance of the organic matrix creates a substantial void. Collagen loss likely affects the bonds between fibrils and crystallites, exposing bone mineral surfaces and facilitating chemical reactivity with the surrounding burial environment. Further, if diagenetic replacement of collagen by secondary apatite is seeded by crystallites within the bone, the original orientation of those crystallites should be preserved in the new apatite growth. The resulting cemented aggregate would exhibit the "single crystal" effect discussed earlier and would yield a low first order birefringence similar to that of collagen, but with reversed optic sign.

Diagenetic replacement is probably common among Near Eastern faunal remains considering the availability in soils of calcium and carbonate ions from the widespread Cretaceous and Tertiary limestones of the ancient Tethys Sea, and the near certain abundance of phosphates in anthropogenic sediment. Alkaline conditions probably favor the growth of secondary apatite because (1) they are destructive to collagen and thus expose crystallite surfaces, and (2) they can produce high ground water saturation levels of apatite constituents, which is necessary for the initiation of mineral precipitation (Nancollas and Mohan 1970:732).

Misaligned crystallites vs. naked crystallites. A final inaccuracy was the explanation given for the wild pattern. The absence of birefringent rims in sections cut from wild animals is not the result of random crystallite orientation. Specimens showing a magenta interference color go completely black in these areas when the gypsum plate is removed. They do not refract transmitted light because they possess insufficient collagen and insufficient secondary apatite. Without collagen or intrusive diagenetic impurities, little if any birefringence due to original or derived components of the specimen occurs, and only the first order red of the gypsum will illuminate the section sufficiently to disclose microstructural features.

Extreme cases of collagen loss without subsequent replacement by apatite to cement the whole together would reduce bone largely to its mineral crystallites. If this process were allowed to continue while the products of organic breakdown were steadily leached out, the bones would become increasingly friable and would eventually disintegrate completely.

Taphonomic implications. Drew, Perkins, and Daly reported finding non-birefringent articular rims on bones possessing thick trabeculae. They concluded that the association was not accidental and probably represented a physiological response by bone to the more vigorous lifestyle of wild animals. If, however, the birefringent patterns resulted from post-depositional influences, then the data could not be used to support an interpretation involving functional adaptation. In order to explore the matter, I surveyed the now expanded Sackler collection of thin sections to determine (1) whether bones from the same site showed the same degree of preservation and (2) whether preservation state correlated in any way with trabecular morphology.

Based on the pattern and intensity of interference colors, the optic sign of the birefringence, and the degree to which histological detail was preserved, it was possible not only to discern different magnitudes of collagen loss and secondary apatite crystallization in bones subjected to different burial conditions, but also to arrange, or seriate, the sections so as to demonstrate hypothetically progressive diagenetic changes.

In fresh bone (as in Fig. 8 above), birefringence of the calcified cartilage layer was always positive and the interference colors were strong—ie., bright second order blue appeared when the collagen bundles paralleled the slow

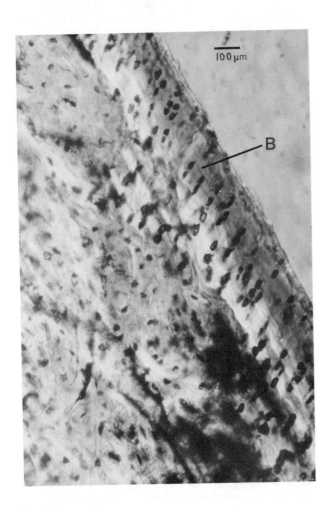

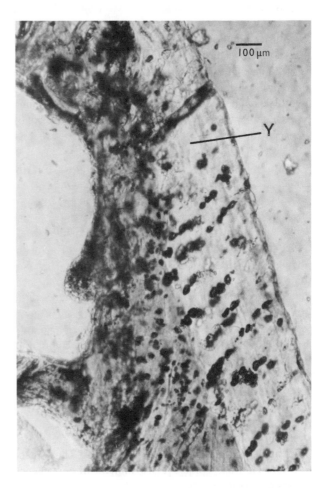

Fig. 11:
Photomicrographs of transverse sections through the distal articular surface of caprine metapodials (*Capra hircus*) oriented similarly but showing differing birefringence; detail of calcified cartilage layer on the axial side of the condyle adjacent to the sagittal notch; crossed nicols with gypsum plate. *a.* Late Neolithic goat from Erbaba (455) displaying positive collagen birefringence: blue (B) rim. *b.* Proto-Neolithic goat from Zawi Chemi Shanidar (459B) displaying reversed, negative birefringence produced by secondary apatite: yellow (Y) rim.

ray of the gypsum plate. Dark organic matter was present in the chondrocyte lacunae, and tidemarks were observed frequently. In sections displaying initial protein loss, the interference colors began to fade and gradually merged with the background magenta as collagen decay proceeded (Fig. 12). Greater protein loss usually coincided with the disappearance of the chondrocyte remains. With their cellular material leached out, the empty lacunae were visible against the magenta only as Becke lines (Fig. 13): thin white refraction blurs marking the boundary between the apatite and the hole that move outward into the mineral as the focus point is raised and move back into the hole when the focus point is lowered (Phillips 1971:50-51; Kerr 1977:75-77; Shelley 1985:57-58). The growth of secondary apatite appeared as a faint glow of negatively birefringent material invading magenta areas. In many sections, the glow was quite strong, signaling denser crystallization. The new interference colors were always typical of apatite.

Subchondral and trabecular areas showed a similar diagenetic progression. In some sections, the positive collagen birefringence had dimmed or disappeared, leaving only the background magenta. In other sections, reversed interference colors emerged and spread commensurate with the growth of secondary apatite. Osteocyte lacunae also lost cellular matter and showed Becke line effects, yet they tended to retain a black organic residue more often, especially in the innermost parts of trabecular intersections where the bone was thickest (Fig. 14a).

A number of slides showed a localized loss of histological detail, which likely resulted from either the partial dissolution of bone mineral prior to the precipitation of secondary apatite, or the erosion and replacement of secondary apatite during a subsequent episode of diagenesis (Fig. 14b). In either instance, enough bone mineral remained to orient the secondary growth along lamellar directions and create a uniformly reversed birefringence, but not enough remained to preserve with clarity the microscopic features of the original bone tissue, such as osteocyte lacunae and lamellar borders. Loss of histological detail in ancient bone has been previously studied (Saloman and Haas 1967; Stout 1978; Sillen 1981).

Occasionally, crystals of calcite—or more rarely gypsum—were found lining or filling the intertrabecular spaces (Fig. 14a, b), or encrusting the periosteal and articular surfaces (Fig. 14c). These accumulations are precipitated out of ground water post-depositionally.

Sections from five sites (Godin Tepe, Erbaba, Suberde, Ali Kosh Tepe, and Beidha) document these changes, showing that diagenesis varied between sites more than it did within them. Sections from each site showed fairly uniform effects that were expressed equally by bones with thick and thin trabeculae, i.e. preservation state correlated more closely with findspot than with trabecular anatomy.

Godin Tepe, a large mound site containing a late

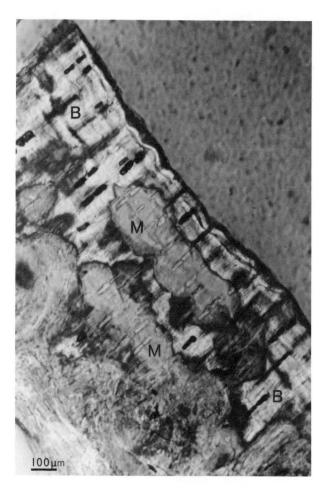

Fig. 12:
Photomicrograph of sagittal section through the distal articular surface of an equine first phalanx (*Equus hemionus* or hybrid) from Bronze Age Godin Tepe (Godin IV) showing collagen birefringence; calcified cartilage reveals blue (B) interference color fading into magenta (M); crossed nicols with gypsum plate.

Neolithic through Iron Age cultural sequence, is located in a highland valley of the central Zagros Mountains in Iran (Young 1969; Young and Levine 1974; Henrickson 1986; Gilbert 1979). Seven Bronze Age equid specimens (ca. 3000-1900 B.C.) were sectioned. Despite the poor prognosis offered for protein survival in buried skeletons (Hedges and Wallace 1978, 1980), all Godin sections revealed some positive birefringence indicative of collagen. Chondrocytes and osteocytes were variably preserved, but histological detail remained sharp. Occasionally, the interference colors appeared dim or faded, and sometimes they blended with the magenta of the gypsum plate indicating initial collagen loss (see Fig. 12). Protein radioimmunoassays performed on the same bones corroborated the optical evidence and demonstrated significant collagen preservation, approaching nearly a 40% reaction in some specimens. Results of the assays suggested that bone proteins

Fig. 13:
Photomicrograph of sagittal section through the distal articular surface of a caprine humerus (*Capra* sp.) from Late Neolithic Suberde (319); detail of calcified cartilage layer showing empty chondrocyte lacunae bounded by Becke lines on magenta background; crossed nicols with gypsum plate.

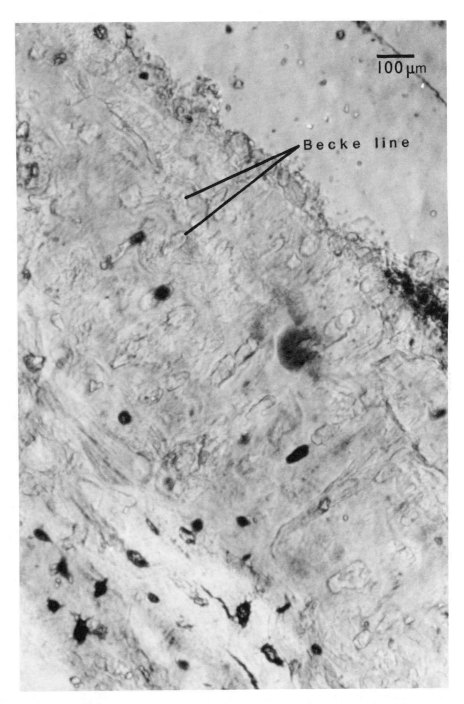

are more likely to survive burial within neutral soils insulated from aeration and moisture and located in regions or elevations with lower mean annual temperatures (Gilbert et al. 1990).

Twenty-one caprine sections from the late Neolithic site of Erbaba (ca. 5600 B.C.) in the Beyşehir valley of south central Turkey also displayed mostly positive collagen birefringence in their calcified cartilage layers (see Fig. 11a). Dark chondrocyte and osteocyte substance remained, and histological structure was unusually well preserved. Magenta and reversed interference colors also appeared, most often within subchondral/trabecular loca-

tions and in bands of adjacent diaphyseal lamellae. Intertrabecular spaces were commonly lined by minute calcite crystals suggesting calcareous ground water flow during some part of the burial interval. In general, compact bone seemed to retain its collagen better than the spongy parts.

Several sections of cattle bone from Erbaba showed heavy replacement by secondary apatite. For now, this contrast with the condition of caprine bone lacks a satisfactory explanation.

The controversial site of Suberde, also late Neolithic (ca. 6500 B.C.) and located in the Suğla basin adjoining Beyşehir, contained bones showing considerable collagen

Fig. 14:
Photomicrographs of sagittal section through the distal humerus of a caprid (*Capra* sp.) from Early Neolithic Beidha (10012); trabeculae and articular surface with secondary apatite replacement and calcite encrustation; crossed nicols with gypsum plate. *a.* Empty osteocyte lacunae along periphery and dark organic matter remaining in lacunae located deeper within trabecular intersections. *b.* Loss of osteocyte lacunae in trabecular struts through secondary apatite recrystallization. *c.* Articular surface showing opaque coating of dirty calcite encrusting calcified cartilage layer, pockets of intrusive calcite crystals (X), tidemarks, and empty chondrocyte and osteocyte lacunae (some of which are obliterated by recrystallization).

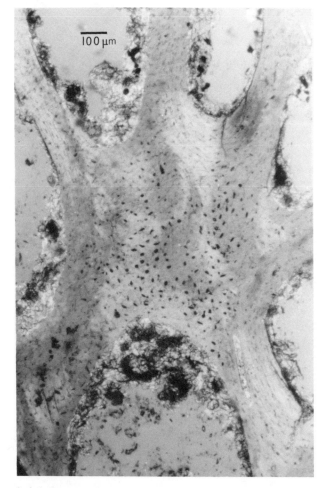

loss but little secondary apatite. The outermost 0.1 mm or so of bone along both articular and periosteal surfaces in over a dozen slides yielded only the magenta of the gypsum plate, suggesting that soil chemistry had been hostile to collagen survival. Protein destruction and leaching were most apparent in these surficial areas of closest contact, and empty chondrocyte and osteocyte lacunae were the rule (see Fig. 13). Collagen birefringence was observable only in the interior of the specimens, where, in addition, histological detail was preserved and dark osteocyte material persisted. Magenta penetration into spongy bone lamellae was fairly common, however, and some specimens also revealed initial growth of secondary apatite within the magenta areas. In contrast to the soils of other sites, the sediments at Suberde may have been deficient in calcium phosphate or lacked sufficient ground water concentrations to enable more thorough secondary crystallization.

Twelve sections (comprising goats and hemiones) from Ali Kosh Tepe, an early Neolithic site (8000-6000 B.C.) in the Deh Luran plain of southwestern Iran (Hole et al. 1969), revealed advanced stages of collagen loss and replacement by secondary apatite. Strong reversed interference colors occurred in the interior as well as along outer surfaces. Chondrocytes were either much reduced within

their lacunae or they were completely leached out (Fig. 15). Though some osteocytes were visible deep within the thicker trabeculae, most were gone in the majority of the sections, and their empty lacunae exhibited Becke line effects against the reversed interference colors. The intertrabecular spaces of some Ali Kosh bones showed substantial calcite encrustation in which masses of minute crystals covered the trabecular surfaces but did not penetrate into the secondary apatite of the bone itself.

Protein assays of Ali Kosh specimens showed virtually no remnant collagen (Gilbert et al. 1990), again corroborating the results of optical examination and suggesting that collagen is not likely to survive in bones deposited within the generally warmer and alkaline soils of semi-arid climate areas.

In the Ali Kosh sections, wild hemiones with sturdy trabeculae and early domestic goats with relatively more delicate spongy architecture both demonstrated the same low organic survival and secondary apatite crystallization. No correlation was apparent between cancellous structure and birefringence.

The village site of Beidha in Jordan (Kirkbride 1966, 1968) represented an extreme case of recrystallization. Among nearly 20 sections inspected from Epipaleolithic

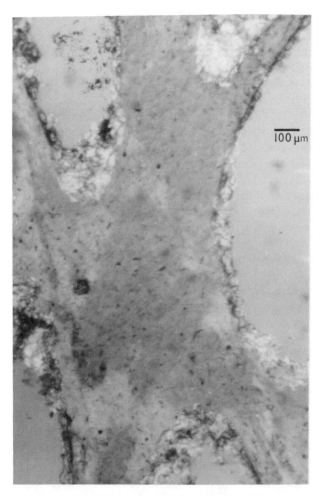 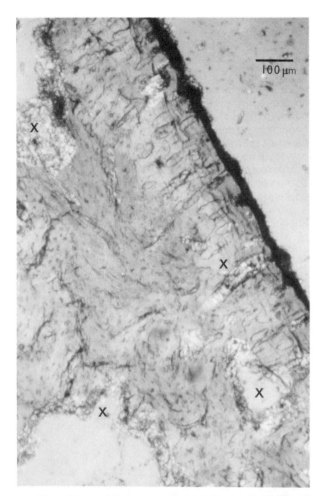

and Early Neolithic deposits (11,000-6500 B.C.), reversed interference colors were universal in both interior and surface areas. As at Ali Kosh, dark osteocyte material tended to survive if it was deeply embedded within trabeculae (see Fig. 14a), but organic loss was everywhere apparent. In some areas, histological detail was either blurred or obliterated by recrystallization at some point during the burial interval (see Fig. 14b). At Beidha, carbonate encrustation was also extreme. It lined intertrabecular spaces, in some cases almost filling the voids completely. It coated most outer surfaces (see Fig. 14c), and even invaded peripheral layers, penetrating into and disrupting the secondary apatite. Sections from wild gazelles exhibited the same diagenetic changes as those from (presumed) early domestic caprids that still possessed fairly sturdy trabeculae.

Obviously, taphonomic considerations must figure importantly in the interpretation of birefringence. Within the range of specimens examined, the freshest bones showed positive collagen birefringence and well preserved tissue structures, whereas the most altered bones showed only reversed negative birefringence and much loss of histological detail.

One might conclude that if bones are fresh or otherwise unaffected by cooking, exposure, or other predepositional deterioration when they are interred, then temperature and ambient soil chemistry in the early stages of burial would probably play the major part in determining the extent of change. If burial conditions are not hostile to preservation, bones would presumably reach equilibrium with the sediments surrounding them during this initial phase of diagenetic transformation and then would remain intact within the ground until their recovery. Preservation would also depend upon a reasonably stable depositional environment. Episodes of flooding, exposure and reburial, chemical variation, and edaphic/climatic fluctuation would likely quicken the pace of diagenesis, possibly with unfavorable consequences for bone survival. The information presently available from the sections examined suggests that the Near Eastern depositional environments sampled affect bone largely in (1) the degree of chemical hostility to protein and (2) the availability of soluble apatite components to fuel secondary crystallization.

The different birefringent patterns cannot be linked to physiological adaptation, but they nevertheless furnish useful information about changes taking place within the bone and their possible stimuli. Such data are of importance in paleodiet research (Price 1989), where chemical

67

Fig. 15:
Photomicrograph of transverse section through the distal
articular surface of a hemione radius (*Equus hemionus*)
from the early Neolithic Ali Kosh phase at Ali Kosh Tepe;
calcified cartilage showing secondary apatite replacement
(Y), and partly empty chondrocyte lacunae; subchondral
plate highly vascularized (X); crossed nicols with gypsum
plate.

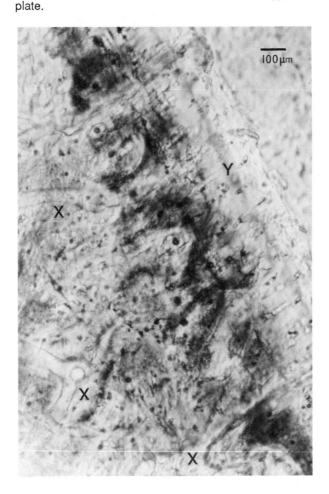

analysis of collagen and bone mineral from ancient human
skeletons is exploited to learn about the dietary factors
metabolized to build those tissue components. Diagenesis
renders the interpretation of such compositional evidence
more complex and demanding.

Lamellar structure in the diaphysis. The layering
observed in long bone shafts is the result of lamellar
ossification (Pritchard 1972a:15). Typical structures in
mature mammalian compact bone, the layers represent
bone laminae laid down in one of three patterns: *circumferential* layering around the periosteal surfaces of compact
bone, *concentric* layering around secondary osteons (or
Haversian systems), and *interstitial* layering representing
the remnants of previous laminae left between more recent
concentric lamellae (Fig. 16). Adhesion and structural
integrity is facilitated by a very thin interlamellar space

filled with cement. The causes of lamellation were long de-
bated, but applications of scanning electron microscopy
have demonstrated that lamellar structure derives principally from abrupt changes in collagen bundle orientation
from layer to layer, much like plywood construction
(Pritchard 1972a:15-16; Boyde 1972).

The different interference colors of adjacent layers that
Isabella found in shaft bone sections also suggested a
plywood-like structure in the circumferential lamellae.
She concluded that diaphyseal cross-sections from wild
animals contained mostly vertically-oriented crystallites
because of the first order red interference color that most
thick layers revealed. She reasoned that polarized light
would pass unrefracted along the optic axis direction of the
crystallites (i.e. of the collagen fibrils). The shaft bones of
domestic animals showed stronger lamellation, with adjacent layers alternating between yellow and blue. This
pattern suggested that the c axes were tilted and possessed
a radial component in one layer, and, in the next, lay more
like a circumferential wrapping around the bone at some
angle to the previous radially-oriented layer (Drew et al.
1971a:280).

Unfortunately, interference colors are not necessarily
indicative of fiber orientation alone. The situation is complex
and not easily interpreted. Though petrographic cross-
sections suggested radial and circumferential fiber directions in long bone shaft lamellae, Drew, Perkins, and Daly
determined through X-ray analysis that diaphyseal crystallites possessed a strong vertical component. Orientation of
a section exactly normal to the collagen bundle direction
should produce magenta under a gypsum plate. Any devia-
tion from normal places the c axis of the collagen at an
angle to transmitted light and permits double refraction to
create interference colors that will depend upon the angle
of c axis inclination.

In diaphyseal cross-sections, then, the interference
colors should be fairly uniform within lamellae in accordance with the generally strong alignment of collagen
bundles. If the interference colors alternate from lamella to
lamella (Fig. 17), they may signal minute changes in
collagen bundle direction, but they may also reflect layers
of positive and negative birefringence. Such an eventuality
would entail collagen loss and secondary apatite replacement within certain lamellae but not others. In this way, the
presence of magenta lamellae could indicate an intermediate stage of organic destruction prior to secondary apatite
precipitation.

It is difficult to decide how to interpret interference
color patterns in diaphyseal cross-sections. In Fig. 17, a
humeral shaft from a Suberde goat, it is safe to assume that,
like the outer margins of other Suberde sections, the
periosteal and endosteal lamellae are magenta because of
collagen loss. The cause of the blue and yellow banding in
the diaphyseal interior is not readily explained, however.

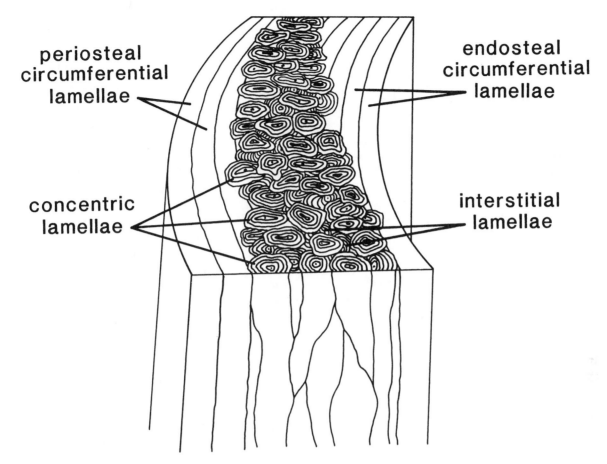

Fig. 16:
Drawing of shaft bone in cross-section showing the three types of lamellar structure.

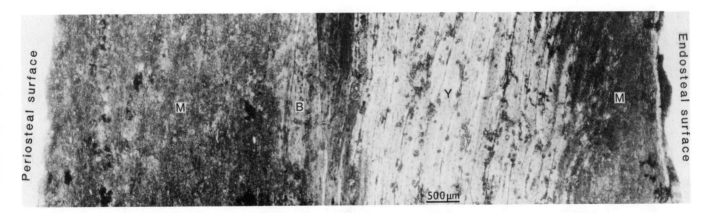

Fig. 17:
Composite photomicrograph of cross-section through the humerus shaft of a late Neolithic goat (*Capra* sp.) from Suberde showing circumferential lamellae; magenta (M) interference color in periosteal and endosteal layers indicates collagen loss; outer blue (B) band and inner yellow (Y) band may represent lamellae with preserved collagen and secondary apatite deposition, or varying angles to the vertical made by collagen bundles running upward within the lamellae; crossed nicols with gypsum plate.

Longitudinal sections through shafts would have avoided these difficulties, but none were cut.

The appearance of diaphyseal lamellae under the microscope as independent layers containing regular internal organization relates only to the bone slice under observation. Throughout the rest of the bone tissue, fiber orientations are variable, and the collagen bundles, together with their associated mineral crystallites, change direction frequently within a single lamella. Bundles also occasionally cross the interlamellar space to join adjacent lamellae, thus creating an overall pattern of interconnectedness and heterogeneous alignment.

Compact, circumferentially lamellated bone may be replaced by secondary osteons, or Haversian systems. These cylinders of concentrically lamellated bone surrounding a central blood vessel are produced through a sequence of cellular activities. A round tunnel is first resorbed from old bone by osteoclast cells (Hancox 1972). Osteoblast cells then initiate the refilling of the tunnel with bone matrix, which ossifies to form concentric lamellae (Pritchard 1972b). Proliferation of secondary osteons obliterates the preexisting pattern of circumferential lamellae (Fig. 18), and it does so more often in older animals at locations of active muscle attachment. Major interpretive difficulties are connected with this adaptive remodeling, but the issue is best taken up in the discussion of spongy bone morphology.

Spongy bone morphology

Differences between the wild and domestic pattern of trabecular architecture are more a matter of gross structure than crystal structure. The wild pattern comprises a thick subchondral plate, thick trabeculae, and zone of gradual transition between the two. With increasingly thick trabeculae, the intertrabecular voids naturally begin to decrease in relative size and grow rounder. The domestic pattern is the opposite: thin subchondral plate, thin trabeculae, little to no zone of transition, and oblong to rectangular voids.

Spongy, or cancellous, bone looks in section like a mass of mutually contiguous alveoli packed together in the manner of soap bubble foam. In reality, there are no alveoli. The voids are the projections onto the section plane of a more or less continuous space crossed by a structural framework of bony struts and plates. Trabecular architecture exhibits a range of morphological variation that can be characterized in three progressive stages (Singh 1978). The first and simplest is a series of interconnecting cylindrical struts composed of remnant primary lamellar or remodeled bone. This condition can evolve to the next stage as some of the struts broaden into small plates that seal off the openings between adjacent struts, creating discontinuous intertrabecular partitions. There may be few plates, or many. Finally in the third stage, the small plates coalesce along preferred directions to form expansive sheets of bone held rigid by many fine struts bridging the intervening space to the adjacent plate or sheet.

The simplest type of cancellous bone is generally found in skeletal locations free of mechanical load. As weight-bearing stress increases on certain bone surfaces, the trabecular structure beneath them tends to become more platey or sheet-like, with the preferred direction of the sheets aligned with the principal stress vectors (Currey 1984:33). From the standpoint of resistance to compressional and tensional forces, the trabeculae demonstrate that bone responds to stress by building firmer supports only in the essential places and directions. The result is a bone that is anisotropic to stress, i.e. better able to withstand it along certain vectors than others. In actuality, bone does not

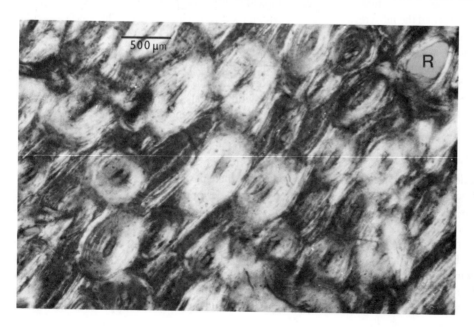

Fig. 18:
Photomicrograph of cross-section through the humerus shaft of a bovine (*Bos taurus*) from Aphrodisias (676W) showing invasion of secondary osteons into the region of circumferential lamellae (which run NE-SW) and an active area of osteoclastic resorption (extreme NE corner at R); crossed nicols with gypsum plate.

respond directly to stress but rather to strain (Kummer 1972; Currey 1984). Stress is effectively the load and is measured as force per unit area of the cross-section upon which the force is applied, kg/mm^2. Strain represents deformation under stress and is measured in alterations in length per unit of original undeformed length, mm/mm.

Given that the shapes of bones and their development from embryonic to fully ossified tissue are genetically determined, it is nevertheless clear that aspects of both compact and spongy bone anatomy are determined by adaptive responses to strains experienced by the skeleton during life. The close correspondence between a bone's cancellous structure and the trajectories of mechanical stresses produced during loading prompted Wolff (1892) to hypothesize, based upon ideas of functional adaptation by Roux (1881) and notions of economy of mass proposed by Bourgery (1832), that bones appear to remodel themselves so as to fit their functions (Roesler 1981, 1987). Wolff's Law, as it is now called, relates form to function but explains nothing about generative and regulatory processes.

Uncertainty still surrounds this remodeling process, for it seems to serve many purposes. It has been thought to (1) replace old dead bone with new, (2) release calcium and phosphorus for other body uses, (3) improve or renew blood circulation, (4) keep the internal and external form of bones anatomically congruent during growth, (5) reduce bone density to make it more resilient, (6) stop microcracking and resist creep, fatigue, and other kinds of failure, and (7) adjust structural "grain" to better withstand mechanical stresses.

Spongy bone is formed through adaptive remodeling (Pauwels 1954, 1965; Sissons 1956:450ff.). Trabecular thickness and organization are determined by osteoclastic and osteoblastic activities so that, in general, the sturdiest dimensions oppose compressive forces and the most resilient dimensions counter flexional and tensional forces. To be specific, trabecular architecture seems designed to provide: (1) the compliance necessary to protect articular cartilage from being crushed during loading, (2) alignment in the direction of the principal stresses acting on the bone to provide support, and (3) provision of stability against shear through a cross-braced framework streamlined by the removal of extraneous bone to achieve minimum weight (Currey 1984:139ff.).

Remodeling may well function in many ways; its peculiar distribution within compact bone remains difficult to explain, however. Secondary osteons replace early-forming woven bone during endochondral ossification, and in so doing, impart greater strength, but invasion of mature circumferential lamellae by Haversian systems seems to bring about a reduction in strength according to Currey (1975, 1984:264ff.). Although remodeled compact bone seems to be structurally inferior to the original circum-ferential lamellar bone, it nevertheless occurs in places associated with mechanical loading (Lanyon et al. 1982; Bouvier and Hylander 1981). Due to their different geometry and density, circumferential and concentric lamellae exhibit different elastic properties (Lipson and Katz 1984) and tensile strength (Reilly and Burstein 1975) so that a structural factor would appear to be involved. On a yet subtler level, remodeling is also viewed as a protective device that maintains a bone's internal organization so that it conforms to a certain margin of safety against failure under habitual or catastrophic strains. Lanyon (1987) suggests that the process is perhaps monitored and directed by osteocytes that sense mismatches between skeletal microarchitecture and the intermittent strains that must be endured during load bearing. Because the pattern of Haversianization is quite similar for left and right body parts yet differs markedly from species to species, and since replacement does not occur in the most highly stressed locations but nearby, Currey (1984:265ff.) adds that remodeling may be to some extent programmatic.

If trabeculae brace the epiphysis against forces tending to deform it, then a sturdier and denser spongy structure in some animals should indicate a greater need on the part of the weight-bearing elements of the skeleton to resist the strains caused by high stress locomotion. A more porous spongy anatomy in other animals suggests that a less massive skeleton was sufficient to support apparently less stressful daily activities.

The observations of Drew, Perkins, and Daly regarding spongy bone architecture hold the greatest promise for illuminating aspects of animal behavior at the dawn of domestication. Specimens in their collection show a fairly strong correlation between high density cancellous tissue, wild morphology of the skeletal part sectioned, and archaeological findspot suggestive of a hunting as opposed to a pastoral food-acquiring strategy. Their early speculations (MASCA 1973:1) linked the density decline in domestic animals to "lack of exercise, poor nutrition, or genetic deterioration" such that they may have "lacked sufficient material ... to form the sturdy bones characteristic of the wild animals." Many factors influence bone growth, including diet, endocrine balance, genetics, mechanical forces, pathology, and ionizing radiation (Sissons 1956). Although mechanical forces (perhaps in combination with other factors) seem to hold the greatest explanatory potential, there has been little zooarchaeological follow-up research designed to test this.

Subsequent research

After 1972, little work was done on bone microstructure by the original investigators. A number of papers appeared in the ensuing years by other individuals who experimented with the microscopic or X-ray diffraction techniques in an attempt to delve deeper into the matter.

Many of these papers were critical, owing to difficulties experienced in duplicating the initial results. The following discussion examines those papers of which the writer is aware. Points raised by their authors are evaluated in the light of present knowledge.

McConnell and Foreman (1971)

Four months after the 22 January 1971 publication in *Science* by Drew, Perkins, and Daly, the first comment emerged in the pages of the 28 May issue of the same journal. Duncan McConnell and Dennis Foreman, Jr. (College of Dentistry, Ohio State University) prefaced their remarks by objecting to what they called an "erroneous" labeling of bone mineral as hydroxyapatite. Isabella responded (Drew et al. 1971b) that use of the term corresponded with acceptable practice, while it circumvented the controversies surrounding the "exact crystallo-chemical nature of bone." As McConnell and Foreman imply, crystallites are perhaps more comparable to dahllite, but bone mineral is in truth a compositionally non-stoichiometric substance that legitimately falls into the taxonomic category of hydroxyapatite.

The thrust of McConnell's and Foreman's criticism was technical and mostly concerned sampling methods. They could not accept, without the assurance of many more X-ray diffraction tests and thin sections, that the wild and domestic patterns were representative. In their judgment, "bone is a complex anatomical structure, and a very small displacement in the position of a section might result in significant textural differences" (p. 971). Their cautionary example was a radiograph of dental enamel from a fetal human in which subparallel crystallites formed aggregates ca. 1 to 2 μm across, but the aggregates were packed together in random alignment thus creating no overall pattern of orientation.

Isabella replied that a sufficient number of sections had been cut along varying planes in both sagittal and transverse directions to establish the fact that crystallite (and collagen) alignment was a widespread phenomenon affecting volumes of bone about 1000 times larger in scale than those of the enamel aggregates.

Drew, Perkins, and Daly assumed that the crystalline orientation in their sections was related to weight-bearing stress, a stimulus which, they pointed out, was unlikely to affect fetal enamel in a similar way. Joint loading influences both the lamellar orientation and cancellous organization of bone, and skeletal growth and remodeling over the life of an animal provide ample opportunity for bone structures to align themselves with the principal load vectors. Enamel, on the other hand, is not as responsive. By the time a tooth is fully developed, its enamel has lost over 90% of its organic matrix, and mineralization accounts for up to 99% of its dry tissue weight (Eastoe 1964:279).

Although enamel layers initiated in the womb appear randomized, more or less oriented crystallites occur in mature enamel prisms (e.g. Darling 1964). The growth process, however, appears the sole source of this internal restructuring. Once formed, enamel must withstand the knocking and grinding of active mastication without the benefit of repair through secondary enamel formation. McConnell and Foreman may not have intended to use fetal enamel as a direct analogy to the dynamic physiological relationship between behavior and skeletal anatomy described by Drew, Perkins, and Daly, but their example was nevertheless based upon an inappropriate scale of variability.

Hecker (1975) and Hesse (1978)

In his dissertation (1975) on the Beidha fauna, Howard Hecker (Franklin Pierce University) reported on the study of 45 humerus and metapodial sections of goat/ibex and gazelle sampled from several cultural levels. His thesis documented only 21 of the sections in detail (pp. 213-221), all of them transversely cut metapodia. The humeri were not discussed as they revealed the same features.

Hecker compared his Beidha sections to a small control group but relied for much of his interpretation on the work done previously at the Sackler Lab. All the Beidha specimens appeared to conform to the wild pattern, having (1) denser spongiosa, (2) generally small intertrabecular spaces, (3) thick periosteal and subchondral bone, and (4) no birefringent effects at the articular rims comparable to those found in the Erbaba sections.

Hecker's assessment of cancellous structure was factual and relevant, but the absence of a conspicuous positive birefringence in the calcified cartilage layer may have led to some confusion. In the Beidha specimens, secondary apatite replacement was complete, cellular matter was generally missing, and calcite encrustation had obscured surficial microstructural features to a great extent. The articular rims appeared much less distinctive as a result of the intrusive calcite crusts. Though the negative birefringence of the apatite precipitate did not correspond to the magenta margins typical of the wild Suberde bones, the Beidha fauna were categorized as wild because the articular rims were not visually well-defined and all other indicators pointed to thicker and sturdier architecture.

Although Hecker felt on the basis of other data that a domestication process was ongoing at Beidha, he concluded that the results of sectioning gave no evidence of it (p. 220). As the birefringent patterns reflect only diagenetic changes and have no necessary relationship with the behavioral states of once-living animals, trabecular anatomy is left as the remaining criterion on which to base a judgment.

Hecker was uncertain what changes would appear first

under the conditions of containment that likely accompanied the earliest attempts at cultural control, and because the Beidha specimens examined gave no clue, two caprid metacarpals from the AMNH were examined. AMNH 19381 was labeled *Capra pyrenaica* and AMNH 54612, *Capra hircus blythi*. Both had been captured and confined in a zoo until their death, but museum records were silent on the length of their captivity. As one would expect, sections from these bones showed positive collagen birefringence and prominent articular rims, but they still displayed a thick trabecular architecture, which suggested to Hecker that trabecular reduction could be a fairly slow process.

In truth, Hecker did not know the duration of confinement, nor even whether the goats underwent a behavioral adjustment to their new, presumably more restricted, habitat. If the zoo animals could retain a sturdy spongiosa, then the Beidha caprids might also have been subject to some form of cultural control without incurring substantial trabecular thinning. Insufficient information rendered the test inconclusive, yet strongly suggested that trabecular architecture does not necessarily reflect the exact nature of the human-animal relationship.

Nine sections were cut from morphologically wild-looking sheep and goat bones of early Neolithic Ganj Dareh Tepe in western Iran by Brian Hesse (University of Alabama-Birmingham). His dissertation included brief mention of the examination (pp. 218-222). Based upon that report, only the goats showed a domestic pattern in the microstructure, which supported other indications of cultural control that appeared in the age and sex profiles of the assemblage as well as in other archaeological finds at the site. Several of the Ganj Dareh goats proved troublesome to characterize, the probable result of an opaque ferrous precipitate obscuring the passage of light through the section (Perkins 1971).

Pollard and Drew (1975)

The last publication of bone section data by Isabella appeared three years after her departure from Columbia (subsequently to join the faculty of Ramapo State College in Mahwah, New Jersey). Her collaboration with Gordon Pollard led to a paper on the bone structure of South American camelids. Pollard's excavations in the Rio Loa valley of northern Chile documented the transition from nomadic hunting to sedentism and pastoralism in habitation sites near the river. Camelid fauna were recovered from two sites representing the early and late ends of this cultural transformation.

For the early end (Vega Alta II, beginning ca. 500 B.C.), 13 sections were cut from 9 lower limb elements out of a total of 114 identifiable bones collected. For the late end (Loa II, ending ca. A.D. 400), 23 sections were cut

from 16 specimens out of the 400 recovered. Because the skeletal effects were clearer in bones lower on the limb, the authors presumed that the microstructural patterns "were intensified as the weight on the bone increased" (p. 300).

A small control group of AMNH zoo specimens (llama, alpaca, guanaco, and vicuña) was also sectioned. Patterns of articular birefringence and open texture were found associated with the first two domestic species, while in the two wild species, the same features were either "missing, discontinuous, or highly anomalous," while fewer and smaller intertrabecular spaces appeared within the spongiosa (p. 300).

Both wild and domestic patterns were observed on bones from Vega Alta II and Loa II phases. In both sites, the domestic animals were identified as "undoubtedly llamas" (p. 303). Another, unidentified camelid species bearing a wild pattern was apparently hunted throughout the cultural sequence. The wild pattern of these individuals differed little from phase to phase, but the pattern identified as domestic was quite variable. Those from the semisedentary Vega Alta II phase possessed a thinner rim and less intense interference colors, which the authors thought might indicate an early stage of domestication. Full sedentism was apparent in the Loa II phase based upon a larger population, locally-made pottery, a llama corral, and a clearer domestic pattern in the microstructure.

Comment on the Chilean material would be premature because only the sections from the Loa II site (RAnL 100) remain in the collection. It seems likely, however, that initial collagen loss may cause the fading of interference color on specimens from the Vega Alta II site (RAnL 273A).

Watson (1975)

The first important challenge came from J.P.N. Watson of the University of London's Institute of Archaeology.

Watson was critical of several things. The first concerned the labels "wild" and "domestic" used to characterize the microstructural patterns. He thought it highly improbable that the terms could be meaningful descriptive labels for the anatomical changes observed and suggested that the many possible varieties of human-animal relationship likely formed a continuum. Domesticates left free to wander over natural terrain might in fact emulate a wild lifestyle more closely than other, more closely confined, domesticates.

Watson proposed in contrast that abrupt osteological changes should not be expected to correlate with the state of domestication per se (p. 375). Though he suggested that such changes might more likely have been a direct result of the selective breeding and genetic modification accompanying the more evolved stages of domestication, he did not, in the end, favor a genetic explanation. In rejecting a biomechanical explanation, however, he missed a major point.

To Dexter and Pat, the microstructural effects reflected biomechanical reactions to changes brought on by the domestication process:

DOMESTICATION
PROCESS
▼
CHANGE IN
ACTIVITY LEVEL
▼
OSTEOLOGICAL
RESPONSE

This is not exactly the same thing as saying what Watson seems to have assumed: that the osteological response was a direct concomitant of being domesticated. Dexter and Pat had hypothesized a preexisting cause for the changes in activity level, which involved their contention that migratory animals hunted during the Upper Paleolithic could be controlled initially in the Epipaleolithic or early Neolithic only by capture and containment. Thus, they suspected that a sudden break with the wild lifestyle took place for certain ungulates when they were confined, perhaps in cul-de-sacs, box canyons, or artificial corrals in various parts of the Near East.

Thin sections made from sheep and goat bones recovered at Zawi Chemi Shanidar and Ganj Dareh had (in their estimation) caught the process at its start, showing the effects of changing behavior in one species but not in the other. Because the Erbaba sections contrasted so dramatically with those from Suberde, they reasoned further that the microstructural patterns (as they interpreted them) remained valid reflections of a wild-domestic dichotomy even in later generations of domesticates.

Unfortunately, Dexter and Pat spoke of the patterns as if they were universal and, in so doing, swept all forms of cultural control into the same category in a manner that Watson found objectionable. With the potential for variability in the earliest pastoral management strategies, Watson was correct to question so all-inclusive an interpretation. Unconvinced that domestication entailed any necessary biomechanical changes, he did not seriously consider the possibility that Dexter and Pat might have correctly surmised a major behavioral shift in animals consequent on the spread of just such a new strategy for animal production.

Watson's second criticism was that independent identification of wild or domestic status was based, in some instances (especially at Suberde), on hypothetical grounds that have not met with widespread approval among zooarchaeologists. Although he did not develop this point

further, others did (see below).

Third, Watson noted with disapprobation that initial concern over soil chemistry did not lead to a consideration of the possibility that differential preservation caused the microscopic changes. He suggested that taphonomic processes might have inflicted variable damage from site to site, and that burial conditions might have been more hostile to bone survival in the past. His points implied that samples should have been screened according to the degree of organic preservation before sectioning.

The question of differential preservation was a crucial one. Drew et al. (1971a:280, n. 3) did control for varying soil chemistry conditions at Suberde, Erbaba, and Shanidar, but Isabella found nothing to suggest major dissimilarities in the sediments themselves, and thus she proceeded on the assumption that the burial interval affected the recovered fauna relatively equally. Testing of the bones to assay their organic content prior to sectioning, or recognition of the significance of reversed birefringence would have shown that this was not the case.

Watson then sought to show how the microstructural orientation effects could be accounted for by differential survival of bone collagen. He proposed, correctly, that interference colors were produced by the collagen matrix, not by the hydroxyapatite crystallites of the bone mineral phase (p. 376). The rest of his paper presented a limited investigation and reinterpretation.

Watson properly cited Rouiller (1956:123-124) and Hancox (1972:10), who state that the birefringence of fresh bone comes largely from collagen. The so-called ground substance of embryonic and interfibrillar tissue is also somewhat birefringent, showing a similarly uniaxial positive effect when constituent hyaluronate fibers are oriented (Sylvén and Ambrose 1955). Watson supposed that the optically negative hydroxyapatite crystallites would oppose the birefringence of the collagen since their c axes are parallel. In reality, though, the crystallites are too small to have any optical effect, though they frequently obscure the collagen patterns in radiographs.

Watson thus concluded that the "domestic" sections of Drew, Perkins, and Daly were likely to be compositionally very similar to those cut from fresh bone (p. 376). Though he correctly identified collagen loss as the cause of the magenta interference color in the "wild" sections, his explanation still included the expectation that the remnant bone mineral would be randomly arranged. He suggested that progressive destruction of organic matrix would lead to disorder in the aligned microstructures that were supported by that collagen network (p. 382). His solution makes sense in the case of crumbling bone leached of its organics, but the thin sections discussed above demonstrate that secondary apatite crystallization frequently maintained fiber orientation while it preserved the physical integrity of the bone and, in many instances, much of the histological detail despite near total annihilation of the protein.

To prove his point about collagen preservation, Watson decalcified two archaeological specimens (a distal humerus and a metatarsal shaft) and one modern metatarsal shaft of caprine bone (p. 379). He provided little information about the archaeological specimens, stating only that they derived from Iron Age to Hellenistic levels of the site of Gravina (Botromagno) in Italy. The distal humerus section (G530-1A) "showed an almost entirely red interference colour, reminiscent of ... the 'wild' sheep humerus from Suberde" (p. 379). Decalcification produced no change in the birefringence and demonstrated that, with the mineral dissolved, only organics could account for the interference colors.

Apparently, the shaft sections showed positive collagen birefringence before and after removal of the apatite, whereas the semiarid climate and Mediterranean soil had eliminated enough protein in the distal humerus to produce only first order magenta.

Watson then treated the sections with stains specific to the collagen and mucopolysaccharide-based cement. His staining revealed the presence of collagen in places where it should have been: mature lamellae that had previously displayed positive birefringence. The staining also revealed cement in the interlamellar spaces of the two shaft sections as well as in the entire subchondral area of the distal humerus. Decalcification of the distal humerus seems to have left behind only the mucopolysaccharides, which absorbed their characteristic stain in the areas where collagen had originally been destroyed diagenetically. Conceivably, it was this remnant cement that held the protein-poor bone together when it was excavated.

Watson's argument about collagen loss was convincing. He did not mention reversed interference colors and thus apparently did not section bones containing secondary apatite crystallization. He also omitted any discussion of the X-ray diffraction results but referred the reader to "certain criticisms" already made by McConnell and Foreman (1971)—who did not object to the diffraction but rather to the inadequacy of the sampling.

After brief mention in his first paragraph, Watson proceeded to ignore another important part of the microstructural patterns. In concentrating solely on birefringence, he never examined trabecular morphology, the matter that bears the most direct connection to a biomechanical stimulus.

From the skeletal collections of the University Museum of Zoology at Cambridge, Watson obtained sagittal sections of distal humeri from wild Anatolian *Capra aegagrus* and Rocky Mountain *Ovis montana* (*canadensis*?), all individuals having been shot in the late 1800s. Between crossed nicols, a thin articular rim with positive collagen birefringence was observed on each, which, as

Watson pointed out, contradicted the association of blue rims with a domestic state. He failed to note, however, that the sections also showed extremely thick subchondral plates with no large oblong lacunae anywhere within the limits of the published photomicrographs. Following Wolff's Law, Watson's wild caprids still reveal a subchondral morphology concordant with expectation.

Wright and Miller (1976) and Binford (1981)

Many of the first sections ground and examined were from Suberde and Erbaba fauna, and it was these observations which first suggested the presence of microscopic differences in the bones of wild and domestic animals. Dexter and Pat had identified the Suberde fauna as wild, but varied reactions elicited by their publication (Perkins and Daly 1968) indicated that many harbored uncertainties about the nature of the ancient animal exploitation at the site.

Drew, Perkins, and Daly also analyzed fauna from other Neolithic sites, and the results generally indicated that morphologically wild-looking animals that could be identified as domestic, or culturally controlled, on independent grounds—e.g. zoogeography, age and sex criteria, and increased recovery frequency compared to earlier periods—showed trabecular thinning, yet other species that could not be so identified revealed the same sturdy trabecular structure as the Suberde specimens. At Zawi Chemi Shanidar, sheep yielded a porous pattern, goats a dense one; at Ganj Dareh Tepe, goats yielded a porous pattern, sheep a dense one. Only at Beidha was the situation unclear. When one challenges the interpretation offered for Suberde, one must also reassess the parallel findings and their implications at other Near Eastern sites.

Only two examples are presented here to illustrate critiques of Dexter and Pat's analysis of the Suberde fauna.

To Gary A. Wright and Suzanne J. Miller (SUNY-Albany), the Suberde sheep were probably domesticated (1976). They constructed survivorship estimates from the meager age and skeletal part frequency data that Dexter and Pat published, and by their reckoning, the curves resembled more closely the harvest profiles of ancient and modern villagers than those generated by prehistoric hunters of the Old World or Rocky Mountains. Demographic compositions of contemporary wild sheep populations were also dissimilar. They used their comparative data, gleaned from faunal reports and ethological studies, somewhat like a touchstone to diagnose faunal residues as those of hunting or herding groups.

Dexter and Pat identified the Suberde fauna as wild using different criteria for each species. In the case of sheep, they compared the ratio of juveniles (0-15 months) to mature specimens (>15 months) with that reported by Higgs for a European Iron Age site and with population figures given by Murie (1944) for wild Dall sheep. In their bar graph (Perkins and Daly 1968:103), the results for epiphyseal fusion (of distal metapodials only) and tooth eruption (for both sheep and goats together) indicated that 28-35% were juvenile and 65-72% were mature. The correspondence was markedly closer to Murie's figures than to Higgs's, allowing Dexter and Pat to posit that a kill-off equally distributed across age cohorts over a long interval of hunting might have made the Suberde refuse look like the demographic profile of its wild prey population. In addition, no conclusive evidence for morphological change in the caprine skeleton could be found. Finally, after publication of their study, the thin section evidence favored the wild identification.

Wright and Miller suspected Murie's statistics to be incorrect and also felt Dexter and Pat had misinterpreted them (p. 307). They judged the Suberde sheep too young for anything but a selective cull of immature and subadult individuals from a domestic village herd because "no sheep specimens represented animals younger than three months or older than three years" (Perkins and Daly 1968:103).

Wright and Miller based their points precariously upon estimates of age alone. Two taphonomic qualifications must guide the use of such data: (1) reliability of the sample and (2) applicability of the death assemblage models used for comparison.

Dexter and Pat estimated age at death for the Suberde caprines based on a very small proportion of the recovered sample, and thus the use of survivorship information to reconstruct ancient harvest profiles must be deemed risky business at best. The Suberde fauna were highly fragmented. Although the recovered sample was enormous (ca. 300,000 pieces), the identifiable fraction came to only 14,000, or 4.7%. Sheep and goats accounted for about 65% of that total, but further separation by species into 85% sheep/15% goats could be done using only certain diagnostic elements, which amounted to only 700 bones. In the end, only 595 bones (700 x .85) could be identified as sheep, which represents only 6.5% of the total caprine material. An even smaller percentage would have been useful for ageing.

At the time, those few skeletal parts that could be identified with certainty as sheep or goat did not provide an epiphyseal fusion sequence for all stages of skeletal maturation. Looking more carefully at the bar graph, the results for distal metapodial fusion and tooth eruption indicated that 28-35% were 15 months or younger, and 65-72% were 15 months *or older*. How much older cannot be determined on the basis of a single element and without a series of occlusal wear stages for the fully erupted teeth. Dexter and Pat may have set a maximum ovine age of three years based upon identifiable sheep parts, but they could never guarantee this cap for other non-diagnostic sheep elements in the collection.

Wright and Miller argued, sensibly, for more exacting use of immature/mature ratios and kill-off estimates as important indicators of the ancient death assemblage. They may have misinterpreted Dexter and Pat, but they appear to have applied Suberde data uncritically when they assumed that no sheep lived beyond three years of age. Summing data from all levels of the site, they concluded that "Suberde fits the model of domesticated herd composition, not the one of a wild herd" (p. 309).

Though informative, their control cases should not have been taken as conclusive diagnostics, nor as the only viable death assemblage models against which to evaluate Suberde. (A more detailed discussion of the interpretive subtleties of age and slaughter pattern data is found in Hesse [1982].) The age-related data from Suberde (and other sites) forming the backbone of their argument were weak, and though they stated at the outset that their focus was on the meaning of age structure in faunal assemblages, they ignored other data pertinent to their interpretation of Suberde, such as meat weight estimates. Dexter and Pat had observed that, if caprines were indeed submitting to domestication at Suberde, their remains suggested diminishing contribution to the total protein intake over time. Caprines were the most commonly recovered taxa in all three Neolithic layers (IV-II), yet their frequency—adjusted for carcass size—dropped from 70% in layers IV-III to 50% in layer II, the difference absorbed in large part by an increase in cattle from 14% in IV-III to about 30% in II.

Finally, Wright and Miller rationalized the microstructural effect by saying that,

> Like other morphological changes, this did not occur immediately or even within the first few generations following domestication. If the Suberde sheep were domesticated recently, there is no conflict between the survivorship curve and the lack of a blue rim (Wright and Miller 1976:311).

They did not consider trabecular architecture at all, and without supportive evidence, they preferred to categorize the microstructural effects together with "other morphological changes" as a genetic byproduct of selective breeding.

Suberde is an unusual site in that its putative hunter inhabitants lived amidst hundreds of Anatolian farming villages and towns at least 3000 years after the earliest evidence for animal domestication in the Near East and at least 500 years after the widespread appearance there of morphologically domestic stock. There is something odd about Suberde. An archaeologist who disregards this peculiarity compromises the evidence considerably. Data from other ancient Near Eastern sites demonstrate clearly that if the inhabitants of Suberde were beginning to domesticate the animals they killed for food, they were still inexplicably out of phase with everyone else. The point to be made here is that a one-dimensional approach based on scanty data does not (necessarily) invalidate conclusions drawn from gross morphological and microstructural evidence.

In his book dealing with myth making in faunal studies, Lewis Binford took Dexter and Pat to task for inventing "a post hoc accomodative argument" to account for the different patterns of caprine and bovine body parts recovered at Suberde (1981:184185). Dexter and Pat had coined the term 'schlepp effect' to describe the distribution of bones at kill sites and habitation sites, the idea for which had been adapted from archaeological reconstructions of Paleo-Indian bison hunter sites in the New World. They supposed that the low recovery of upper limb bones from cattle in the Suberde assemblage indicated that muscle bundles had been filleted at the kill site and the meat dragged home in the hide. The foot bones were retained either because they were useful as handles for the hide sack or because lower limbs were valued for their sinew. The Suberde caprine remains, on the other hand, possessed the proper anatomical proportions of upper to lower limb bones, suggesting that their smaller size had rendered field butchery unnecessary, making them immune to the schlepp effect (Perkins and Daly 1968:104).

Binford did not object so much to the attempted reconstruction as to the lack of effort expended to document related ethnographic instances, substantiate the meat procurement strategy using other archaeological indicators, or otherwise evaluate the proposition in continued scientific investigation (1981:244-245). Indeed, the Suberde faunal report read as if no other interpretation of the bone recovery patterns existed. Although the reconstruction may be correct as is, the evidence can, in truth, fit other scenarios. Binford's criticism does not invalidate the hypothesis of wild fauna at Suberde; it was leveled at the methods Dexter and Pat used to authenticate the hypothesis as historical truth. The matter reflects upon aspects of Dexter's character as scholar and teacher.

Dexter led a life of relative leisure. He held no full-time positions but worked long and hard on subjects of interest to him. His father, Dexter Perkins, Sr., was an internationally known professor of American diplomatic history at the University of Rochester, and his paternal grandmother, Cora D. Farmer, was the sister of Fanny Merritt Farmer, the renowned Boston Cooking School chef. Dexter's mother, Wilma Lord Perkins, edited and enlarged the *Fanny Farmer Cookbook* after the original *Boston Cooking School Cookbook of 1896*. By 1959, when Dexter completed his Ph.D. in zoology at Harvard, the cookbook was already in its 11th edition and accounted for a large part of the family fortune that supported him. After his mother's death in 1976 and his father's confinement to a nursing home, Dexter continued to live on the family estate in Harvard, Massachusetts, venturing out on a weekly basis to teach during the academic year at Harvard, Columbia, and the University of Pennsylvania, logging thousands of highway miles in the process.

As Dexter lived, so did he do science. Innovative and indefatigable in his approach to faunal studies, he nevertheless took an easier path in much of his interpretive work. He spent months in painstaking field and lab analysis on the masses of skeletal material from numerous sites of the late prehistoric Near East. Charged by the intellectual challenge, his explanations incorporated intricate arguments based often upon pioneering applications of new ideas in ethology, statistics, and pastoral evolution. Except for the problems of faunal quantification, which he examined continually throughout his life with Columbia statistician Burton H. Singer, his conclusions stood mostly unverified by independent, well-designed hypothesis testing, and were only validated in his own mind by data taken from the next collection on which he worked. He taught his students to think independently, encouraged new avenues of inquiry, and stimulated creative interdisciplinary thinking, for which we remain much in his debt. Yet, many of us had to develop on our own a sense of discipline for the laborious task of reevaluating, testing, and refining exploratory data into established knowledge.

The admittedly perplexing problem of Suberde remains unresolved. With the quantitative data encumbered by scholarly disagreement, the microstructural aspect may take on even greater importance as a potentially illuminating tool once the systemic cause and effect mechanisms are better understood.

Zeder (1978)

Melinda A. Zeder (Smithsonian Institution) accepted the hypothesis that anatomical responses to differences in locomotor stress were mirrored in the wild and domestic patterns, and she proceeded to test it against independent data. Assuming that the effects might map out a continuum corresponding to the magnitudes of stress experienced by an animal through its participation in a given ecosystem, she collected bones from animals for which some information was available on lifetime activities.

While in Iran in 1973, Zeder purchased twelve domestic sheep under a grant from the University of Michigan. Four animals were selected from each of three transhumant routines of the south central Zagros region: (1) lowland sedentary herds from the Deh Luran and Susiana plain areas of Khuzistan, (2) lowland transhumant herds moving seasonally between the piedmont plains and the first Zagros ranges to the north and east, and (3) highland transhumant herds moving seasonally between localities in the more elevated fold belt of Luristan near Khorramabad. In addition, a fourth group of four specimens was acquired from the skeletal collections of the Field Museum of Natural History in Chicago, consisting of wild sheep (*Ovis ammon orientalis*) collected by Douglas Lay (p. 70).

Zeder compared the collected specimens microstructurally and chemically, repeating the work of Drew, Perkins, and Daly with a sample more or less controlled for activity level and differentiated to some extent by habitat. Presuming that bone microstructure would vary according

77

to the degree of locomotor stress, her expectation was that sedentary life would impose the least, while a wild lifestyle would impose the most strain on limb bones. Highland transhumance was expected to produce patterns close to those of wild animals, based on the roughness of the terrain, and lowland transhumance was expected to fall somewhere in between. The project was intended only as a pilot study, results from which would establish the merits of collecting a larger and statistically more reliable sample.

Three standard petrographic thin sections were cut from a distal humerus of each individual: a sagittal and transverse section of the articular surface, and a sagittal cut along the shaft (p. 72). Use of distal humeri was intended to reproduce as closely as possible the methods used in the initial Sackler research. No information was provided on the age of the individuals, or whether the specimens had been pretreated prior to sectioning.

Zeder correctly pointed out the confusion over optic sign in the early publications of Drew, Perkins, and Daly but still assumed that the hydroxyapatite crystallites produced the interference colors (p. 81, n. 3). Also correctly, she labeled section illustrations as having blue rims in layers "with crystals perpendicular to the articular surface of the bone" (p. 75, caption to figure 2A). Yet, with the articular surface oriented perpendicular to the slow ray of the gypsum plate as the illustration suggests, such blue rims denote the positive birefringence characteristic of collagen.

The sections revealed multiple banding at the articular surfaces (p. 72). Only the innermost band—labeled 'A' in Zeder's published photomicrographs—displayed birefringence (p. 75, caption to figure 2A). Zeder found the multiple bands a mystery, as Drew, Perkins, and Daly did not encounter them (p. 81, n. 8), but because the birefringent rims represent the innermost layer of calcified cartilage (Zone IV), the darker banding above the calcified layer in Zeder's fresh bone sections is likely to be the dried remnants of synovial cartilage from Zones I-III.

Like Watson, Zeder found that both wild and domestic specimens exhibited birefringent layers near the articular surfaces. On the shaft sections, she was unable to find any characteristics to distinguish one group from the other (p. 72). In short, her examination did not reproduce the birefringent patterns obtained in the Neolithic specimens from Erbaba, Suberde, and other sites because her specimens had not undergone the diagenetic transformations that produce those patterns.

To measure trabecular thickness, Zeder enlarged photomicrographs of spongy bone sections and measured intertrabecular area in five to eight places using a polar planimeter. Results of several independent measurements were averaged to produce a bone to space (B/S) ratio. Overall averages calculated for each bone and each group revealed tight clustering of B/S ratios for the wild and lowland transhumant animals, but very wide and variable results for the lowland sedentary and highland transhumant animals (p. 73). The thickest trabeculae were observed among the wild sheep, and the thinnest generally were observed among the lowland transhumant sheep. Ratios for lowland sedentary and highland transhumant fell in between but with substantial overlap. As might be anticipated, wild specimens possessed generally more robust trabeculae. No intelligible pattern emerged among the groups of domestic sections, however. Likewise, the shape of intertrabecular spaces was quite variable across the groups (p. 82, n. 12). In addition, Zeder found no osteometric distinctions, discovering only that the B/S ratio showed a weakly inverse relationship with a depth x breadth index of shaft ovalness (p. 75). The trabecular density findings of Drew, Perkins, and Daly were but poorly apparent, and only in Zeder's wild specimens. The domesticates did not demonstrate any clear stress-related clines.

Interviews with shepherds convinced Zeder that differences in nutritional intake existed between the wild and domestic groups sampled. Hypothesizing that feed variability might lead to differences in bone chemistry, she employed atomic absorption spectroscopy to determine the levels of calcium, magnesium, and zinc. Zeder recognized that her analysis would not pick up subtle differences in bone chemistry the way a more extensive roster of trace elements would, but she expected that elements representing the gross composition of bone mineral might reflect aspects of skeletal density.

Table 1 displays the averages and ranges in calcium content and B/S ratio of porosity, and Fig. 19 is a bivariate plot of the chemical vs. density-related data. Variability is substantial both within and between groups, yet their mean values are suggestive. Wild sheep produce the highest average B/S ratio, while the lowland sedentary sheep have the lowest average calcium content. The average score of the highland transhumant sheep lies midway between, but the lowland transhumant group is skewed higher in calcium content and lower in B/S ratio for no intuitively obvious reason.

Zeder concluded that, although her results did not conform to expectations, the failure to confirm the findings of Drew, Perkins, and Daly did not necessarily invalidate them. She felt that continued investigation might yield better results if several complicating issues were addressed first: (1) how bone reacts to different levels of stress (i.e. strain), (2) whether levels of stress commonly encountered by transhumant and migratory animals are sufficient to effect significant microstructural changes, (3) which skeletal loci are most useful for differentiating animals according to which kind of stress, and (4) what modifications can be expected from differences in age, health, or other factors in the specimens analyzed.

Table 1. Trabecular bone to intertrabecular space (B/S) ratios calculated by Zeder (1978:table 2) for modern Iranian sheep; calcium content determined for the same samples (1978:table 6). High B/S ratio means thick trabeculae relative to intertrabecular space.

Sample Group	B/S Ratio		Calcium Content (%)	
	Average	Range	Average	Range
Lowland sedentary	1.14 ± 0.26	0.85-1.31	53.25 ± 6.1	46.33-59.67
Lowland transhumant	0.92 ± 0.08	0.83-0.98	68.50 ± 4.8	62.00-73.00
Highland transhumant	1.26 ± 0.22	1.00-1.39	55.50 ± 11.0	40.67-67.00
Wild	1.33 ± 0.06	1.27-1.38	61.50 ± 10.3	47.00-71.00

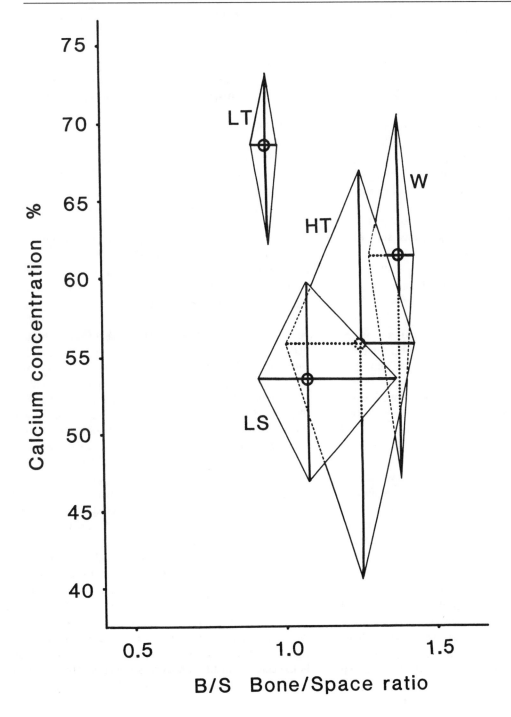

Fig. 19:
Bivariate plot of Zeder's B/S ratio against calcium content using grouped data from Table 1; group ranges are indicated by bold lines, averages are marked by a circle.

Clearly, experimentation to establish parameters for these variables must be more tightly controlled than was the case for Zeder's investigation. Her project had good scientific form and, at least initially, focused on the crucial aspects of the microstructural issue. The results demonstrate the magnitude of variability.

Østergård (1980)

The most recent paper on the skeletal microstructure of wild and domestic animals of which I am aware is that of Morten Østergård of the Zoological Museum, Copenhagen. His contribution was an attempt to verify the orientation of crystallites in epiphyseal and diaphyseal locations.

To avoid the problem of collagen preservation and address directly the problem of crystallite orientation, Østergård used X-ray diffraction analysis. The wavelength of the Cu Kα radiation employed is about 1.54 Å, much smaller than that of light and therefore capable of providing information about the structure of particles as small as bone crystallites, which average 50 Å thick by 400 Å long. Although X rays are also affected by the organic matrix of bone, the mineral phase gives a stronger signal due to its more highly ordered atomic lattice planes and the ability of its calcium and phosphate ions to scatter incoming X rays more effectively than the carbons and hydrogens of the protein.

Østergård selected bones from Museum collections, pairing a mature (fused) specimen of a domestic species with the same element of its wild counterpart: dog (*Canis familiaris*) and wolf (*C. lupus*), cattle (*Bos taurus*) and aurochs (*B. primigenius*), pig (*Sus domesticus*) and boar (*S. scrofa*). The specimens, all with museum numbers, derived from both recent and subfossil (archaeological?) sources.

For the suids, Østergård sampled humeri, radii, and metacarpals; for the others, either humeri or femora. Twenty bone disks, comprising a first series, were drilled from the bone surface at both articular and diaphyseal locations, and a second series of 12 cross-sections was cut in the same places perpendicular to the first series.

Each of the small bone disks and slices was embedded in the mounting medium Araldite, ground flat on a slide, and oscillated for three hours under an X-ray beam at the Geological Institute of the University of Copenhagen. Østergård concluded that the orientation of crystallites at a given point on the skeleton was more or less the same in each taxon and did not vary with respect to wild or domestic state.

Preferred orientation was judged by measuring the amplitudes of X-ray reflection peaks. Reflection intensities for the (002) basal pinacoid and for the (300) prismatic faces were compared in the same manner that Isabella had earlier done. The (002) planes register a strong reflection when the angle of incidence $2\Theta = 25.9°$, and the (300) faces reflect most strongly at $2\Theta = 32.9°$ A peak more intense

(higher in amplitude) than that of a standard powder pattern was interpreted to mean that more pinacoids or prismatic faces were aligned in the plane of the oriented section.

Østergård presented little data. Only a few poorly labeled plots of canid specimens were published as representative, together with a powder pattern to show the relative amplitude of the reflections. Though they are arbitrary values, the amplitudes themselves were not given, making it impossible for the reader to calculate peak ratios. Drew, Perkins, and Daly did not provide amplitudes either, but calculated and reported typical I_{002}/I_{300} ratios (1981a).

Unfortunately, neither the X-ray examinations of Østergård nor the original ones of Drew, Perkins, and Daly included controls to insure that the peak intensity ratios measured were directly related to crystallite orientation as opposed to other factors. The most important potential complication arises with changes in the shape or average size of crystallites.

The ideal size of particles in diffraction analysis is between 10^{-2} and 5×10^{-4} mm, which is 10^{6} to 5×10^{4} Å (Azároff 1968:549). Bone crystallites fall well below this range and therefore do not furnish a sufficient number of lattice planes per particle to generate well-defined diffraction maxima. With secondary apatite crystallization, however, larger growths can result, and peak intensities can rise sharply as crystallites attain more favorable dimensions to produce stronger X-ray reflections. Crystal habit also makes a difference. In tabular crystals, (300) planes will tend to increase in area more rapidly than (002) planes. The (300) reflection peak can thus display greater variability in bone that has undergone diagenesis. Conversely, loss of crystallites or crystal size reduction through partial dissolution and leaching will work in the opposite sense to yield flattened, poorly-defined reflection peaks. Diagenetic change may, however, involve only proliferation of crystallites rather than increase or decrease in their absolute size, and in such cases, transformed bone could yield diffraction patterns similar to those of fresh bone.

Put plainly, the amplitude of an X-ray reflection is a function of a crystal's size and habit. If one is uncertain about these as well as the character and extent of diagenetic modification, then reflection intensity ratios cannot automatically be assumed to indicate crystallite orientation. Without additional information, the different peak amplitudes generated by modern and archaeological bone are not necessarily comparable. The special application of texture analysis in X-ray crystallography (Azároff 1968:531ff.), a more appropriate and effective way to study orientation, has confirmed the alignment.

Despite the imprecision inherent in the peak amplitudes, X rays did demonstrate some of the main directions of crystallite alignment. Both Isabella and Østergård recorded emphasized (300) prismatic reflections when a longitudinal section of shaft bone was the target, and higher (002) pinacoidal reflections when a cross-section was analyzed (Table 2). Collagen bundles and crystallites do show a strong vertical orientation within diaphyseal lamellae.

At the epiphyses, the situation was complicated. Østergård found more (002) reflections in his bone disks (Table 2). The vertical alignment of crystallites in the calcified cartilage layer would likely boost pinacoidal reflections from X rays advancing perpendicular to the articular surface. The results of Drew, Perkins, and Daly were similar when the articular surface of a domestic animal was the target, but they differed in wild animals for reasons that are as yet unclear.

In the end, however, X-ray diffraction was marshaled to address the wrong question. Alignment of hydroxyapatite and collagen at the fibrillar-crystallite interface is a normal aspect of bone microstructure. Uniform interference colors in fresh bone sections indicate alignment of the collagen within lamellae, and many studies have demonstrated that the c axes of both organic and inorganic phases coincide.

Østergård was unable to find differences in crystallite orientation among wild and domestic carnivores, ruminants, and omnivores. This evidence, if it is unaffected by diagenesis, contradicts (as expected) the hypothesis posed by Drew, Perkins, and Daly about crystallite alignment being a functional adaptation. The crystalline organization of bone is a genetically controlled feature of endoskeletons and has a more ancient origin.

Summary

The research of Drew, Perkins, and Daly accomplished a number of things. It introduced an innovative analytical approach to the study of animal remains at a time when faunal analysis was itself still an innovative analytical approach in archaeology. It represented an emerging trend, still developing today within the varied subfields of archaeological science, that considered composition and internal structure to be potentially informative dimensions of artifacts in the same way as the traditional aspects of frequency and gross morphology. It suggested further that the behavior of ancient animals—observable through its influence upon skeletal structure—might provide clues to the as yet unknown management strategies accompanying the earliest attempts at pastoral control. In these respects, the work on bone microstructure was both pioneering and revealing.

The researchers erred on some technical matters. Misinterpretation of interference colors obscured the significance of the crystalline characteristics of archaeological bone. The errors included:

1. failure to control for factors of post-depositional diagenesis (i.e. by analyzing bones previously screened according to degree of protein retention);

2. incorrect attribution of birefringence to bone mineral crystallites when interference colors were in reality produced by preserved collagen and secondarily deposited apatite;

3. inaccurate assumption that the birefringences showing reversed polarity indicated crystallites in opposing orientations as a consequence of physiological adjustment to weight-bearing stress.

The birefringence of archaeological bone sections indicates the extent of diagenetic change and may, by extension, suggest something of the nature of predepositional events or the physico-chemical conditions of the burial environment. The impact of diagenesis can be slight or considerable, ranging from near complete preservation of both organic and inorganic phases, through various

Table 2. Comparison of X-ray reflection peak ratios in caprine bones from Suberde and Erbaba (Drew et al. 1971a) and canid bones from wolves and dogs (Østergård 1980).

Skeletal locus	Drew, Perkins, and Daly* I_{002}/I_{300}	Østergård** I_{002}/I_{300}
articular surface wild	0.70-0.80	>1.00
articular surface domestic	1.60-1.90	>1.00
articular cross-section wild		>1.00
articular cross-section domestic		>1.00
diaphyseal cross-section wild	2.80-3.30	>1.00
diaphyseal cross-section domestic	1.40-1.70	>1.00
diaphyseal longitudinal section wild	0.53-0.57	<1.00
diaphyseal longitudinal section domestic	0.35-0.41	<1.00

* calculated ratios provided by authors
** calculated ratios not published; estimated from text

stages of protein loss, to partial dissolution of the bone mineral with recrystallization. The degree of protein loss and secondary apatite replacement is discernible from the polarity and intensity of the interference colors, while the extent of recrystallization can be judged mainly by the preservation of histological detail.

Drew, Perkins, and Daly correctly noted the biomechanical sensitivity of trabecular architecture. The morphology of spongy bone underlying weight-bearing articular surfaces does appear to behave in accordance with Wolff's Law and should be susceptible to further analysis.

Initial study of fauna from the Anatolian sites of Suberde and Erbaba yielded models of skeletal microstructure that were perhaps too quickly dichotomized into "wild" and "domestic." The microstructural patterns were assumed to reflect antecedent behavioral energetics that were distinctive of wild and domestic animals, but Watson rejected the "wild" and "domestic" labels, pointing out that such broad categories of cultural control encompassed too much internal variability. As it is still unclear precisely how early domesticates were confined, treated, and exploited, it seems premature to presume specific activity levels as direct correlates. Terms such as "dense" and "porous" or "sturdy" and "delicate" ("robust" and "gracile"?) are better descriptive rubrics for trabecular characterizations.

The fact that the interrelationships between locomotor routines and osteological response are complex was made apparent by Zeder. Her inability to reproduce in modern animals the anatomical differences found by Drew, Perkins, and Daly in ancient ones implies either that we do not yet understand the remodeling process sufficiently to sample and measure the relevant dimensions properly; or that, in contrast to their wild and domestic ancestors, contemporary wild and domestic sheep experience relatively similar skeletal stresses.

For the present, controlled experimental investigation of the effects of locomotor stress on the bones of modern animals is a prerequisite to continued pursuit of meaning in the skeletal data from the Neolithic. Researchers investigating the biomechanics of calcified tissues are still very much concerned to find confirmation of the sensory network within bones responsible for transducing physical forces into morphological changes. Zooarchaeologists will need to follow developments in this field closely, for without some ideas to suggest which threshold levels of strain activate which kinds of osteological response, further work with thin sections of ancient bone will probably remain largely descriptive.

In the coming years, a more detailed picture of trabecular variability will be culled from the nearly 240 slides of the expanded Sackler collection. Armed with trabecular maps to help evaluate objectively the organization of spongy bone, and in collaboration with biologists probing the systemics of skeletal biomechanics, the initial steps taken by Drew, Perkins, and Daly will perhaps lead to a better understanding of the activities responsible for microstructural patterns in the weight-bearing bones of the earliest domesticates.

Acknowledgments

The writer is grateful to the editors of this volume for the opportunity to honor the memory of Dexter and Pat, and pay tribute to the insight of Isabella Drew, by reopening the investigation they began about twenty years ago.

Appreciation for help rendered is expressed to many, including Isabella M. Drew (Ramapo College), William Samolin (Farmington, CT), Ralph S. Solecki (Texas A & M University), Brian C. Hesse (University of Alabama-Birmingham), Howard M. Hecker (Franklin Pierce University), Jacques Bordaz (New York, NY), and Fred Roberts (Monterey Park, CA).

Anatomical and physiological details, as well as much technical assistance, were provided during invaluable consultations with biomedical professionals: Robert J. Pawluk (College of Physicians and Surgeons, Columbia University), Aaron S. Posner (Scarsdale, NY), Peter G. Bullough (Hospital for Special Surgery, NY), Foster Betts (Hospital for Special Surgery, NY), and J. Lawrence Katz (Case Western Reserve University). With cautious presumption, I have applied the knowledge gained from their wise counsel to bones of the long dead. As the scientific process has done to the original research of Drew, Perkins, and Daly, so may it continue to remodel primary hypotheses on the behavior of bone under strain into sturdier theory that will help explain early domestication.

References

Anonymous. 1971. 'Psychedelic' Colors Show Differences Between Domestic and Wild Animals. *Columbia University Newsletter* 12(16):1-2.

Azároff, L.V. 1968. *Elements of X-Ray Crystallography.* McGraw Hill, New York.

Azároff, L.V., and M.J. Buerger. 1958. *The Powder Method in X-Ray Crystallography.* McGraw Hill, New York.

Bassett, C.A.L., and R.O. Becker. 1962. Generation of Electrical Potentials by Bone in Response to Mechanical Stress. *Science* 137:1063-1064.

Bassett, C.A.L., R.J. Pawluk, and R.O. Becker. 1964. Effects of Electrical Currents on Bone *in vivo. Nature* 204:652-654.

Bear, R.S. 1952. The Structure of Collagen Fibrils. *Advances in Protein Chemistry* 7:69-160.

Beevers, C.A., and D.B. McIntyre. 1946. The Atomic

Structure of Fluor-apatite and its Relation to that of Tooth and Bone Material. *Mineralogical Magazine* 27:254-257.

Benninghoff, A. 1925. Form und Bau der Gelenkknorpel in ihren Beziehungen zur Funktion. II. Der Aufbau des Gelenkknorpels in seinen Beziehungen zur Funktion. *Zeitschrift für Zellforschung und mikroskopische Anatomie* 2:783.

Berry, L.G., and B. Mason. 1959. *Mineralogy: Concepts, Descriptions, Determinations.* Freeman, San Francisco.

Binford, L.R. 1981. *Bones: Ancient Men and Modern Myths.* Academic Press, New York.

Bocciarelli, D.S. 1970. Morphology of Crystallites in Bone. *Calcified Tissue Research* 5:261-269.

Bökönyi, S. 1969. Archaeological Problems and Methods of Recognizing Animal Domestication. In *The Domestication and Exploitation of Plants and Animals*, ed. P.J. Ucko and G.W. Dimbleby, pp. 219-229. Aldine Atherton, Chicago.

Bökönyi, S., L. Kakkai, J. Matolsci, and R. Tarjan. 1965. Vergleichende Untersuchungen am Metacarpus des Ursund des Hausrindes. *Zeitschrift für Tierzüchtung und Züchtungsbiologie* 18(4):330-347.

Bordaz, J. 1968. The Suberde Excavations, Southwestern Turkey: An Interim Report. *Türk Arkeoloji Dergisi* 17(2):43-71.

_____ 1969. A Preliminary Report of the 1969 Excavations at Erbaba, a Neolithic Site near Beyşehir, Turkey. *Türk Arkeoloji Dergisi* 18(2):59-64.

_____ 1973. Current Research in the Neolithic of South Central Turkey: Suberde, Erbaba and their Chronological Implications. *American Journal of Archaeology* 77:282-288.

Bourgery, J.M. 1832. *Traité complet de l'anatomie de l'homme. 1: Osteologie.* Paris.

Bouvier, M., and W.L. Hylander. 1981. Effect of Bone Strain on Cortical Bone Structure in Macaques (*Macaca mulatta*). *Journal of Morphology* 167:1-12.

Boyde, A. 1972. Scanning Electron Microscope Studies of Bone. In *The Biochemistry and Physiology of Bone.* Vol. I: *Structure*, 2nd ed., ed. G.H. Bourne, pp. 259-310. Academic Press, New York and London.

Bullough P.G., and A. Jagannath. 1983. The Morphology of the Calcification Front in Articular Cartilage: Its Significance in Joint Function. *Journal of Bone and Joint Surgery* (London) 65B:72-78.

Carlström, D., and A. Engström. 1956. Ultrastructure and Distribution of Mineral Salts in Bone Tissue. In *The Biochemistry and Physiology of Bone*, ed. G.H. Bourne, pp. 149-178. Academic Press, New York.

Carpenter, G.B. 1969. *Principles of Crystal Structure Determination.* W.A. Benjamin, New York.

Cuisinier, F., E.F. Brès, J. Hemmerle, J.-C. Voegel, and R.M. Frank. 1987. Transmission Electron Microscopy of Lattice Planes in Human Alveolar Bone Apatite Crystals. *Calcified Tissue International* 40:332-338.

Currey, J. 1975. The Effect of Strain Rate, Reconstruction and Mineral Content on Some Mechanical Properties of Bovine Bone. *Journal of Biomechanics* 8:81-86.

_____ 1984. *The Mechanical Adaptations of Bones.* Princeton University Press, Princeton, NJ.

Dallemagne, M.J. 1964. Phosphate and Carbonate in Bone and Teeth. In *Bone and Tooth*, ed. H.J.J. Blackwood, pp. 171-174. Macmillan, New York.

Daly, P., D. Perkins, Jr., and I.M. Drew. 1973. The Effects of Domestication on the Structure of Animal Bone. In *Domestikationsforschung und Geschichte der Haustiere*, ed. J. Matolsci, pp. 157-161. Akadémiai Kiadó, Budapest.

Darling, A.I. 1964. The Structure of Human Dental Enamel. In *Bone and Tooth*, ed. H.J.J. Blackwood, pp. 129-134. Macmillan, New York.

De Jong, W.F. 1926. La substance minérale dans les os. *Receuil Travail Chimiques Pays-Bas* 45:445-448.

Deer, W.A., R.A. Howie, and J. Zussman. 1962. *Rock Forming Minerals.* Vol. V: *Non-Silicates.* Longmans, London.

DeNiro, M.J. 1985. Postmortem Preservation and Alteration of *in vivo* Bone Collagen Isotope Ratios in Relation to Paleodietary Reconstruction. *Nature* 317:806-809.

Drew, I.M. 1966. *Properties of the Bootlegger Cove Clay of Anchorage, Alaska.* Ph.D. dissertation, Columbia University, New York.

Drew, I.M., D. Perkins, Jr., and P. Daly. 1971a. Prehistoric Domestication of Animals: Effects on Bone Structure, *Science* 171:280-282.

_____ 1971b. Response to McConnell and Foreman. *Science* 172:972-973.

Eanes, E.D., and A.S. Posner. 1970. Structure and Chemistry of Bone Mineral. In *Biological Calcification: Cellular and Molecular Aspects*, ed. E.H. Schraer, pp. 1-26. Appleton Century Crofts, New York.

Eastoe, J.E. 1956. The Organic Matrix of Bone. In *The Biochemistry and Physiology of Bone*, ed. G.H. Bourne, pp. 81-105. Academic Press, New York.

_____ 1964. Recent Studies on the Organic Matrices of Bone and Teeth. In *Bone and Tooth*, ed. H.J.J. Blackwood, pp. 269-281. Macmillan, New York.

Engström, A. 1972. Aspects of the Molecular Structure of Bone. In *The Biochemistry and Physiology of Bone.* Vol. I: *Structure*, 2nd ed., ed. G.H. Bourne, pp. 237-257. Academic Press, New York and London.

Enlow, D.H. 1963. *Principles of Bone Remodeling.* C.C.

Thomas, Springfield, IL.

Freeman, M.A. 1979. *Adult Articular Cartilage*. Pitman Medical, London.

Frey-Wyssling, A. 1953. *Submicroscopic Morphology of Protoplasm*, 2nd Engl. ed. Elsevier, Amsterdam.

Frost, H.M. 1964. *The Laws of Bone Structure*. C.C. Thomas, Springfield, IL.

Ghadially, F.N. 1983. *Fine Structure of Synovial Joints: A Text and Atlas of the Ultrastructure of Normal and Pathological Articular Tissues*. Butterworths, London and Boston.

Gilbert, A.S. 1979. *Urban Taphonomy of Mammalian Remains from the Bronze Age of Godin Tepe, Western Iran*. Ph.D. dissertation, Columbia University. University Microfilms, Ann Arbor, MI.

Gilbert, A.S., J.M. Lowenstein, and B.C. Hesse. 1990. Biochemical Differentiation of Archaeological Equid Remains: Lessons from a First Attempt. *Journal of Field Archaeology* 17:39-48.

Gilbert, A.S., B.H. Singer, and D. Perkins, Jr. 1981. Quantification Experiments on Computer-simulated Faunal Collections. *OSSA* 8:79-94.

Green, W.T., G.N. Martin, E.D. Eanes, and L. Sokoloff. 1970. Microradiographic Study of the Calcified Layer of Articular Cartilage. *Archives of Pathology* 90:151-158.

Hancox, N.M. 1972. *Biology of Bone*. Cambridge University Press, Cambridge.

Hare, P.E. 1980. Organic Geochemistry of Bone and Its Relation to the Survival of Bone in the Natural Environment. In *Fossils in the Making*, ed. A.K. Behrensmeyer and A.P. Hill, pp. 208-219. University of Chicago Press, Chicago and London.

Hare, P.E., G.H. Miller, and N.C. Tuross. 1975. Simulation of Natural Hydrolysis of Proteins in Fossils. *Carnegie Institution of Washington Year Book* 74:609-612.

Hecker, H.M. 1975. *The Faunal Analysis of the Primary Food Animals from Pre-Pottery Neolithic Beidha (Jordan)*. Ph.D. dissertation, Columbia University. University Microfilms, Ann Arbor, MI.

Hedges, R.E.M., and C.J.A. Wallace.1978. The Survival of Biochemical Information in Archaeological Bone. *Journal of Archaeological Science* 5:377-386.

_____ 1980. The Survival of Protein in Bone. In *Biogeochemistry of Amino Acids*, ed. P.E. Hare, T.C. Hoering, and K. King, pp. 35-40. John Wiley, New York.

Henrickson, R.C. 1986. A Regional Perspective on Godin III Cultural Development in Central Western Iran. *Iran* 24:1-55.

Herring, G.M. 1972. The Organic Matrix of Bone. In *The Biochemistry and Physiology of Bone*. Vol.I: *Structure*, 2nd ed., ed. G.H. Bourne, pp. 127-189.

Academic Press, New York and London.

Hesse, B.C. 1978. *Evidence for Husbandry from the Early Neolithic Site of Ganj Dareh in Western Iran*. Ph.D. dissertation, Columbia University. University Microfilms, Ann Arbor, MI.

_____ 1982. Slaughter Patterns and Domestication: The Beginnings of Pastoralism in Western Iran. *Man* 17:403-417.

Hicks, N. 1971. Bones of Animals Clue to Cultures. *The New York Times* January 23:26.

Hodge, A.J. 1967. Structure at the Electron Microscopic Level. In *Treatise on Collagen*. Vol. 1: *Chemistry of Collagen*, ed. G.N. Ramachandran, pp. 185-205. Academic Press, London and New York.

Hole, F., K.V. Flannery, and J.A. Neely. 1969. *Prehistory and Human Ecology of the Deh Luran Plain*. Memoirs No. 1. Museum of Anthropology, University of Michigan, Ann Arbor.

Kerr, P.F. 1977. *Optical Mineralogy*, 4th ed. McGraw Hill, New York.

Kirkbride, D. 1966. Five Seasons at the Pre-pottery Neolithic Village of Beidha in Jordan. *Palestine Exploration Quarterly* 98(1):872.

_____ 1968. Beidha: Early Neolithic Village Life South of the Dead Sea. *Antiquity* 42:263-274.

Kummer, B.K.F. 1959. *Bauprinzipien des Säugerskeletes*. Thieme, Stuttgart.

_____ 1972. Biomechanics of Bone: Mechanical Properties, Functional Structure, Functional Adaptation. In *Biomechanics: Its Foundations and Objectives*, ed. Y.C. Fung, N. Perrone, and M. Anliker, pp. 237-271. Prentice-Hall, Englewood Cliffs, NJ.

Lane, L.B., and P.G. Bullough. 1980. Age-related Changes in the Thickness of the Calcified Zone and the Number of Tidemarks in Adult Human Cartilage. *Journal of Bone and Joint Surgery* (London) 62B:372-375.

Lanyon, L.E. 1987. Functional Strain in Bone Tissue as an Objective, and Controlling Stimulus for Adaptive Bone Remodelling. *Journal of Biomechanics* 20:1083-1093.

Lanyon, L.E., A.E. Goodship, C.J. Pye, and J.H. MacFie. 1982. Mechanically Adaptive Bone Remodelling. *Journal of Biomechanics* 15:141-154.

LeGeros, R.Z., O. Trautz, J.P. LeGeros, and E. Klein. 1968. Carbonate Substitution in Apatite Structure, *Bulletin, Société Chimique de France*, Special Number:1712-1718.

Lipson, S.F., and J.L. Katz. 1984. The Relationship Between Elastic Properties and Microstructure of Bovine Cortical Bone. *Journal of Biomechanics* 17:231-240.

MASCA. 1970. Bone from Domestic and Wild Animals: Crystallographic Differences. *MASCA Newsletter*

6(1):2.

———. 1973. Technique for Determining Animal Domestication Based on a Study of Thin Sections of Bone under Polarized Light. *MASCA Newsletter* 9(2):1-2.

Mateescu, C.N. 1975. Remarks on Cattle Breeding and Agriculture in the Middle and Late Neolithic on the Lower Danube. *Dacia* (n.s.) 19:13-18.

Mayne, R., and M.H. Irwin. 1986. Collagen Types in Cartilage. In *Articular Cartilage Biochemistry*, ed. K.E. Kuettner, R. Schleyerbach, and V.C. Hascall, pp. 23-38. Raven Press, New York.

McConnell, D., and D.W. Foreman, Jr. 1971. Texture and Composition of Bone. *Science* 172:971-972.

Miller, E.J. 1985. The Structure of Fibril-Forming Collagens. In *Biology, Chemistry, and Pathology of Collagen*, ed. R. Fleischmajer, B.R. Olsen, and K. Kühn, pp. 113. Annals of the New York Academy of Sciences 460.

Müller-Gerbl, M., E. Schulte, and R. Putz. 1987. The Thickness of the Calcified Layer of Articular Cartilage: A Function of the Load Supported? *Journal of Anatomy* 154:103-111.

Murie, A. 1944. *The Wolves of Mount McKinley. Fauna of the National Parks of the United States.* Fauna Series No. 5. U.S. Government Printing Office, Washington, DC.

Nancollas, G.H., and M.S. Mohan. 1970. The Growth of Hydroxyapatite Crystals. *Archives of Oral Biology* 15:731-745.

Østergård, M. 1980. X-ray Diffractometer Investigations of Bones from Domestic and Wild Animals. *American Antiquity* 45:59-63.

Pauwels, F. 1954. Über die Verteilung der Spongiosadichte im coxalen Femurende und ihre Bedeutung für die Lehre vom funktionellen Bau des Knochens. Siebenter Beitrag zur funktionellen Anatomie und kausalen Morphologie des Stützapparates. *Morphologisches Jahrbuch* 95:35-54.

———. 1965. *Gesammelte Abhandlungen zur funktionellen Anatomie des Bewegungsapparates.* Springer Verlag, Berlin, Heidelberg, and New York.

Perkins, D., Jr. 1959. *The Post-Cranial Skeleton of the Caprinae: Comparative Anatomy and Changes Under Domestication.* Ph.D. dissertation, Harvard University, Cambridge, MA.

———. 1964. Prehistoric Fauna from Shanidar, Iraq. *Science* 144:1565-1566.

———. 1971. The Beginnings of Animal Domestication in the Near East. Paper presented at the Columbia University Seminar on the Archaeology of the Eastern Mediterranean, Eastern Europe, and the Near East.

Perkins, D., Jr., and P. Daly. 1968. A Hunters' Village in Neolithic Turkey. *Scientific American* 219(5):96-106.

Phillips, W.R. 1971. *Mineral Optics: Principles and Techniques.* Freeman, San Francisco.

Pollard, G.C. 1970. *The Cultural Ecology of Ceramic Stage Settlement in the Atacama Desert.* Ph.D. dissertation, Columbia University. University Microfilms, Ann Arbor, MI.

Pollard, G.C., and I.M. Drew. 1975. Llama Herding and Settlement in Prehispanic Northern Chile. *American Antiquity* 40:296-305.

Posner, A.S. 1985. The Mineral of Bone. *Clinical Orthopedics* 200:87-99.

———. 1987. Bone Mineral and the Mineralization Process. *Bone and Mineral Research* 5:65-116.

Price, T.D. (editor). 1989. *The Chemistry of Prehistoric Human Bone.* Cambridge University Press, Cambridge.

Pritchard, J.J. 1972a. General Histology of Bone. In *The Biochemistry and Physiology of Bone.* Vol. I: *Structure*, 2nd ed., ed. G.H. Bourne, pp. 1-20. Academic Press, New York and London.

———. 1972b. The Osteoblast. In *The Biochemistry and Physiology of Bone.* Vol. I: *Structure*, 2nd ed., ed. G.H. Bourne, pp. 21-43. Academic Press, New York and London.

Reed, C.A. 1960. A Review of the Archeological Evidence on Animal Domestication in the Prehistoric Near East. In *Prehistoric Investigations in Iraqi Kurdistan*, ed. R.J. Braidwood and B. Howe, pp. 119-145. Studies in Ancient Oriental Civilization 31, University of Chicago Press.

Reilly, D.T., and A.H. Burstein. 1975. The Elastic and Ultimate Properties of Compact Bone Tissue. *Journal of Biomechanics* 8:393-405.

Robinson, R.A. 1952. An Electron Microscope Study of the Crystalline Inorganic Component of Bone and Its Relationship to the Organic Matrix. *Journal of Bone and Joint Surgery* (American) 34A:389-434.

Robinson, R.A., and M.L. Watson. 1952. Collagen-Crystal Relationships in Bone as Seen in the Electron Microscope. *Anatomical Record* 114:383-409.

Roesler, H. 1981. Some Historical Remarks on the Theory of Cancellous Bone Structure (Wolff's Law). In *Mechanical Properties of Bone*, ed. S.C. Cowin, pp. 27-42. American Society of Mechanical Engineers, New York.

———. 1987. The History of Some Fundamental Concepts in Bone Biomechanics. *Journal of Biomechanics* 20:1025-1034.

Rouiller, C. 1956. Collagen Fibers of Connective Tissue. In *The Biochemistry and Physiology of Bone*, ed. G.H. Bourne, pp. 107-147. Academic Press, New York.

Roux, W. 1881. *Der züchtende Kampf der Teile, oder die 'Teilauslese' im Organismus. (Theorie der 'funktionellen Anpassung').* Wilhelm Engelmann, Leipzig.

Saloman, C.D., and N. Haas. 1967. Histological and Histochemical Observations on Undecalcified Sections of Ancient Bones from Excavations in Israel. *Israel Journal of Medical Sciences* 3:747-754.

Schenk, R.K., P.S. Eggli, and E.B. Hunziker. 1986. Articular Cartilage Morphology. In *Articular Cartilage Biochemistry*, ed. K.E. Kuettner, R. Schleyerbach, and V.C. Hascall, pp. 3-22. Raven Press, New York.

Shelley, D. 1985. *Optical Mineralogy*, 2nd ed. Elsevier, New York.

Shimokomaki, M., D.W. Wright, M.H. Irwin, M. Van Der Rest, and R. Mayne. 1990. The Structure and Macromolecular Organization of Type IX Collagen in Cartilage. In *Structure, Molecular Biology, and Pathology of Collagen.* ed. R. Fleischmajer, B.R. Olsen, and K. Kühn, pp. 1-7. Annals of the New York Academy of Sciences 580.

Sillen A. 1981. Post-depositional Changes in Natufian and Aurignacian Bones from Hayonim Cave. *Paléorient* 7/2:81-85.

_____ 1989. Diagenesis of the Inorganic Phase of Cortical Bone. In *The Chemistry of Prehistoric Human Bone,* ed. T.D. Price, pp. 211-229. Cambridge University Press, Cambridge.

Singh, I. 1978 The Architecture of Cancellous Bone. *Journal of Anatomy* 127:305-310.

Sissons, H.A. 1956. The Growth of Bone. In *The Biochemistry and Physiology of Bone*, ed. G.H. Bourne, pp. 443-474. Academic Press, New York.

Smith, P.E.L. 1976. Reflections on Four Seasons of Excavations at Tappeh Ganj Dareh. In *Proceedings of the IVth Annual Symposium on Archaeological Research in Iran,* ed. F. Bagherzadeh, pp. 11-22. Muzehe Irane Bastan, Tehran.

_____ 1990. Architectural Innovation and Experimentation at Ganj Dareh, Iran. *World Archaeology* 21:323-335.

Solecki, R.L. 1981. *An Early Village Site at Zawi Chemi Shanidar.* Bibliotheca Mesopotamica 13, Undena, Malibu, CA.

Stockwell, R.A. 1979. *Biology of Cartilage Cells.* Cambridge University Press, Cambridge and New York.

Stougård, J. 1974. The Calcified Cartilage and the Subchondral Bone Under Normal and Abnormal Conditions. *Acta Pathologica et Microbiologica Scandinavica* Section A 82:182-188.

Stout, S.D. 1978. Histological Structure and Its Preservation in Ancient Bone. *Current Anthropology* 19:601-604.

Sylvén, B., and E.J. Ambrose. 1955. Birefringent Fibres of Hyaluronic Acid. *Biochimica et Biophysica Acta* 18:587.

Trelstad, R.L., K. Hayashi, and J. Gross. 1976. Collagen Fibrillogenesis: Intermediate Aggregants and Suprafibrillar Order. *Proceedings, National Academy of Science* 73:4027-4031.

Vignoles, M., G. Bonel, D.W. Holcomb, and R.A. Young. 1988. Influence of Preparation Conditions on the Composition of Type B Carbonated Hydroxyapatite and on the Localization of the Carbonate Ions. *Calcified Tissue International* 43:33-40.

Watson, J.P.N. 1975. Domestication and Bone Structure in Sheep and Goats. *Journal of Archaeological Science* 2:375-383.

White, E.M., and L.A. Hannus. 1983. Chemical Weathering of Bone in Archaeological Soils. *American Antiquity* 48:316-322.

Wolff, J.D. 1892. *Das Gesetz der Transformation der Knochen.* A. Hirschwald, Berlin.

Wright, G.A., and S.J. Miller. 1976. Prehistoric Hunting of New World Wild Sheep: Implications for the Study of Sheep Domestication. In *Cultural Change and Continuity*, ed. C.E. Cleland, pp. 293-312. Academic Press, New York.

Young, T.C., Jr. 1969. *Excavations at Godin Tepe: First Progress Report.* Art and Archaeology Occasional Paper 17, Royal Ontario Museum, Toronto.

Young, T.C., Jr., and L.D. Levine. 1974. *Excavations of the Godin Project: Second Progress Report.* Art and Archaeology Occasional Paper 26, Royal Ontario Museum, Toronto.

Zeder, M.A. 1978. Differentiation Between the Bones of Caprines from Different Ecosystems in Iran by the Analysis of Osteological Microstructure and Chemical Composition. In *Approaches to Faunal Analysis in the Middle East*, ed. R.H. Meadow and M.A. Zeder, pp. 69-84. Peabody Museum Bulletin No. 2. Harvard University, Cambridge, MA.

Zeuner, F.E. 1963. *A History of Domesticated Animals.* Harper and Row, New York.

STRATEGIES OF RISK REDUCTION IN HERDING AND HUNTING SYSTEMS OF NEOLITHIC SOUTHEAST ANATOLIA

Gil Stein

Anthropology Department, Northwestern University, Evanston, IL 60208

Dedication

This paper is dedicated to the memory of Dexter Perkins, Jr. and Patricia Daly. Dexter Perkins taught the class at the University of Pennsylvania which introduced me to zooarchaeology. Dexter Perkins and Patricia Daly's thought provoking 1968 Scientific American *article concerning the Suberde fauna first called my attention to the importance of studying the role of hunting in sedentary Near Eastern communities.*

Research problem: Hunting in food-producing communities

In studying the early food-producing communities of the Near East, most archaeologists have tended to compartmentalize their research, focusing on either a single data category, such as ethnobotanical or faunal remains, or on a single subsistence strategy, such as hunting, herding, gathering, or farming. However, it has become clear that Near Eastern village communities in the seventh millennium B.C. practiced all four subsistence strategies as part of an integrated economic system. The seasonality and scheduling of each of these four strategies imposes constraints on the choice and organization of the other three (e.g. Flannery 1968; Kent 1989); for this reason, none of these subsistence pursuits can be understood in isolation.

This paper examines the relationships among hunting, herding, and plant cultivation in the Aceramic Neolithic food-producing communities of southeast Anatolia. Available evidence suggests that villagers in this area continued to hunt, even after domesticated cereals and caprines came into widespread use. How and why were these different, and often conflicting, subsistence activities combined into a single, well-integrated economic system?

The persistence of hunting and its role as a secondary element within a predominantly agro-pastoral economy can best be understood by considering the role of risk aversion as an organizing principle underlying Neolithic subsistence. Risk is commonly defined as the known or estimable probability of loss and is distinguished from the related concept of "uncertainty"—in which the chances of loss cannot be accurately estimated due to lack of information (e.g. Hegmon 1989:90). Risk and uncertainty in subsistence economies have both cultural and environmental components. The environmental component stems from the existence of variation in factors such as rainfall, temperature, disease, or predators—all of which affect the spatial and temporal availability of plant and animal resources. However, risk and uncertainty are also *culturally* defined constructs, deriving from shared human perceptions about the predictability and severity of environmental variation and its consequences (Douglas and Wildavsky 1982:8).

Risk and uncertainty can be expected to play a particularly important role in human decision-making about subsistence, since food is necessary for survival, while at the same time highly variable in its availability. People can avoid or minimize the risk of subsistence failure through a number of different strategies such as mobility, resource diversification, storage, or exchange (Halstead and O'Shea 1989:3-4). In subsistence economies which use domesticated resources, people can also minimize risk and uncertainty by relying on "conservative" production strategies. Food producers in these conservative or risk-averse systems eschew high levels of output, focusing instead on maximizing the capacity of their crops or herds to survive and recover from serious environmental perturbations (e.g. Adams 1978; Sandford 1982:62).

This discussion focuses on the roles of resource diversification and conservative management strategies as two important means of risk reduction in the subsistence economies of Neolithic southeast Anatolia in the later seventh millennium B.C. This argument has two parts. The first discusses the evidence for herding and hunting at the Aceramic Neolithic site of Gritille in southeast Anatolia, comparing it with contemporaneous faunal data from other Taurus piedmont sites such as Hayaz and

Çayönü. The second part discusses the role of hunting as a strategy to cope with pronounced seasonal variation in levels of risk and uncertainty in sedentary food-producing economies. I suggest that seventh millennium villagers at Gritille and possibly other sites supplemented lower levels of winter consumption of domesticated cereals and caprines by engaging in a highly localized "least effort" hunt that focused on species whose predictable seasonal migratory patterns brought them into the immediate vicinity of the Neolithic settlements.

Aceramic Neolithic subsistence in southeast Anatolia

The earliest known excavated villages in the Taurus piedmont zone of southeast Anatolia are the sites of Çayönü (Braidwood et al. 1981; Braidwood and Braidwood 1982) and Cafer Höyük (Cauvin 1985), dating to the eighth and early seventh millennia B.C. (Cauvin 1988:69; Aurenche and Calley 1988:19). A second, chronologically overlapping, set of settlements at Gritille (Voigt and Ellis 1981; Voigt 1985, 1988), Hayaz (Roodenberg 1980), and Nevali Çori (Hauptman 1988; Schmidt 1988) provide evidence for the mid-to-late seventh millennium B.C. Several researchers have characterized these assemblages as the Early- and Late- "Taurus PPNB," citing stylistic similarities with Levantine Pre-Pottery Neolithic B sites such

as Jericho, Byblos, Bouqras, Mureybit, and Abu Hureyra (Voigt 1985:19; Cauvin 1988:74-77).

Ethnobotanical and faunal data from Çayönü and Cafer indicate that these earliest Taurus PPNB villages grew domesticated cereals such as emmer wheat, while continuing to gather wild cereals and legumes (Van Zeist 1988:58). However, these settlements had no domesticated food animals, relying instead on red deer, aurochs, wild pigs, and wild caprines (Braidwood et al. 1981:250; Helmer 1988:42). Domesticated sheep and goats do not appear until the later Taurus PPNB phases at Çayönü (Lawrence 1982:189), Hayaz (Buitenhuis 1985:67), and Gritille (Stein 1986a:39; 1986b:7). Thus, in southeast Anatolia, animal domestication must be seen as a secondary development within an agriculturally based economic system. Even after the development of herding as a major economic focus, hunting persisted in a small-scale subsistence role, accounting for roughly 3 to 19 percent of the identified animal bones (NISP) at these sites during the later seventh millennium B.C.

Gritille Höyük

Faunal remains from the site of Gritille Höyük in southeast Turkey provide the primary data set for this examination of the relationship between herding and

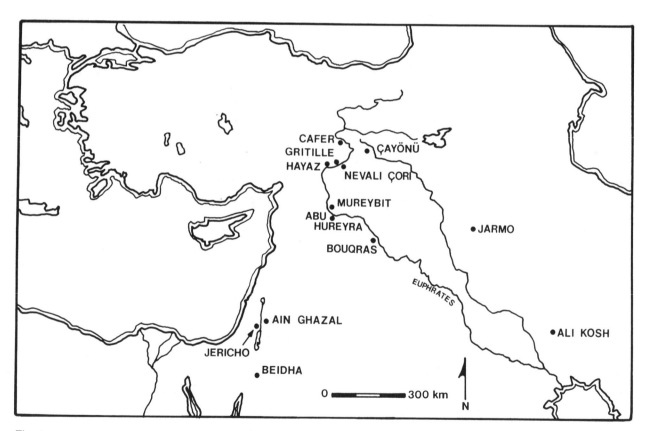

Fig. 1:
Map showing location of Gritille in Karababa basin, Euphrates river valley, southeast Turkey.

hunting in the food-producing village economies of the later Taurus PPNB. Gritille is a small, 1.5-hectare mound, lying ca. 8 km northeast of the modern town of Samsat in the Karababa basin of the Euphrates river valley (Fig. 1). In this region the Euphrates cuts through a piedmont area at the interface between the north Syrian steppe and the eastern Taurus mountains. Mean annual rainfall varies from 400-600 mm, which is sufficient to support dry farming of cereals and pulses on the relatively wide and flat river terraces. The combination of rainfall, groundwater, and river resources also sustains the grazing needed for large numbers of animals, whether wild or domestic. In terms of topography, climate, vegetation, and fauna, the Karababa basin forms part of the "hilly flanks" of the Taurus and Zagros mountains—the foothill zone in which some of the earliest known domestication of plants and animals took place.

As part of the Turkish government-sponsored Lower Euphrates Archaeological Salvage project, from 1981 to 1984 four seasons of excavation were carried out at Gritille by an expedition under the direction of Richard S. Ellis, Bryn Mawr College. This fieldwork recovered a 9000-year discontinuous occupation sequence extending from the seventh millennium B.C. through a 12th-13th century A.D. Medieval Crusader/Ayyubid settlement (Ellis and Voigt 1982; Redford 1986; Stein 1986a, 1986b, 1987; Voigt and Ellis 1981). The earliest occupation of the mound is a 3-4 meter thick deposit of well preserved houses, open areas, and associated artifacts dating from the mid-to-late seventh millennium B.C., corresponding to the "later Taurus PPNB" (Voigt 1985, 1988).

Gritille fauna

Aceramic Neolithic faunal remains were recovered from Gritille by three collection procedures:
1. Recovery during the course of excavation. After being checked by the excavators, all excavated sediments were sieved as follows:
2. Dry sieving of 80% of excavated sediments in 0.5 cm mesh;
3. Wet sieving of the the remaining 20% of sediments in 2 mm (window) mesh.

These procedures were followed to ensure that small mammals and juveniles would be accurately represented in the faunal sample (Payne 1975; Meadow 1980). All recovered animal bone was saved for analysis.

At least 120,000 fragments were recovered from the 350-m² exposure of Neolithic deposits. This discussion focuses on a sample of 8,590 fragments from the late Aceramic phase B at Gritille, dating to the late seventh millennium B.C. (Table 1; see also Voigt 1988:227). Of these, 1,395 fragments, about 16%, were identified to genus. Sheep and goats predominate in the sample, forming 76% of the identified fragments (NISP) (Table 2).

Pigs are second most common at 18%, and cattle the third most common at 3%. The remainder of the sample is composed of gazelle (*Gazella*), red deer (*Cervus*), fallow deer (*Dama*), roe deer (*Capreolus*), dog, hedgehog (*Erinaceus*), hare (*Lepus*), and rodents. Although the majority of caprines, cattle, and pigs seem to have been domesticated, several lines of evidence suggest that wild forms of these animals were hunted as well.

Sheep and goats

Caprines, apparently domesticated, form the largest part (approximately 76%) of the Gritille Aceramic phase B faunal assemblage. In most cases, it was not possible to determine whether the caprine remains represent sheep or goats. When a distinction could be made between the two taxa, 81 fragments were identified as sheep, and 28 as goats, yielding a sheep:goat ratio of 2.89:1.

In the absence of well-preserved horn cores, ages at death provide the best available criterion for determining the domestication status of sheep and goats at Gritille. Ages were calculated from mandibular tooth eruption and wear using Payne's (1973) age estimation system. The mortality data show that 65% of all Neolithic phase B caprines were killed before an age of 3 years (Figs. 2 and 3).

The predominance of young sheep and goats in a faunal sample is generally interpreted as reflecting domestication (Perkins 1964; Hole et al. 1969; Wright and Miller 1977; Hesse 1982). Herders would be expected to keep young male sheep and goats alive only until they reach their maximum meat weight, at an age of 2-3 years, or slightly earlier, when the growth curve begins to level off. At this point, most of the males would be killed, since they contribute nothing further to the herd, and only compete for fodder with the more productive and valuable females. Females would then be kept alive in the domesticated herd until their reproductive abilities begin to decline, at an age of 6-7 years (e.g. Payne 1973:301-302). For this reason, the mortality pattern of a domesticated herd raised as a source of meat (since we have no evidence for dairy or wool production as a principal herding goal until the fourth millennium B.C.: Sherratt 1983) would have mostly young males, with a secondary peak of adult females. Although we lack sufficient data on sex

Table 1. Radiocarbon dates, Gritille Aceramic Neolithic phase B (later Taurus PPNB) (Voigt 1988:227, table 1).

Laboratory no.	5568 B.P.	5730 B.C.	Calibrated B.C.
Beta-8240	7770 ± 150	6050 ± 150	6780 - 6450
Beta-8241	7860 ± 80	6150 ± 80	6810 - 6600
Beta-13218	7950 ± 120	6240 ± 120	7060 - 6645

Table 2. Fragments identified to genus: fragment counts (NISP) and Minimum Number of Individuals (MNI), Gritille Aceramic Neolithic phase B (later Taurus PPNB).

Taxon	Fragment count	Fragment %	MNI	% MNI
Ovis/Capra	952	68.24	29	64.44
Ovis	81	5.81	*	*
Capra	28	2.01	*	*
Gazella	15	1.08	1	2.22
Bos	48	3.44	1	2.22
Cervus	5	0.36	1	2.22
Capreolus	2	0.14	1	2.22
Dama	4	0.29	2	4.44
Sus	249	17.85	5	11.11
Canis sp.	1	0.07	1	2.22
Canis familiaris	2	0.14	*	*
Vulpes	1	0.07	1	2.22
Erinaceus	1	0:07	1	2.22
Lepus	5	0.36	1	2.22
Potamon	1	0.07	1	2.22
TOTAL	1,395	100.00	45	100.00

*Omitted from MNI calculations to maintain mutual exclusivity of classifications.

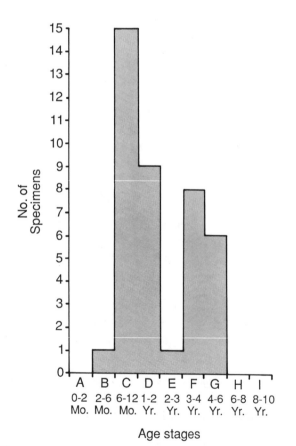

Fig. 2:
Caprine mortality from mandibular tooth eruption and wear (n=40), Gritille Aceramic phase B. Age stages follow the coding system in Payne (1973).

ratios, the ages at death of the Gritille sheep and goats conform to this bi-modal, juvenile-oriented pattern, strongly suggesting that these were domesticated animals (Fig. 2).

It is especially significant that the Gritille caprine survivorship pattern also accords well with Redding's (1981) expected population structure for a domesticated herd managed with the goal of "herd security" (Fig. 3). Redding defines this strategy as the minimization of fluctuations in yield below the subsistence needs of the herding group. Herd security can be measured in terms of the ability of the animal population to maintain itself, minimizing the effects of deaths due to natural hazards such as climatic extremes, disease, predation, and parasitism (Redding 1981:187). Focusing on herd security is thus a risk-averse production strategy. Under the herd security model, it is expected that 52.4% of the caprines will be culled between the ages of 6 months and 2 years (Redding 1981:table X-3). At Gritille, 60% of the sheep and goats were culled within this age range, closely conforming to the predictions of the model. Thus the currently available data on the Gritille phase B caprine mortality suggest that risk aversion (i.e. herd security) was a primary principle structuring meat production for the most abundant domesticated animals at this settlement during the late seventh millennium B.C.

The inhabitants of Gritille apparently minimized subsistence risk in other ways as well, by maintaining a diversified resource base which included not only caprine herding, but also the hunting of wild caprines. Metric data suggest that small numbers of wild caprines are present in the Gritille assemblage. Measurements of sheep and goat distal humeri show a clear size break between a cluster of relatively small sheep and goats (the majority of the measured sample), and a few outlying data points for larger goats (Fig. 4). As Lawrence (1982:180) notes, one must be very careful in using sheep and goat measurements to infer domestication because the size overlap between the wild and domestic forms is quite appreciable. However, the clear size difference in the Gritille caprine humeri may well reflect an assemblage dominated by domesticated sheep and goats, with the larger specimens indicating that wild caprines continued to be hunted.

Pig (Sus)

Pigs form the second largest part of the Gritille Aceramic phase B assemblage. Although the number of measurable specimens is quite limited, the currently available metric data suggest that both domestic and wild forms were exploited by the Neolithic villagers.

Domesticated pigs are significantly smaller and have shorter faces than their wild ancestors. Since this shortening of the snout involves a reduction in tooth size as well, measurements of the second and third molars are generally used to determine whether pigs were wild or domesticated (Flannery 1983; Lawrence 1980). Five pig molars from Gritille Aceramic phase B were complete enough to be measured (Table 3).

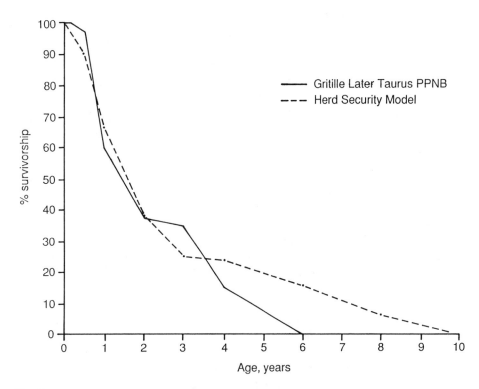

Fig. 3:
Caprine survivorship curve from mandibular tooth eruption and wear (n=40), Gritille Aceramic phase B, compared to predicted survivorship under herding strategies emphasizing herd security (after Redding 1981).

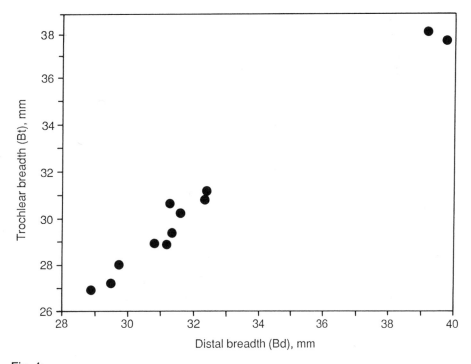

Fig. 4:
Caprine distal humerus measurements, Gritille Aceramic phase B: distal breadth and trochlear breadth (after von den Driesch 1976).

Two differing sets of tooth measurements have been proposed to mark the dividing line between wild and domestic pigs. Based on the analysis of pig teeth from Europe, Stampfli has proposed a set of minimum molar lengths for wild pigs (Stampfli, cited in Lawrence 1980:299, 307). A second set of tooth measurements was provided by Flannery (1983), based on the analysis of 21 modern Near Eastern wild pigs. Flannery's data suggest that Near Eastern wild pigs are smaller than the minimum measurements given by Stampfli for the dentition of European wild pigs.

When compared with these measurements, the Gritille pig teeth suggest that both wild and domesticated pigs played a role in the late Aceramic economy. Three of the five molars fall within the domesticated size range by both Flannery's and Stampfli's criteria (Table 3 and Fig. 5). The remaining two teeth are in a size range which is domesticated by Stampli's criteria, but wild according to Flannery's measurements. These results might mean that the pigs at Gritille were at a relatively early stage of domestication. However, since Flannery's domestication indices are based on local Near Eastern wild pig populations, they would be most applicable to the Gritille data; it thus appears more likely that the inhabitants of Gritille kept some domestic pigs while continuing to hunt wild pigs, perhaps as a winter food source. Clearly, a much larger sample of teeth is needed in order to clarify the range of variation for wild and domesticated pigs in southeast Anatolia.

Table 3. Gritille Aceramic Neolithic phase B pig molar tooth measurements and published pig domestication indices.

A. Gritille data:

Specimen no.	Tooth	Length (mm)	Width (mm)
7839	M^3	34.04	20.35
7836	M^2	22.08	18.95
7930	M^2	22.60	18.10
8252	M^2	20.45	15.49
8845	M_2	19.95	12.66

B. Pig domestication indices (European population) (Stampfli in Lawrence 1980:299, 307):

Tooth	Minimum length for wild (mm)	Maximum length for domestic (mm)
M^3	34.5	36.5
M^2	23.5	25.5
M_3	37.0	39.0
M_2	20.5	22.5

C. Population parameters for Near Eastern wild pigs (n=21) (Flannery 1983):

Tooth	Mean length	Std. dev.	Maximum length	Minimum length
M^3	37.4	2.51	42.8	34.1
M^2	23.3	1.65	26.3	20.7
M_3	41.3	2.43	49.3	37.6
M_2	23.4	1.29	26.4	21.0

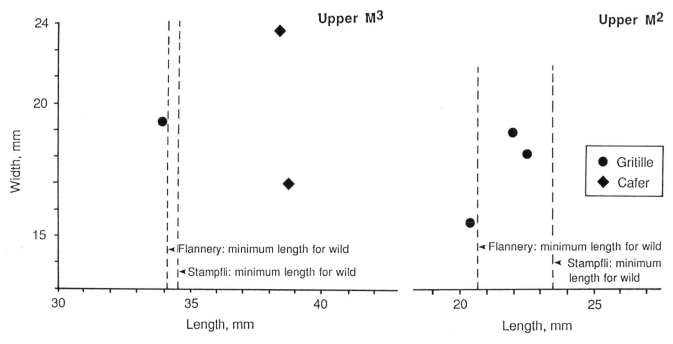

Fig. 5:
Pig molar tooth measurements, Gritille Aceramic phase B, and suggested size ranges for domesticates. Parameters for wild pig measurements from Flannery (1983) and Stampfli in Lawrence (1980). Data points for Cafer show dimensions of wild *Sus*.

Cattle (Bos)

Cattle form the third most commonly occurring animal in the analyzed sample. As with caprines and pigs, the available sample suggests that both domesticated and wild cattle were used by the Neolithic villagers at Gritille. Only a few cattle bones were complete enough for measurement (Table 4). Cattle domestication involves a size reduction that can be detected in the dimensions of foot bones such as the first and third phalanges. Studies of the Deh Luran Neolithic sites in southwestern Iran suggest that the length of wild cattle third phalanges ranges from 81-109 mm (Hole et al. 1969:306-307). By the Deh Luran criteria, one of the Gritille third phalanges falls in the size range of domesticated *Bos taurus*, while the other lies in the range of the wild *Bos primigenius*. As with the pig data, the Gritille cattle measurements are ambiguous. If the Deh Luran domestication criteria are applicable to southeast Anatolia, then both wild and domesticated cattle were exploited at Gritille. If wild cattle in southeast Anatolia were smaller than Iranian wild cattle, however, then the Deh Luran domestication criteria would be inapplicable, and the Gritille cattle could easily be wild. A larger sample of measurable bones must be analyzed to determine whether the Gritille Neolithic cattle represent either a small wild population in the process of domestication, or else a mixed subsistence strategy which exploited both wild and domesticated cattle. In either case, it is clear that at least some wild cattle were present in the late Taurus PPNB at Gritille.

To summarize, the later Taurus PPNB villagers of Gritille practiced a mixed economy of hunting and herding within the broader framework of cereal-based agriculture. Culling patterns suggest that they followed risk-averse herding strategies which focused on herd security in their management of domesticated sheep and goats. The villagers also apparently minimized risk by exploiting a diversified set of resources. Domesticated pigs and cattle were kept in the Aceramic phase B settlement. As a supplement to these domesticates, the inhabitants of Gritille also hunted small numbers of caprines, cattle, and pigs, along with cervids and small mammals.

Comparison of Gritille with Hayaz and Çayönü

This risk-averse emphasis on wild/domestic resource diversification and caprine herd security may have characterized the other late Taurus PPNB communities as well. The Gritille Aceramic phase B faunal sample analyzed to date shows striking similarities with the published fauna from the contemporaneous nearby site of Hayaz Höyük (Buitenhuis 1985) and the slightly earlier material from the uppermost Aceramic levels (the "large-room sub-phase") at Çayönü (Lawrence 1980, 1982). In all three sites, domesticated caprines are the most common animals, with pigs second, and cattle the third most frequent among identified fauna (Fig. 6).

Table 4. Cattle third phalanx measurements (after von den Driesch 1976), Gritille Aceramic Neolithic phase B.

Specimen no.	DLS (mm) greatest length	Ld (mm)	MBS (mm)
8043	69.15	56.26	23.04
8887	92.10	—	30.31

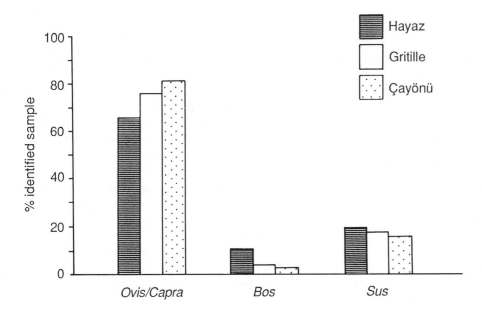

Fig. 6: Comparison of main taxa at Hayaz, Gritille, and Çayönü, later Taurus PPNB. Hayaz percentages of NISP calculated from raw counts in Buitenhuis (1985:table 1). Çayönü percentages of "relative frequency" from Lawrence (1982:table 4). "Uppermost sub-phases" refers to the building levels also called "large-room sub-phase" in earlier publications (Braidwood and Çambel 1982:7; Lawrence 1982:175-176).

In addition, Hayaz, Çayönü, and Gritille all show clear evidence for hunting as a secondary, subsistence activity. Like Gritille, the nearby contemporaneous site of Hayaz has both domesticated and wild forms of sheep, goats, cattle, and probably pigs (Buitenhuis 1985:67; Helmer 1988:48). Although domesticates form the main part of the later PPNB sample, wild game comprises at least 9.2% of all identified bone (see fragment counts in Buitenhuis 1985:table 1). The hunted species are aurochs, wild caprines, boar, cervids, and small mammals—a range virtually identical to the spectrum of prey at Gritille.

The "uppermost levels" (also known as the "large-room sub-phase": Lawrence 1982:175; Braidwood and Çambel 1982:7) at Çayönü are slightly earlier than Gritille and Hayaz. Domesticated sheep and goats form 81.3% of the faunal remains from these levels. In descending order, pigs (15.2%), cattle (2.2%), and red deer (1.3%) account for almost all of the remainder. Based on preliminary analyses, Lawrence has suggested that both cattle and pigs are apparently wild in the Çayönü uppermost levels (Lawrence 1982:184-185; Helmer 1988:48), although the domestication status of pigs remains problematic (cf. Stampfli, cited in Lawrence 1980:299, 307; Kuşatman 1990). If both pigs and cattle were wild, then hunting accounted for almost 19% of the animals used in the late Taurus PPNB occupation at Çayönü. This figure is much higher than the percentages of wild fauna at Hayaz and Gritille. This difference might partially reflect chronological factors such as a long term decline in hunting over the course of the seventh millennium. Alternatively, if, as Stampfli and Kuşatman have suggested, pigs were actually domesticated, then only 3.5-4.0% of the Çayönü fauna would have been wild, a proportion much closer to the figures for Gritille (ca. 3%) and Hayaz (ca. 9%).

The evidence from Gritille, Hayaz, and Çayönü makes it clear that these communities followed similar strategies of subsistence diversification in which hunting continued as a secondary form of animal exploitation even after caprine domestication was well established. Clearly, wild game would have provided only a small fraction of the total biomass or meat weight consumed at these settlements. However, if wild game were selectively consumed only in certain seasons, then the relative importance of these resources would have been considerably greater. It is suggested here that hunting played an important role as a winter supplement to domesticated resources, as part of an overall strategy of risk avoidance.

Risk and uncertainty in Near Eastern sedentary food-producing communities

Why did the Neolithic villagers of southeast Anatolia continue to hunt, even after they had domesticated animals and crops as reliable sources of food? What was the relationship between herding and hunting within the over-

all context of the sedentary agricultural economies of the late Taurus PPNB? In trying to answer these questions, it helps to look at two very different sets of schedules: 1) the seasonal cycle of agriculture and herding, and 2) the seasonal cycle by which wild animals such as deer or mountain goats migrate from summer to winter grazing areas. Briefly, these schedules suggest that the villagers hunted in the winter and relied much more on domesticated crops and animals for the rest of the year.

The production of domesticated crops and mammals in the Near East follows a consistent seasonal round. In southeastern Turkey, cereals are planted in October or early November, and harvested in June or July. In the herding cycle, sheep and goats are born in the winter, usually between January and March. Although the semi-arid region of southeast Turkey has a predictable cycle of dry summers and winter rainy seasons, the high degree of inter-annual variability in rainfall (Beaumont et al. 1976:70) gives rise to great uncertainty in both agricultural and pastoral yields.

For both the agricultural and herding cycles, winter is the season of greatest uncertainty. For the herds, the winter birthing season is a period of heightened susceptibility to disease and relatively harsh weather conditions. Herd losses can vary widely from winter to winter. Similarly, villagers do not know how the crops will survive, or how long they will have to live off their stocks of stored grain. If crops fail or are badly damaged, then supplies of currently stored cereals will also have to be stretched to provide seed grain for the next planting, thereby cutting even further into the amount available for human consumption. It is important to note that, for the villagers, the main question is not "how much food is currently available in storage?" but rather "for how long do available stocks of food have to last?"

Winter "least effort" hunting

In short, winter is the season when farmers and herders are most reluctant to consume their stored crops or animals. For this reason, winter is also the time of year when one would expect wild resources to play the greatest role as dietary supplements to domesticated plants and animals. In particular, the seasonal cycle of wild animals in the oak-pistachio woodlands zone would have provided a valuable added resource to the Neolithic villagers of Gritille at just the time when it would provide the most benefit. Animals such as red deer, fallow deer, wild goats, and wild sheep have a fairly predictable seasonal migratory pattern in which they spend summer in the uplands and winter in the lowlands.

Gritille is located at an elevation of 400 m in the largely snow-free flood plain of the Euphrates river valley, while the immediately neighboring mountains and plateau are snow covered in winter (Fig. 7). In a situation like this, deer, wild goats, and probably wild cattle (au-rochs) as well would have come out of the hills into the Euphrates river valley as a relatively sheltered, prime winter-grazing area. In other words, every winter, relatively dense concentrations of these wild animals would have been coming straight toward Gritille at precisely the time when the villagers were most reluctant to consume their domesticated animals or stored crops. Along with the advantages of predictability and dense concentrations, winter hunting would also have minimized scheduling conflicts with the labor requirements of the agro-pastoral economy, since the latter are greatest during the summer. Finally, winter hunting would have been a particularly safe supplementary subsistence strategy because the pattern of inter-annual variability in the availability of migratory wild game in snow-free lowland areas is largely independent of the factors affecting yields of agricultural and pastoral products (cf. O'Shea 1989:59). If this suggestion is correct, then hunting emerges as an important seasonal component of the Neolithic economy. It would have reduced subsistence risk by 1) providing an easily available and reliable "least effort" source of winter food,

while 2) permitting longer term storage of domesticates through to the spring, when villagers would have been able to make more accurate assessments of how well their crops and herds would survive and produce that year.

Conclusions

I suggest that risk aversion played a major role in shaping the strategies by which both domesticates and wild resources were used in late Taurus PPNB village economies. Archaeobotanical and faunal data from Gritille, Hayaz, and Çayönü suggest that villagers sought to minimize the risk of subsistence failure through five main strategies:

a. Diversification of the food supply among several different activities such as cereal agriculture, wild plant gathering, herding, and hunting;

b. Within each activity, diversification of plant and animal species exploited—e.g. the reliance on a combination of domesticated sheep, goats, cattle, and pigs instead of an exclusive dependence on caprines;

c. the pursuit of caprine herding strategies in which culling patterns maximized herd security;

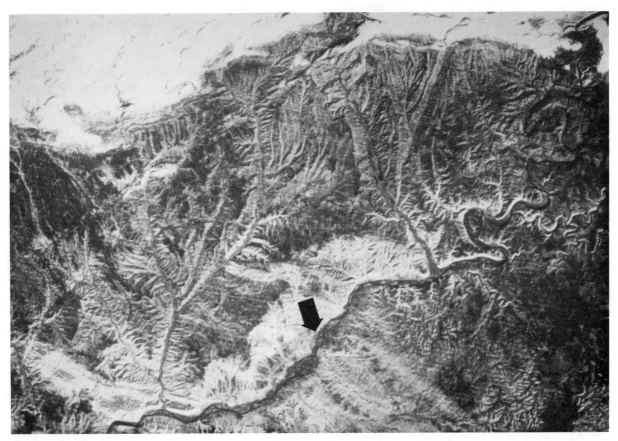

Fig. 7:
LANDSAT satellite image of the Euphrates river valley in the Gritille area (arrowed). This image, taken in February 1975, shows the concentration of heavy snows in the Taurus mountains (the white area at the top left), while the river valley itself remains largely snow free. Snows would have forced wild mammals into the lower elevations, allowing for a localized "least effort" winter hunt by villagers in the flood plain.

d. seasonal variation in subsistence emphasis, so as to minimize the consumption of domesticated plants and animals during the periods of greatest uncertainty about their future productivity;

e. the use of hunting as a seasonal (winter) dietary supplement, in a "least effort" strategy which focused on locally available species whose seasonal movements were highly predictable.

The development of sheep and goat domestication cannot be understood without reference to other parts of the later Taurus PPNB subsistence system. The Gritille data suggest that herding and hunting were organized as complementary strategies of animal use within a diversified, risk-averse economy.

Acknowledgments

Excavations at Gritille were directed by Dr. Richard Ellis and sponsored by Bryn Mawr College with the cooperation of the University of North Carolina and the participation of The University Museum, University of Pennsylvania. Analysis of the Gritille fauna has been funded by a Fulbright-IIE grant, MASCA Research Fellowships at the University of Pennsylvania, and by a Wenner-Gren Post-Doctoral grant. I am grateful to Dr. Mary M. Voigt for discussions of the Gritille Neolithic stratigraphy and its periodization. Pam Crabtree, Richard Redding, and Patricia Wattenmaker provided helpful critiques of earlier drafts of this paper. Final responsibility for the content of this paper rests with the author.

References

Adams, R.M. 1978. Strategies of Maximization, Stability and Resilience in Mesopotamian Society, Settlement, and Agriculture. *Proceedings of the American Philosophical Society* 122(5):329-335.

Aurenche, O., and S. Calley. 1988. L'architecture de l'Anatolie du Sud-est au Néolithique Acéramique. *Anatolica* 15:1-24.

Beaumont, P., G. Blake, and M. Wagstaff. 1976. *The Middle East. A Geographical Study.* John Wiley, London.

Braidwood, L., and R. Braidwood (editors). 1982. *Prehistoric Village Archaeology in Southeast Turkey. The Eighth Millennium B.C. Site at Çayönü: Its Chipped and Ground Stone Industries and Faunal Remains.* BAR International No. Series 138, Oxford.

Braidwood, R., and H. Çambel. 1982. The Çayönü Excavations: Overview through 1981. In *Prehistoric Village Archaeology in Southeast Turkey. The Eighth Millennium B.C. Site at Çayönü: Its Chipped and Ground Stone Industries and Faunal Remains,* ed. L. and R. Braidwood, pp. 1-15. BAR International Series No. 138, Oxford.

Braidwood, R., H. Çambel, and W. Schirmer. 1981. Beginnings of Village Farming Communities in Southeastern Turkey: Çayönü Tepesi, 1978 and 1979. *Journal of Field Archaeology* 8(3):249-258.

Buitenhuis, H. 1985. Preliminary Report on the Faunal Remains from Hayaz Höyük from the 1979-1983 Seasons. *Anatolica* 12:61-74.

Cauvin, J. 1985. Le Néolithique de Cafer Höyük (Turquie): Bilan provisoire après quartre campagnes (1979-1983). *Cahiers de l'Euphrate* 4:123-133.

_____ 1988. La Néolithisation de la Turquie du Sud-est dans son contexte Proche-Oriental. *Anatolica* 15:69-80.

Douglas, M., and A. Wildavsky. 1982. *Risk and Culture.* University of California Press, Berkeley.

Driesch, A. von den. 1976. *A Guide to the Measurement of Animal Bones from Archaeological Sites.* Peabody Museum Bulletin No. 1. Harvard University, Cambridge, MA.

Ellis, R., and M. Voigt. 1982. 1981 Excavations at Gritille, Turkey. *American Journal of Archaeology* 86:319-332.

Flannery, K. 1968. Archaeological Systems Theory and Early Mesoamerica. In *Anthropological Archaeology in the Americas,* ed. B. Meggars, pp. 67-87. Anthropological Society of Washington, Washington, DC.

_____ 1983. Early Pig Domestication in the Fertile Crescent: A Retrospective Look. In *The Hilly Flanks. Essays on the Prehistory of Southwestern Asia Presented to Robert J. Braidwood, November 15, 1982,* ed. T.C. Young, Jr., P.E.L. Smith, and P. Mortensen, pp. 163-188. Studies in Ancient Oriental Civilization 36. Oriental Institute, University of Chicago, Chicago.

Halstead, P., and J. O'Shea. 1989. Introduction: Cultural Responses to Risk and Uncertainty. In *Bad Year Economics, Cultural Responses to Risk and Uncertainty,* ed. P. Halstead and J. O'Shea, pp. 1-7. Cambridge University Press, Cambridge.

Hauptmann, H. 1988. Nevali Çori: Architektur. *Anatolica* 15:99-110.

Hegmon, M. 1989. Risk Reduction and Variation in Agricultural Economies: A Computer Simulation of Hopi Agriculture. *Research in Economic Anthropology* 11: 89-121.

Helmer, D. 1988. Les animaux de Cafer et des sites preceramiques du Sud-est de la Turquie: Essai de synthèse. *Anatolica* 15:37-48.

Hesse, B. 1982. Slaughter Patterns and Domestication: The Beginnings of Pastoralism in Western Iran. *Man* (n.s.) 17(3):403-417.

Hole, F., K. Flannery, and J. Neely. 1969. *Prehistory and Human Ecology of the Deh Luran Plain*. Memoir No. 1. Museum of Anthropology, University of Michigan, Ann Arbor.

Kent, S. (editor). 1989. *Farmers as Hunters: The Implications of Sedentism*. Cambridge University Press, Cambridge.

Kuşatman, B. 1990. The Origins of Pig Domestication. Paper presented at the Sixth International Conference of the International Council for Archaeozoology (ICAZ), Washington, DC.

Lawrence, B. 1980. Evidences of Animal Domestication at Çayönü. In *The Joint Istanbul-Chicago Universities Prehistoric Researches in Southeastern Anatolia*, ed. H. Çambel and R. Braidwood, pp. 285-308. Istanbul University Faculty of Letters Publication No. 2589. Istanbul.

_____ 1982. Principal Food Animals at Çayönü. In *Prehistoric Village Archaeology in Southeast Turkey. The Eighth Millennium B.C. Site at Çayönü: Its Chipped and Ground Stone Industries and Faunal Remains*, ed. L. and R. Braidwood, pp. 175-199. BAR International Series No. 138, Oxford.

Meadow, R. 1980. Animal Bones: Problems for the Archaeologist Together with some Possible Solutions. *Paléorient* 6:65-77.

O'Shea, J.M. 1989. The Role of Wild Resources in Small Scale Agricultural Systems: Tales from the Lake and the Plains. In *Bad Year Economics, Cultural Responses to Risk and Uncertainty*, ed. P. Halstead and J. O'Shea, pp. 57-67. Cambridge University Press, Cambridge.

Payne, S. 1973. Kill Off Patterns in Sheep and Goats: The Mandibles from Asvan Kale. *Anatolian Studies* 23:281-303.

_____ 1975. Partial Recovery and Sample Bias. In *Archaeozoological Studies*, ed. A.T. Clason, pp. 1-17. Elsevier, Amsterdam.

Perkins, D., Jr. 1964. Prehistoric Fauna from Shanidar, Iran. *Science* 144:1565-1566.

Perkins, D., Jr., and P. Daly. 1968. A Hunters' Village in Neolithic Turkey. *Scientific American* 219(5):96-106.

Redding, R. 1981. *Decision Making in Subsistence Herding of Sheep and Goats in the Middle East*. Ph.D. dissertation, University of Michigan. University Microfilms, Ann Arbor, MI.

Redford, Scott. Preliminary Report on the Medieval Settlement at Gritille. *Anatolian Studies* 36:103-136.

Roodenberg, J.J. 1980. Premiers résultats des recherches archéologiques à Hayaz Höyük. *Anatolica* 7:1-10.

Sandford, S. 1982. Pastoral Strategies and Desertification: Opportunism and Conservatism in Dry Lands. In *Desertification and Development: Dryland Ecology in Social Perspective*, ed. B. Spooner and H.S. Mann, pp. 61-80. Academic Press, London.

Schmidt, Klaus. 1988. Nevali Çori: Zum Typenspektrum der Silexindustrie und der Übrigen Kleinfunde. *Anatolica* 15:161-201.

Sherratt, A. 1983. The Secondary Exploitation of Animals in the Old World. *World Archaeology* 15(1):90-104.

Stein, G. 1986a. Herding Strategies at Neolithic Gritille: The Use of Animal Bone Remains to Reconstruct Ancient Economic Systems. *Expedition* 28(2):35-42.

_____ 1986b. Village Level Pastoral Production: Faunal Remains from Gritille Höyük, Southeast Turkey. *MASCA Journal* 4(1):2-11.

_____ 1987. Regional Economic Integration in Early State Societies: Third Millennium B.C. Pastoral Production at Gritille, Southeast Turkey. *Paléorient* 13(2):101-111.

Van Zeist, W. Some Aspects of Early Neolithic Plant Husbandry in the Near East. *Anatolica* 15:49-67.

Voigt, M. 1985. Village on the Euphrates: Excavations at Neolithic Gritille in Turkey. *Expedition* 27(1):9-24.

_____ 1988. Excavations at Neolithic Gritille. *Anatolica* 15:215-232.

Voigt, M., and R. Ellis. 1981. Excavations at Gritille, Turkey: 1981. *Paléorient* 7:87-100.

Wright, G., and S. Miller. 1977. Prehistoric Hunting of New World Wild Sheep: Implications for the Study of Sheep Domestication. In *Cultural Change and Continuity. Essays in Honor of James Bennett Griffin*, ed. C. Cleland, pp. 293-317. Academic Press, New York.

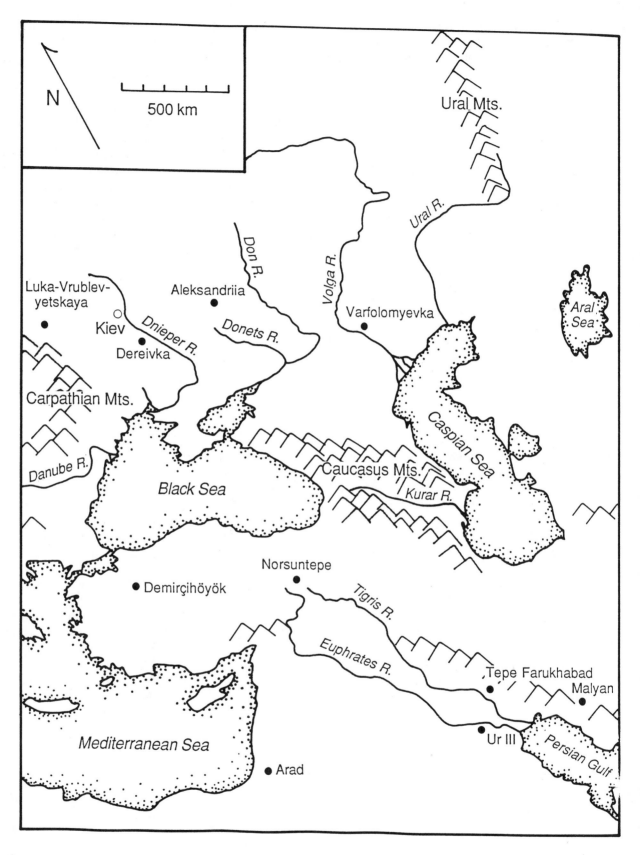

Fig. 1:
Map of sites referred to in text.

LOOKING A GIFT HORSE IN THE MOUTH:

IDENTIFICATION OF THE EARLIEST BITTED EQUIDS

AND THE MICROSCOPIC ANALYSIS OF WEAR

David W. Anthony
and
Dorcas R. Brown

Hartwick College, Oneonta, NY 13820

A remembrance

I shall always remember Pat Daly sitting on the end of a University of Pennsylvania lab table, shrouded in smoke, with a pie tin full of lipstick-stained cigarette butts beside her, illustrating and/or punctuating Dexter Perkins' lectures with characteristically acerbic comments. When she took the podium (figuratively) she was subjected to an equivalent bombardment from the Perkins sidelines. Neither could stand to let the other speak uninterrupted for long, and the result was the ideal team-taught course, in which argument, exposition, and analysis were stressed equally. (Well, perhaps not equally.) They encouraged me to pursue the subject that began as a paper for their course and became a doctoral dissertation and a long-term research project: the domestication of the horse and the origin of riding. Inspired partially by their insistence on the integration of cultural and zoological data, I concentrated on questions of cultural process—modeling the social and economic implications of domestication and riding (Anthony 1985, 1986). A renewed concern over the nature of the basic faunal evidence subsequently brought me into collaboration with my co-author on the present project. Whether Perkins and Daly would wish to claim me now is anyone's guess, but I salute them wholeheartedly.

Horse domestication and riding

The earliest documented method of control for equids was the nose-ring, a device borrowed from ox driving and pictured on asses in Mesopotamian artistic representations of Early Dynastic III (Littauer and Crouwel 1979:35). No actual bit is dated earlier than 1600-1500 B.C., although it is generally assumed that the bit must have been used with true horses, which first appeared in southwest Iran and Mesopotamia about 2100 B.C. (late ED III), presumably

from domesticated stock in Anatolia and/or the Caucasus. Horses appear to have been domesticated much earlier, by about 4000 B.C., in the Ukrainian steppes north of the Black Sea. It is not known how horses were used between 4000 and 2100 B.C. other than as food, nor is it known where the use of the bit began. Soviet scholars often assume that riding began with domestication at about 4000 B.C., but the fourth-millennium evidence for riding is only circumstantial.

This paper describes the earliest direct evidence for bitting yet obtained anywhere, based on the newly developed technique of microscopic bit wear analysis applied to horse teeth. The experiment described was conducted on equid teeth from Malyan, Iran, and the technique will soon be applied to the teeth of the earliest claimed domesticates, in the Ukraine.[1]

The Ukrainian evidence

The faunal evidence relating to the earliest domestication of the horse in the Ukraine has been published in only a preliminary fashion (Bibikova 1967, 1969, 1970; Nobis 1971). Bibikova's initial analysis (1967) was based upon a single skull and mandible selected from an assemblage of 2,555 identifiable horse bones excavated at the Ukrainian Copper Age Sredni Stog culture site of Dereivka (Fig. 1), dated about 4000 B.C. (Telegin 1973:28-59; 1986). The skull was that of a stallion, 7-8 years old, discovered in a "cult" deposit containing a horse head-and-hoof assemblage, probably representing a hide with the head and left lower leg attached (cf. Piggott 1962). Found with the horse bones were two fragmentary articulated dog skeletons, two ceramic figurine fragments, and an antler "cheekpiece." Nearby was another perforated antler tine identified as a mattock by the excavator (Telegin 1973:47), but possibly representing a second cheekpiece for a soft bit. The entire assemblage was discovered at the periphery of a Sredni Stog culture occupation site that yielded 3,938 identifiable animal bones, of which 2,555 (61%) came from horses, representing at least 52 animals.

Bibikova's cranial analysis compared the Dereivka stallion with skulls of domesticated and wild horses, both ancient and modern, using 20 cranial measurements. Seven of the Dereivka skull measurements were larger than those of any of the comparative specimens consulted, including measurements of overall and basal skull length, skull height, and width of the nasals. The metacarpals associated with the Dereivka skull suggested an animal that stood approximately 144 cm at the withers—the tallest animal documented at Dereivka, therefore atypically large even within its own population (which averaged 136 cm withers height). Conclusions drawn from measurements of this single animal cannot be reliably generalized (Anthony in press); however, Bibikova (1967:113) felt that several cranial traits suggested a domesticated status: a large, lightly built cranium, a very long nasal portion, a short tooth row, and a wide occiput.

Bibikova has also published an analysis of the Dereivka metacarpal and phalange dimensions (1970) and a more general discussion (1969) that includes partial data on the age and sex characteristics of the horses. The latter discussion includes statements indicating that 15 of the 17 sexable mandibles represented males, and that there were no old individuals in the assemblage. The great majority were young adults or juveniles, predominantly juvenile males.[2] Juvenile males are precisely the individuals one would first select for slaughter in a managed herd (they are disruptive and do not contribute significantly to the increase of the population), while they are unlikely targets of human predation in the wild (the largest, most predictable, and therefore most vulnerable social group being the harem band consisting primarily of adult females).

Although the faunal samples are small and widely scattered, horse bones are consistently present as food remains in Sredni Stog sites at about twice the frequency documented in earlier Dnieper-Donets sites (ca. 4500-4000 B.C.) in the same region. This doubling in the frequency of excavated horse remains (to an average of about 13% MNI, representing 48% of the minimum meat weight), combined with the Dereivka age and sex data and the extension of horse exploitation even to well-watered catchments that had not previously produced horse remains suggests that the exploitation of horses had become greatly intensified in the Ukrainian steppes north of the Black Sea during the period 4000-3500 B.C. The Sredni Stog culture also exhibits a constellation of new social and economic patterns that are consistent with the adoption of riding (Anthony 1985).

The social and economic effects of the adoption of riding can be modeled based upon the acquisition of horses by Indians in North and South America (Anthony 1985, 1986). Riding introduced a radically new type of rapid, long-distance transport that effectively reduced the distance between critical resources and permitted the efficient exploitation of the grassland environment. The American model suggests that the results of riding in the Ukraine should have included a greatly increased ability to exploit systematically the grassland environment, an expansion of territorial ranges, increases in warfare associated with these territorial readjustments, changes in settlement and trading patterns, related increases in social differentiation, and a heightened emphasis on the social role of warfare. Changes in warfare required no actual fighting from horseback, but depended solely on the novelty of horse-aided rapid transport as a means of approach and retreat. Most of these changes appear to be documented archaeologically during the Sredni Stog period, although the full development of the predicted pattern occurs only after about 3500 B.C., with the emergence of the Yamna horizon across the northern Black Sea/Caspian steppes.

The Sredni Stog culture possessed two parts of the triad that would make possible the efficient exploitation of the steppes: horses and domestic grazing stock (cattle and sheep). The Yamna horizon represents the archaeological expression of the initial *intensive* occupation of the Eurasian grasslands, a penetration made possible by domestic grazing stock and horse transport (rapid, long-distance), combined with ox-cart transport (slow, high-volume). When the latter technology appeared in the Black Sea/Caspian steppes at about 3500-3300 B.C., an explosive movement into the Eurasian grasslands followed. This peopling of the steppe laid the foundation for the development of all later Central Asian pastoralist societies.

If the adoption of riding is to be assigned such great importance in this sequence of events, then the quality of the archaeological evidence for riding becomes a critical issue. The evidence for riding during the Sredni Stog and Yamna periods in the Ukraine (approximately 4000-2800 B.C.) is entirely circumstantial. There are three categories of evidence: objects interpreted as cheekpieces for soft bits of rope or leather; carved stone horse-head effigies—apparently mace heads—that seem to display harness straps; and the changes in cultural patterns mentioned above that are consistent with the adoption of riding.

The antler-tine one-hole or two-hole cheekpieces are found in pairs, as in the Sredni Stog grave #18 at Aleksandriia (Telegin 1973:137; 1959), in contemporary Trichterbecher (TRB) funnel beaker sites in East Germany (Lichardus 1980), and perhaps at Dereivka (Fig. 2a). They have saucer-like worn areas near the perforations that suggest wear by cordage or thongs. At least one specimen (perhaps

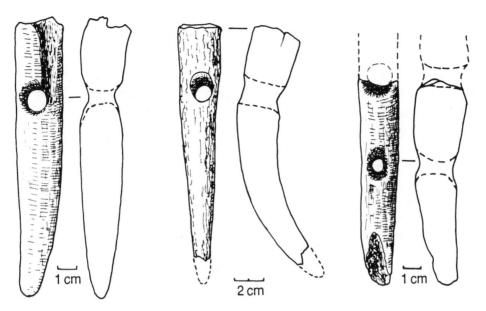

Fig. 2a:
Perforated antler tines—possible cheek pieces—from Dereivka, ca. 3600 B.C.
After Telegin 1986.

a pair) was found in direct association with the skull of the "cult deposit" stallion at Dereivka. This class of objects bears a strong morphological resemblance to antler artifacts known to have functioned as cheekpieces in later periods (Moszolics 1953; Smirnov 1961:52). Their function would have been to prevent a soft bit from sliding sideways out of the horse's mouth, and to apply pressure against the muzzle when the rein was pulled on the opposite side. Experimental use by Lichardus (1980:16-19) has established that one-hole crescentic antler tines could have functioned effectively as cheekpieces. Although the circumstantial evidence for Sredni Stog cheekpieces is strong, it is impossible to demonstrate conclusively that this was indeed the function of these artifacts.

The horse-head effigies are of two types: an earlier "stylized" type that is not zoomorphic and might not in fact have any connection to horses, and a later zoomorphic type that appears to portray horse heads, possibly with harness straps (Fig. 2b) (Danilenko and Shmagli 1972; Telegin and Anthony 1987). The latter are found in Sredni Stog and Yamna burial sites from the lower Volga westward to the lower Danube and Yugoslav Macedonia. They are made of porphyry, a raw material with a restricted distribution generally associated with "status" objects, suggesting a linkage between horses, symbols of power (the effigy mace itself), and access to rare or exotic materials. This association might be expected if horses were used as transport and riding animals, but would be less easily explained if horses were used only for food. (Why are there no cattle or sheep maces?)

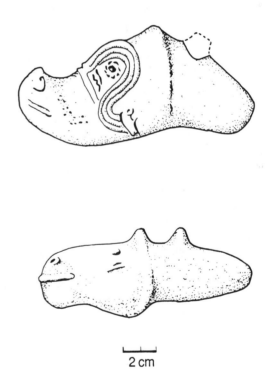

Fig. 2b:
Horse head effigy maces, from the region of the mouth of the Danube river, ca. 3000 B.C. Casimcea, top, and Suvorovo, bottom.
After Telegin 1986.

The Near Eastern evidence

The Near Eastern evidence for horse riding has been summarized by Littauer and Crouwel (1979). The earliest actual horse remains in the Near East appear to date to about 2000-2200 B.C. Horse bones have been recovered from the Old Elamite levels of Tepe Farukhabad on the Deh Luran plain, dated to about 2200-2000 B.C. (Redding 1981:243-244), from the Early Bronze Age levels of Arad in the northern Negev, dated about 2200-2000 B.C. (Davis 1987), and from the Kaftari phase of Malyan in Fars province, Iran, dated to about 2000 B.C. (Zeder 1986, 1988). These horses were introduced, probably as domesticates. Earlier horse remains are known from Late Chalcolithic Anatolia, at Norsuntepe and Demirçihöyök, dated to approximately 3500-3000 B.C. (Yakar 1985:374-375). Given the complete absence of horses from earlier Anatolian settlements, it seems likely that these also were introduced, again probably as domesticates from the north (Bökönyi 1978:54, figures 8-10). Earlier Caucasian horses have been recovered from Eneolithic levels (approximately 4000 B.C.) in Armenia and in a few settlements in the steppe-zone of the lower Kura River valley in what is now Soviet Azerbaijan, at the northeastern (Caspian) border of Transcaucasia (Mezhlumian 1990; Munchaev 1975:387). A trans-Caucasian route of transmission seems probable.

The earliest unarguable textual reference to horses occurs in Ur III contexts, roughly contemporary with direct physical evidence for horses at Tepe Farukhabad and Malyan (Littauer and Crouwel 1979:43). The textual term is translated ANSE.KUR.RA, or "equid (ass?) from the mountains," reinforcing the impression that horses were introduced into Mesopotamia from Iran and/or Anatolia. Riding of equids is depicted on Ur III and Akkadian seals and Old Babylonian terracotta plaques, and several Ur III texts might refer to mounted officials or couriers. (Prior to 2000 B.C. most equid transport involved wheeled vehicles—"battle wagons" or "platform cars"—pulled by either asses or hemion-ass hybrids [Littauer and Crouwel 1979:46].) A terracotta equid figurine from Ur III Selenkahiyeh in Syria shows a headstall with cheekstraps, noseband, and browband. Nose-rings also were used to control equids well into the second millennium (Littauer and Crouwel 1979:60-61).

If horses were used as mounts in the Black Sea/Caspian steppes and were introduced as domesticates to the south, then one would expect to find the northern practice of riding diffusing with the horse. It is not clear whether or not this happened. Certainly the circumstances of horse exploitation were quite different in the cities of Mesopotamia. In the northern steppes an animal that could rapidly transport a group of raiders to and from an unsuspecting enemy village might have been extremely useful even if the actual fighting was conducted on foot (as often occurred in the warfare of the American Plains Indians). The more formal military campaigns and the walled cities of Mesopotamia would have rendered this tactical usage ineffective. The economic stability provided by horse transport in the grassland environment might also have been a negligible factor in the agricultural lowlands of Mesopotamia. Riding might still have been useful to Mesopotamian messengers and couriers, and it is in this context that riding seems to have been most often employed (Littauer and Crouwel 1979:67).

Riding, particularly horse riding, seems to have been regarded as an undignified and lower-status means of transport in the Near East. Attached to the chariot, however, horses were so desirable that they displaced asses during the early second millennium B.C. Control mechanisms included the traditional Mesopotamian nose-ring, inappropriate for the effective control of equids, but retained and used nevertheless. Nose-rings were often used to direct the equid team (as well as horses that were ridden), although effective control would have been minimal. The metal bit might have been developed in conjunction with the development of the war chariot, as a means to more effectively maneuver equid chariot teams in battle (Littauer and Crouwel 1979:70). The oldest actual metal bits preserved do not predate 1500 B.C., but there are sealings and metal rein terrets from earlier contexts in Syria and Anatolia that portray or imply the existence of right and left reins passing on either side of the horse's head (Littauer and Crouwel 1979:60). Such an arrangement implies the use of either a dropped noseband, which applies pressure to the animal's nose, or a bit. While a noseband would be effective as a braking device, it, unlike a metal bit, would provide little directional control. The existence of bits as early as 1650 B.C. has been suggested on the basis of unusual premolar tooth wear on a Middle Kingdom horse mandible excavated at the fortress of Buhen in northern Sudan (Clutton-Brock 1974), but at the time the suggestion was offered no experimental evidence supported the identification. If metal bits were indeed in use before 1500 B.C., those who possessed them would have gained a distinct advantage in maneuverability.

Bit wear analysis

This project began as an effort to identify the earliest horses used as mounts through a microscopic examination of bit wear on teeth. The principal problem in investigating bit wear was that no previous research concerning the effects of bits on horses' teeth existed. Early conversations with veterinarians suggested that there was considerable uncertainty as to whether bits even came into contact with horse teeth. A properly adjusted bit placed on a well-trained horse ideally will remain on the soft tissues of the mouth (Figs. 3 and 4b, 4e). If the horse can lift the bit back onto its premolar teeth the rider cannot cause pain to the

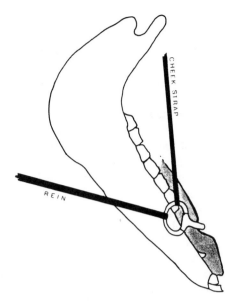

Fig. 3:
Proper position of jointed snaffle bit with horse's head down (horse's tongue shaded). No bit-tooth contact.

Fig. 4:
a. Jointed snaffle bit. *b.* Correctly fitted and adjusted jointed snaffle bit on modern horse. *c.* Mouth-piece of the bit, raised by the tongue back to the cheek teeth. *d.* Mullen mouth loose ring snaffle bit. Arrows point to tooth-wear on the bit. *e.* Proper position of mullen mouth snaffle. *f.* Mullen mouth snaffle being grasped between the cheek teeth.
After Clayton 1984, 1985.

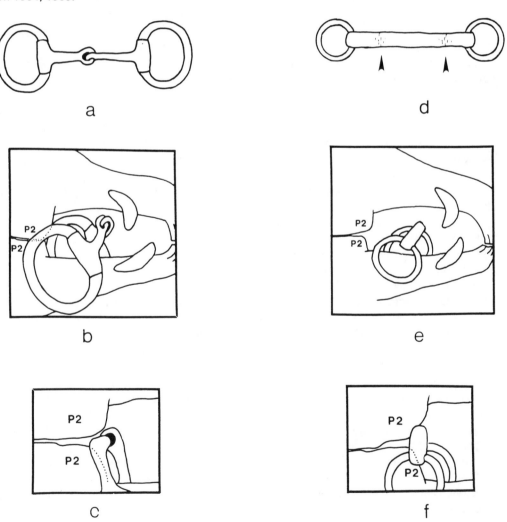

tongue and gums, and must attempt to control the horse through strength alone. Archaeozoologists (Payne in press) have questioned whether horses actually chew bits regularly enough to cause bit wear. Thus, the first step in examining bit wear was to determine whether or how bits affect horse teeth. Rope and leather bits are no longer used exclusively by any population, so metal bit wear became the focus of the initial research.

Fortunately, the action of the bit in a horse's mouth has been studied previously, though not with the objective of defining bit wear. Hillary Clayton (1984, 1985) has published the only relevant research in this area. Her horses were bitted, restrained in stalls, and the reins manipulated while fluoroscopic X-ray photographs were taken of the horse's mouth. Drawings made from these photographs are presented in Fig. 4. Clayton demonstrated that horses often take the bit in their teeth, to the extent that tooth wear is sometimes visible on the metal bit (Fig. 4d). Conversations with trainers and horse behavior specialists reinforced Clayton's findings that even the best-arranged bit will very often end up on the teeth.[3] Moreover, the fleshy corners of the mouth are sufficiently far forward so that the bit is prevented from moving back farther than the anterior half of the first lower premolar (P2). The bit therefore repeatedly moves onto a limited part of the occlusal (biting) surface of the lower P2 (Figs. 4c, 4f), and must be held between the teeth with considerable force to prevent it from slipping back onto the gums.

The method

For the purposes of this study only the mandibular premolar teeth were examined. Most horses have a slight molar overbite, so that when the bit is gripped between the teeth it sits between the middle of the upper premolar and the anterior edge of the lower premolar. This precarious position on the lower premolar contributes to slippage back and forth over the rostral (anterior) edge or prow of the tooth. Bit wear is therefore likely to be more pronounced on the mandibular premolars.

The premolars were examined under an incident light microscope and a scanning electron microscope (SEM). The incident light microscope was used to study internal fracture patterns beneath the surface of the translucent enamel. The SEM was used to study surface topography. Because metal bit wear is caused by compression fractures, both techniques were productive. Most examinations were conducted at low magnifications (10-35X), since the diagnostic features of metal bit wear are relatively large.

Because the project is directed towards research on archaeological specimens that cannot be altered, high-resolution casts were made of many study specimens, including the Kaftari phase equids from Malyan. Casting techniques followed the methods described by Rose (1983). Impressions were made with Express 3M, a vinyl polysi-

loxane, and casts were made with Tapox epoxy resin. Casts were compared with the originals under the SEM, and are highly accurate. At magnifications of 10-75X (the extreme ranges used in this study) there was no detectable loss of resolution.

Mandibular premolars were collected from a variety of horses, including some that had been habitually bitted with metal bits up to the time of death, some that had been bitted on an irregular basis (a brood mare, a research horse), and a large assemblage of unbitted feral horses from two environments: the eastern barrier islands of Maryland/ Virginia, and the high plains of western Nevada. In some cases whole mandibles were collected, and in others only the first premolars (P2). The feral horses provided the baseline against which the bitted horses were compared.

Comparisons involved macroscopic as well as microscopic features. The beveling of the anterior P2 that is associated with metal bit wear is quite visible without a microscope. The degree of beveling was measured by placing a right-angle ruler horizontally across the two highest cusps on the lingual side of the tooth and fitting the vertical scale against the front of the tooth. The millimeter measurement is taken from the horizontal edge down to the point at which the base of the bevel intersects the vertical edge (Fig. 5). For all domesticated horses that exhibit the diagnostic microscopic traits of bit wear, this measurement averaged 3.52, meaning that 3.52 mm of the anterior corner of the tooth had been worn away. For feral horses that had never been bitted this measurement averaged 0.82, meaning that there was usually less than a millimeter of natural beveling under wild conditions (Fig. 6). These two groups are significantly different according to a t-test (t=-2.34, df=9.05, 2-tailed probability=.044), suggesting that there is more than a 95% probability that beveling alone can separate bitted and feral horses.

The sample

Mandibles of thirty horses were examined for this study. Ten of these were from domestic horses submitted to metal bits under a variety of circumstances.[4] Twenty were from feral horses that had never been bitted.[5] All of this comparative evidence was utilized in the examination of a single set of oddly worn equid teeth from the Kaftari phase at Malyan (Table 1).

The sample includes a wide range of domestic breeds and usages, and feral horses from two markedly different environments (eastern barrier islands and western high plains grassland). Continuing study of these teeth will provide important data during later phases of the project.

Horse teeth and the mechanics of metal bit wear

Horse teeth are composed of an exterior mantle of cementum surrounding a core of dentine containing interior ridges of enamel. The enamel ridges are exposed on the

LINGUAL PROFILE   OCCLUSAL SURFACE

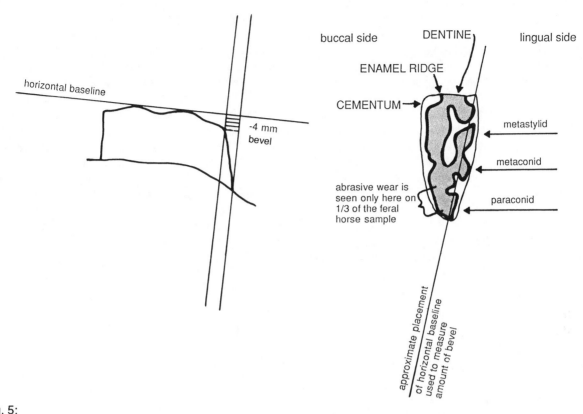

Fig. 5:
The bevel measurement is taken from a horizontal baseline defined by the highest points on the metaconid and metastylid cusps, down to the base of the bevel on the rostral prow. Wear must appear over the entire paraconid enamel surface to conclusively prove bit wear.

Fig. 6:
Degree-of-bevel measurements. Range (horizontal bar) and mean (vertical bar) measurements are illustrated. Sample size is indicated in parentheses.

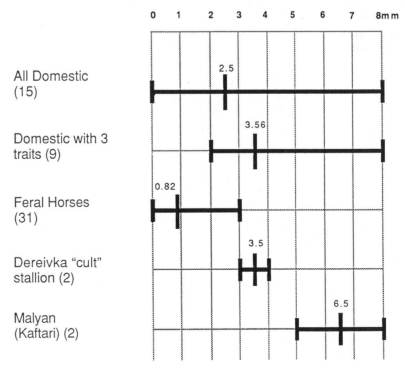

occlusal surface of a tooth, but generally not on the sides. Cementum is a bone-like material that will form scar tissue in response to injury if a blood supply is available. The exterior cementum near the crown of a tooth should form scar tissue much less rapidly (if at all) than the cementum near the gum line, where the blood supply is concentrated. However, the details of tooth injury and repair in horses have not been adequately studied. Figure 7 shows a healed tooth injury of the cementum near the crown of the tooth of a four-year-old harness racer. A scar-like tissue appears to have partially covered the injury even at this location well removed from the gum line. It is likely that the scar tissue was formed when this area was nearer the gum line, and subsequent tooth growth raised the scarred area nearer to the crown. On the other hand, it might be that the exterior cementum can form scar tissue in response to injury even at locations near the crown of the tooth. Scratches and spalls removed from the exterior cementum by the bit might therefore be modified by scar tissue under some (most?) circumstances.

Enamel has much more limited healing capabilities. It is likely that recrystallization does not occur significantly after episodes of surficial scarring or spalling. Bit wear is therefore likely to remain unmodified by healing on the enamel ridges that are exposed on the occlusal surface of the tooth. Horse teeth are hypsodontic, however, which means the occlusal surface of the tooth is continuously being worn away by abrasion, and is continuously being replaced by growth. This process persists until the available tooth length is entirely worn away, at which point the animal dies of starvation. An episode of bit-related spalling on the occlusal enamel will therefore be worn away relatively rapidly by occlusal abrasion and regrowth. Experiments with dental microwear in vervet monkeys (Teaford 1988:1155) suggest that scratches in enamel two microns in depth may be entirely obliterated by more recent scratches and/or occlusal abrasion within six weeks.

Recent research with bovids (Alan Walker, pers. com. 1988) indicates a much more rapid wear rate on hypsodontic teeth. Individual enamel scars caused by bit wear will

Table 1. Characteristics of study horses.

Specimen #	Age	Sex	Usage	Breed
1	4	F	Harness Racer	Standard
2	14	M	Dressage	Thoroughbred
3	4	M	Draught	Belgian workhorse
4	8	F	Feral	Barrier Island Pony
5	20	F	"	"
6	20	F	"	"
7	6	F	"	"
8	6	F	Brood Mare	Thoroughbred
9	10	M	Racer	"
10	7	F	Dressage	Appaloosa
11	mature	F	Research	Thoroughbred
12	10	M	Racer	"
13	5	F	Racer	"
14	5	M	Hunter	"
15	3	?	Feral	Nevada Mustang
16	8	M	"	"
17	4	M	"	"
18	6	F	"	"
19	3	?	"	"
20	12+	F	"	"
21	1-2	?	"	"
22	4	M	"	"
23	1-2	?	"	"
24	6	F	"	"
25	1-2	?	"	"
26	6-8 mo.	?	"	"
27	very old	M	"	"
28	9	M	"	"
29	8	M	"	"
30	7	F	"	"

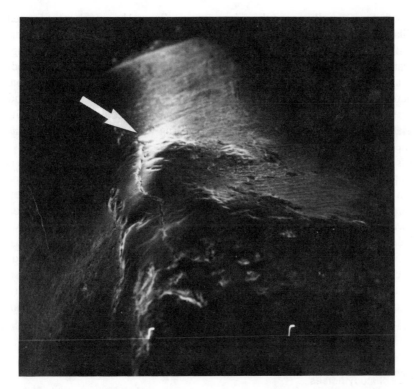

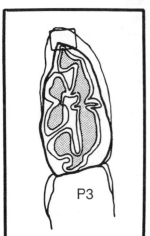
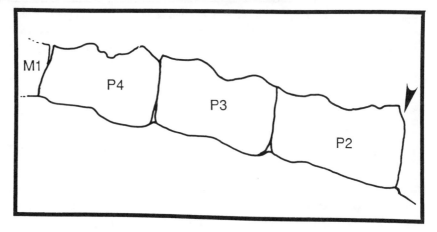

Fig. 7:
Specimen 1, 4-year-old harness racer. Magnified 35x. Buccal profile of right side. This permanent P2 erupted no more than 1 1/2 years before this animal died. Micrograph looking down the rostral edge from the occlusal surface shows a healing scar (white arrow) in the cementum. The profile shows incipient bit wear; the rostral point (black arrow) is just starting to wear down.

therefore have a short life unless they are relatively massive. Bit wear detected on the occlusal enamel ridges of a horse's tooth will represent only the wear produced relatively recently before the animal's death. The rate of normal occlusal abrasion varies depending on age and diet (Silver 1970:294). It seems likely that a young horse left unbitted would lose most or all traces of occlusal bit wear within three to six months; an older horse (8+ years) with a slower rate of tooth growth would retain dental scars longer.

The mechanical causes of bit wear were entirely a matter of speculation when this project began. Some questions remain, but important mechanisms have been identified, particularly in relation to metal bit wear. Soft (rope and leather) bit wear is the focus of ongoing research.

It was initially thought that bit wear would be caused by the rider jerking the bit back against the leading or rostral edge of the premolar, producing impact fractures and scratches. A similar human-induced cause of bit wear was suggested by Clutton-Brock (1974:93). This does occur, but the most significant metal bit wear appears to be produced by the horse itself. By elevating and retracting the tongue, the horse is able to raise the bit to a position between the forward premolars (Clayton 1984:193). The massive pressure applied by the horse's jaws then appears to be the primary mechanical agent causing metal bit wear. The unyielding metal bit apparently causes compression fractures that weaken the internal structure of the occlusal enamel. For the purposes of this analysis the important point is that bit wear is likely to be most pronounced on the occlusal surface of the tooth, where the enormous strength of the horse's jaw bears on the metal bit, rather than on the rostral edge, where only infrequent bit-tooth contacts would occur, most often in connection with sharp turning maneuvers.

These observations suggest that the metal bit acts as a pressure-flaking tool that weakens and then splits off spalls of enamel. Once the enamel is removed the bit begins to grind against dentine and cementum, which are much softer and spall rapidly. The anterior third (or perhaps half, on some individuals) of the occlusal surface of the lower P2 receives all of this damage. With continous usage, particularly in a horse that habitually chews the bit, the anterior third of the lower P2 is worn down into a smoothly rounded inclined plane. This beveling is strongly indicative of metal bit wear even without microscopic examination. Of course, if the horse is young and is left unbitted for a long period of time, extreme beveling will eventually be obliterated by growth and occlusal abrasion.

Microscopic and macroscopic evidence

The macroscopic traits of metal bit wear can be seen in the profile views of specimens 13 and 12 (Figs. 8b and 9b respectively). Specimen 13 was a five-year-old race horse and specimen 12 was a ten-year-old racehorse. Both were bitted right up until the time of their deaths. The beveling or rounding of the anterior of the P2 (arrowed on the figures) is evident in both horses, as is the variation in this kind of wear. Specimen 13 exhibits a rounded worn area affecting only the anterior quarter of the tooth. Specimen 12 is a much older horse and the classic beveling of the anterior third of P2 can be seen. Some younger horses show just the tip of the rostral point crushed or flaked off (Fig. 7). This is attributed to the lack of long-term consistent use of a metal bit prior to death.

The feral specimens illustrated in Figs. 8a and 9a show no beveling. Marked beveling of P2 was not evident in any of the 20 wild horse mandibles examined. In a few cases malocclusion produced a slight inclination in the anterior part of the P2. When this occurred (rarely), it was not a smoothly rounded inclination, but displayed an uneven surface. Moreover, the incline was not evident on *both* lower P2s. A pair of P2s with the anterior third uniformly

rounded and smoothed into an inclined plane occurred only in the bitted sample of horses.

Not all bitted horses exhibit classic anterior beveling. Two horses that were probably only intermittently bitted, a brood mare and a laboratory research animal (specimens 8 and 11), exhibited little or no beveling. In addition, one other domestic specimen (10, the Appaloosa) exhibited an unusual wear pattern in which there was no anterior beveling of P2, but there was significant spalling and even a trough-like worn feature across the metaconid portion of the occlusal surface, approximately one cm back from the anterior edge. This pattern of wear might have been caused by an underbite or an unusually wide mouth, permitting the bit to sit farther back on the tooth in a more secure position.

The microscopic traits of metal bit wear are quite distinctive. They can be described under three headings: 1) *Spalling that covers much of the tooth enamel*. The spalls and fractures associated with metal bit wear typically cover the majority of the occlusal enamel surface on the anterior third of the P2. The enamel occlusal surfaces of a feral horse are quite smooth, even polished in places. Fractures from dietary roughage or malocclusion are isolated in a smooth field. In a bitted horse, the metal bit roughens the entire surface of the occlusal enamel and causes dense extensive spalling on the lingual, buccal, and anterior enamel surfaces of at least the first cusp (compare Figs. 8a and 8b or 9a and 9b).
2) *A predominace of center-origin spalls*. The mechanical cause of this trait is unknown, but it is one of the best designators of metal bit wear. Spalls and chips on the enamel of feral horse premolars tend to be small and are concentrated on the edge of the enamel ridge, "nibbling" at the edge of the occlusal surface (Fig. 8a). Center-origin spalls occur, but are small, sparsely encountered, and do not carry to the edge of the enamel ridge. Metal bit wear produces a predominance of spalls that begin in the center of the flat occlusal surface of the enamel ridge and often carry to the edge, removing large chunks of enamel. In some cases where the spalls do not carry to the edge, the enamel occlusal surface actually becomes V-shaped rather than flat, with a trench of joined spalls running longitudinally down the enamel ridge. When a long trench feature of this type does break toward the edge, a long section of enamel will spall away. Many of these center-origin spalls are visible in Figs. 8b and 9b.
3) *Abraded fractures within spall scars*. Spalls and chips removed naturally from the enamel of unbitted feral horses leave a scar that has a fairly "clean" conformation, with distinct scar edges. The scar edges are geometrically serrated in some cases, as if the integrity of the crystalline enamel structure were being expressed even as a piece of enamel broke away. The spall scars left by metal bit wear are rough and uneven in appearance, possibly because the

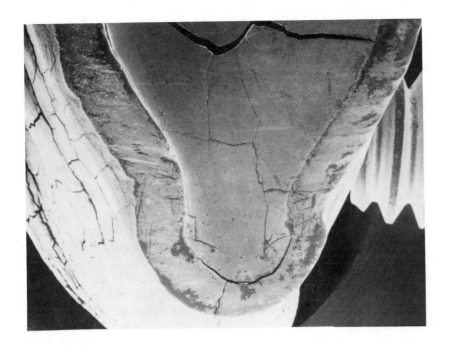
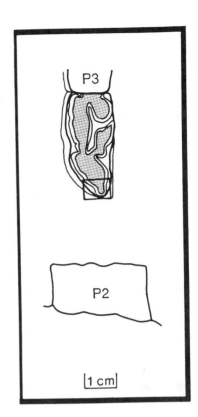

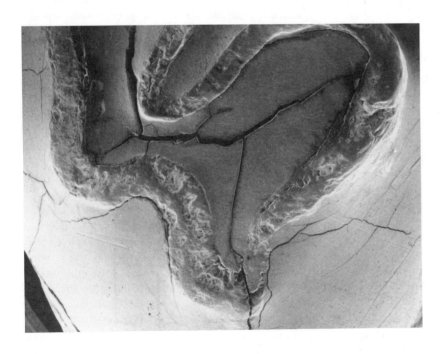
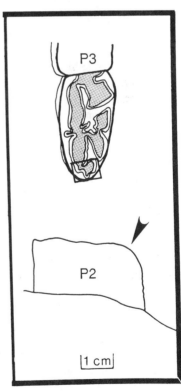

Fig. 8:
Comparison of unbitted (top) and bitted (bottom) horse premolars.
a. Specimen 4, 8-year-old Barrier Island Pony. Magnified 13x. Buccal profile of right side. *b.* Specimen 13, 5-year-old racing horse. Magnified 14.125x. Buccal profile of right side. Bevelling arrowed.

internal integrity of the enamel was weakened by compression fractures prior to the removal of the spall. In addition, the repeated movement of the bit over the broken enamel abrades the enamel surface, leaving smooth polished patches within the fracture scar (Figs. 8b and 9b).

Taphonomic processes

Taphonomic effects on horse teeth have not been adequately studied. A variety of post-mortem and post-depositional processes might produce spalling of the tooth enamel. Post-mortem processes should affect the entire tooth surface, or at least affect the occlusal and non-occlusal surfaces equally. When a particular type of surficial damage is confined to either the side or the occlusal surface, a pre-mortem agent can be suspected. For example, some of the feral horses from the Assateague and Chincoteague barrier islands exhibited a peculiar pitting that affected the sides, but not the occlusal surfaces of the premolar teeth. The agent that caused the pitting is unknown, but it is probable that the pitting occurred while the animals were alive, and that the occlusal surface was either protected from the pitting agent or that occlusal abrasion wore away the pits as they were formed. A post-mortem pitting agent should have affected the occlusal surface as well as the side.

Some of the feral specimens used in this study had been exposed to the elements for perhaps two years, but no specimen in our original sample was truly archaeological. It was therefore very enlightening to have the opportunity to examine four Upper Paleolithic lower P2s from Solutré, kindly provided by Sandra Olsen. The Solutré horse teeth were not affected by bits, but were subjected to millennia of post-depositional soil abrasion. It was hoped that they would help to differentiate taphonomic spalling from bit wear. No firm generalizations concerning taphonomic spalling can be offered on the basis of these four specimens. All exhibit extensive scarring of the occlusal enamel, the occlusal dentin, and the exterior cementum, caused by millennia of movement downslope within a coarse, heavy soil matrix. Sections of occlusal enamel up to a millimeter in length have been chipped away entirely. However, this simple spalling does not resemble metal bit wear as it has been described above. The Solutré teeth are so extensively abraded, their comparative value for microwear study is minimal. Until more work has been done on unbitted wild horse teeth from archaeological contexts, the effects of taphonomic processes cannot be fully accounted for.

The Malyan equids

The equid teeth from the Kaftari phase at Malyan have been a focus of casual curiosity because of the unusual wear they exhibit. Similar wear has been called bit-wear by Clutton-Brock (1974), but this has been questioned by Payne (in press). During the Kaftari phase (at Malyan, ca.

2100-1800 B.C.) Malyan was a 135-hectare city, probably the center of the kingdom called Anshan in the Mesopotamian records, and the largest and most powerful urban center in western Iran. At this time equids (apparently asses) had long been used to pull wheeled wagons and carts in military contexts in Mesopotamia, and were used by messengers as riding animals. The introduction of the horse provided an animal of greater speed and strength that rapidly replaced the ass and ass-hemione hybrid in draught and riding.

The evidence presented here suggests that the introduction of the horse may have coincided with the earliest appearance of metal bits. It is possible that metal bits were developed in Western Iran or Mesopotamia in conjunction with the arrival of horses and improvements in chariot technology—all of these factors interacting in a burst of military innovation. It is also possible that metal bits were developed elsewhere, in the hinterlands of Iran, Anatolia, or the Caucasus, and were introduced fully developed to Mesopotamia, with the horse. On the other hand, metal bits might have been in use even earlier, and if Zarins' (1978) reading of the textual evidence is correct, horses might also have been introduced centuries before 2100 B.C. At this time, however, the earliest firm osteological evidence for horses and bit-wear evidence for metal bits both come from the Ur III period.

The Malyan equid remains have been fully described (Zeder 1986), and the animal butchering and processing patterns at Malyan have been analyzed (Zeder 1988). The specimens examined for this study are a horse mandible from the Kaftari phase deposits in area GGX98 (possibly a domestic residential area with some small scale craft production), and a probable mule or possibly a horse from area F26 (a portion of the city with an unknown function).

The lower premolar teeth (specimens 70058 and 70065) of the equid from area F26 exhibit the classic traits of metal bit wear. The anterior third of *both* lower premolars is quite smooth and uniformly rounded into a beveled inclined plane (Fig. 10). No feral horse examined in this study exhibited this trait, but it was commonly encountered among bitted horses (see Fig. 6). The SEM micrograph shows tooth surfaces greatly damaged by pitting caused by the matrix in which the specimen was found. However, within the worn enamel ridges there are numerous center-origin spalls, some of which are postmortem, but some of which have the distinctively rough, fibrous appearance of bit wear. The extensive post-mortem damage to the tooth renders the microscopic evidence somewhat less than conclusive, but the macroscopic evidence is convincing by itself. This equid, which was either a horse or a mule (Zeder 1986:393-394), was bitted with a metal bit. It is the earliest equid known to have been guided with a metal bit anywhere in the world. Incidentally, the data presented here

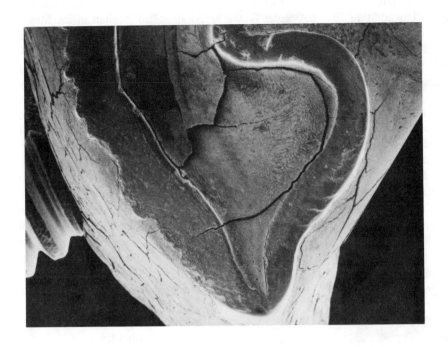
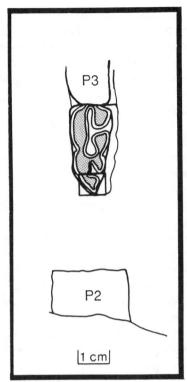

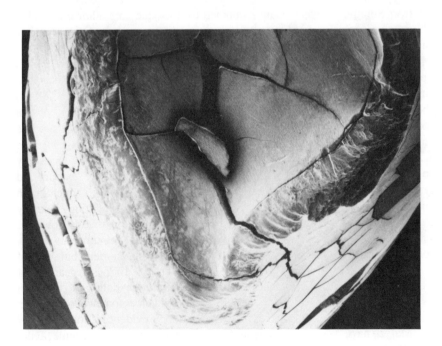
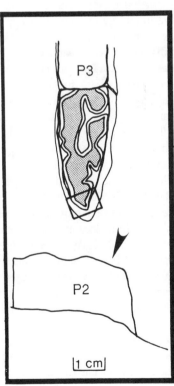

Fig. 9:
Comparison of unbitted (top) and bitted (bottom) horse premolars.
a. Specimen 7, 6-year-old Barrier Island Pony. Magnified 14.125x. Buccal profile of right side. *b.* Specimen 12, 10-year-old racing horse. Magnified 13x. Buccal profile of right side. Bevelling arrowed.

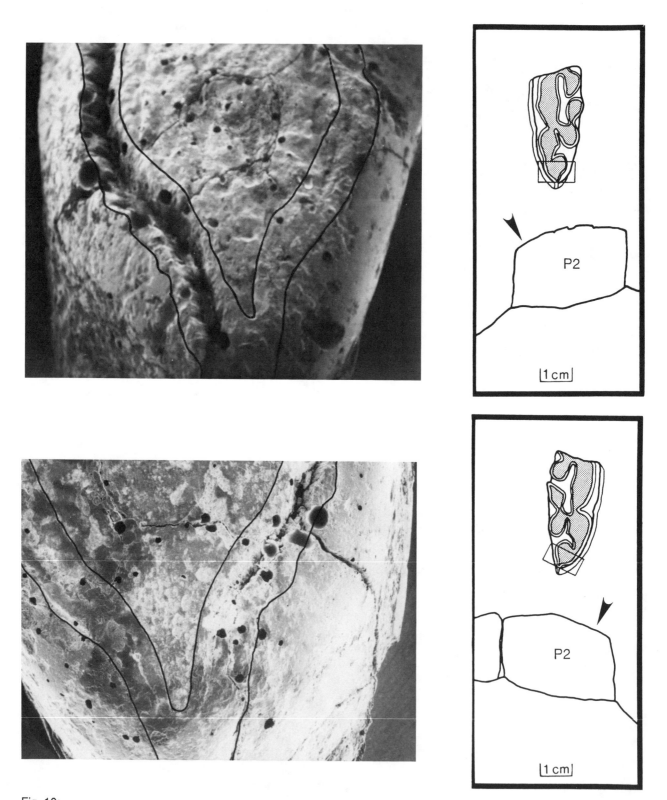

Fig. 10:
a. Cast of Malyan specimen 70065, F26, Lot 5. Magnified 10x. Lingual profile of right side. *b.* Cast of Malyan specimen 70058, F26, Lot 5. Magnified 13x. Lingual profile of left side.

Enamel ridges are outlined in black ink. Small black holes are bubbles from the casting process. Pitting is a result of taphonomic processes and obscures microscopic detail. However, the center spalling and trenching seen here is not apparent on the posterior of these P2s nor on the rest of the molar tooth row. Macroscopically, both profiles show the classic bevelling (arrowed) seen only in horses regularly using metal bits.

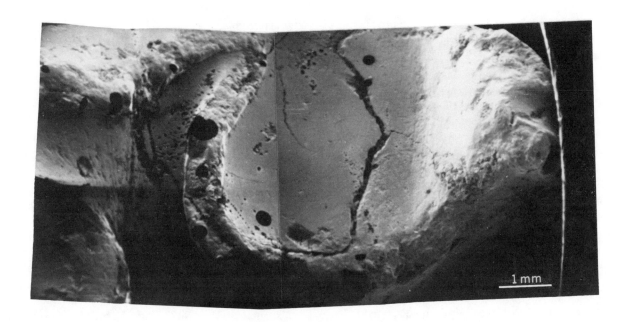

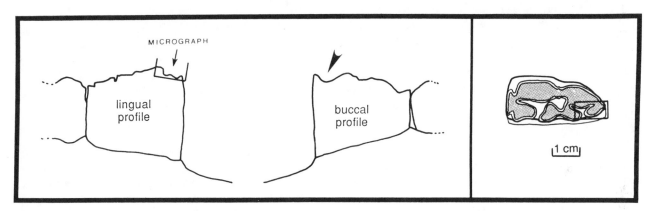

Fig. 11:
Cast of Malyan specimen 70051, GGX98, Lot 22. Left side.
Unusual groove is worn just behind the rostral prow (arrowed). Micrograph shows the smooth interior of the groove, and battering on the tip. This type of wear has not been encountered in any of our wild or metal bitted specimens.

also support the identification of metal bit wear on the 1650 B.C. horse from Buhen (Clutton-Brock 1974).

The second equid examined was a horse from area GGX98. The lower left molar row was preserved, including the lower left P2 (specimen 70051). The matching right mandible was not recovered. This P2 exhibited a type of wear that was not encountered during the present study in any horse, wild or domestic. It is possible that it represents rope bit wear, which has not yet been studied, or either an unusual type of metal bit or, less likely, very unusual occlusal wear. In profile (Fig. 11) the tooth exhibits a pronounced groove worn into the anterior occlusal surface behind the rostral prow of the tooth. The groove crosses the entire occlusal surface, isolating the high prow in front of the worn area. The maximum width of the groove is 0.55 cm. across its upper edges. The groove is asymmetrical,

with a shallow posterior and a steep anterior slope. The isolated prow of the tooth is extensively battered and chipped, but possibly by post-mortem agents. Other raised portions of the tooth are also heavily scratched and battered by post-mortem agents.

Within the groove, however, there is no evidence for such post-depositional abrasion. The soft dentin that surrounds the worn enamel ridges within the groove is not scarred, as it would be if solifluction or some other agent had abraded this area. Only the raised enamel ridge is extensively scarred. The pattern of enamel spalling conforms to that seen in metal bit wear: extensive spalls; many center-origin spalls, some of which carry to the edge and remove relatively large chunks of enamel; and uneven, fibrous spall scars. Because these microscopic features occur within a macroscopic feature (the groove) that is previously undocumented, their cause cannot be firmly identified. It seems likely that the feature represents some kind of bit wear, but a final identification awaits further comparative study.

Conclusions

It is possible that the examination of other equid teeth from the Near East will demonstrate an even earlier date for metal bits. In the meantime, questions are raised about the origins and usage of these particular animals. Were horses and metal bits introduced to the Near East simultaneously? If metal bits were available, why did nose-rings continue to appear in representations of ridden and driven equids for centuries afterwards? Were nose-rings actually used as late as 1500 B.C., or was this a conservative artistic convention? If they were used (as seems likely), was there a difference in function or context between bitted and non-bitted equid transport?

The metal bit wear study has demonstrated the usefulness of an analytical technique that can be applied to the study of horse remains from any post-Neolithic period. It has laid the groundwork for the next step in the bit wear project, which is the study of soft bit wear and the analysis of the use of the earliest domesticated horses in the U.S.S.R. Dexter Perkins and Pat Daly pioneered this general approach to faunal/cultural analysis with their microscopic studies of bone density in relation to domestication. We hope that they would have appreciated this application.

Notes

1. Examination of the Ukrainian horse teeth occurred in Kiev in March and April of 1989, and a description of the preliminary results is now in press (Anthony and Brown 1990). Mandibular premolars from Ukrainian sites ranging from the Upper Paleolithic (23,000 B.P.) to the Slavic Iron Age (A.D. 900) were examined. Bitwear is present on the teeth of the "cult stallion" from Dereivka, but seems to be absent on the other four mandibular premolars from Dereivka. The Dereivka "cult stallion" is now the earliest horse known to have been bitted anywhere in the world. Our research in Kiev was made possible by the hospitality and cooperation of the Ukrainian Institutes of Zoology and Archaeology. Our special thanks to Dr. N. Belan and Dr. D. Telegin.

2. Preliminary results from a new study of the Dereikvka horse teeth by Marsha Levine of Cambridge University indicate that over half of the Dereivka horses were killed at age 6-9 (Levine 1990). This suggests to her a wild population, exploited with hunting techniques that focused on bachelor bands or on mature stallions. The latter do challenge predators, so might fall prey preferentially to stalking techniques. However, one would expect ambush techniques to be more productive with wild herd animals of highly predictable habits like horses, particularly in the marsh and forest river-edge environment near Dereivka, where hunters might be easily concealed. Ambushing of entire bands should yield a broader age and sex structure. The authors have examined

Acknowledgments

This project has been supported by a Research Grant from the American Philosophical Society, a Trustees Summer Research grant from Hartwick College, and grant #5033 from the Wenner-Gren Foundation for Anthropological Research. In addition, many individuals helped generously. Mary Littauer provided invaluable advice on horse bits and handling and on the archaeology of equids in the Near East. Melinda Zeder and Kate Gordon of the Smithsonian Institution were largely responsible for the encouragement and advice that got us off the ground. Art Smith (West Chester University) provided initial access to an SEM. Janet Monge (University of Pennsylvania), Pat Shipman, Alan Walker, and Sandi Olsen (Johns Hopkins University) taught us how to make high-resolution casts and gave us advice on dental microwear and SEM techniques. Kathleen Ryan (University of Pennsylvania) and John Hunt (Cornell University) helped with additional SEM access and training. Domestic specimens were provided by John King, Mark Cline (Cornell University), and Helen Acland (University of Pennsylvania). Feral specimens were collected and documented under difficult field conditions by Ron Keiper (Penn. State University), Roger Bryant, and Dick Wheeler (B.L.M./Nevada). Julie Hartman conducted most of the 35 mm recording photography and helped with research. We are deeply grateful for the help provided by these individuals and institutions. Any errors are entirely our own.

six mandible fragments from Dereivka that contained incisors (providing rough age data) attached to the part of the jaw where canines should grow (providing sex data: canines are absent in most females). These six pieces represent all the preserved mandibular fragments that contain sex and incisor-age information for the same individual. All six have canines, therefore are probably male; and the mean age is between 4 and 5, significantly younger than Levine's mean, which was calculated from crown heights on a different group of specimens. A cull of males at 3-5 years of age, just after the testicles drop permanently on modern Przewalski colts (Mohr 1971:92), conforms to the pattern predicted in this paper. It should be noted that Levine's age data indicate 17% of the Dereivka horses were killed at age 4 or under. Our mandibular fragments might represent a sample from this group. It is possible that Dereivka contains the mixed remains of both wild and domesticated horses.

3. Thanks particularly to Dr. Chris Uhlinger, North Carolina State University and Dr. Stephen Mackenzie, State University of New York at Cobleskill.

4. The domestic horses were acquired with the help and cooperation of the autopsy laboratories at the New Bolton Center, University of Pennsylvania Veterinary School (thanks to Dr. Helen Acland); and the Cornell University Veterinary School (thanks to Dr. John King and Dr. Mark Cline).

5. The wild horses were more difficult to locate. Part of the sample was obtained by the authors during a field trip to the feral horse preserve at Chincoteague, Virginia. Dr. Ron Keiper of the Pennsylvania State University provided our first eagerly-sought feral specimens from Assateague, Maryland. A large and ex-tremely well-documented feral sample was provided by Dr. Roger Bryant and Dr. Richard Wheeler, of the Bureau of Land Management in Nevada. Without the cooperation of these individuals, the project would not have succeeded.

References

Anthony, D. 1985. *The Social and Economic Implications of the Domestication of the Horse.* Ph.D. dissertation, Department of Anthropology, University of Pennsylvania. University Microfilms, Ann Arbor, MI.

_____ 1986. The "Kurgan Culture," Indo-European Origins, and the Domestication of the Horse: A Reconsideration. *Current Anthropology* 27(4):291-313.

_____ In press. The Domestication of the Horse. In *Equids in the Ancient World*, ed. R.H. Meadow and H.-P. Uerpmann, Beihefte zum Tübinger Atlas des Vorderen Orients 19/1. Ludwig Reichert Verlag, Wiesbaden.

Anthony, D., and D. Brown. 1990. The Origins of Horseback Riding. *Antiquity* 64:in press.

Anthony, D., and B. Wailes. 1988. Review of *Archaeology and Language: The Puzzle of Indo-European Origins*, by C. Renfrew. *Current Anthropology* 29(3):441-445.

Bahn, P.G. 1980. Crib-biting: Tethered Horses in the Paleolithic? *World Archaeology* 12(2):212-217.

Bibikova, V.I. 1967. Kizucheniiu drevneishikh domashnikh loshadei vostochnoi evropy. *Biulleten Moskovskogo Obshchestva Ispytatelei Prirodi, Otdel Biologicheskii* 72(3):106-117.

_____ 1969. Do istorii domesticatsii konya na pivdennomu skhodi Evropy. *Arkheologiia* (Kiev) 22:55-67.

_____ 1970. Kizucheniiu drevneishikh domashnikh loshadei vostochnoi evropy. Soobshchenie 2. *Biulleten Moskovskogo Obshchestva Ispytatelei Prirodi, Otdel Biologicheskii* 75(5):118-126.

Bökönyi, S. 1978. The First Waves of Domestic Horses in Eastern Europe. *Journal of Indo-European Studies* 6:17-76.

Clayton, H.M. 1984. A Fluoroscopic Study of the Position and Action of the Jointed Snaffle Bit in the Horse's Mouth. *Equine Veterinary Science* 4(5):193-196.

_____ 1985. A Fluoroscopic Study of the Position and Action of Different Bits in the Horse's Mouth. *Equine Veterinary Science* 5(2):68-77.

Clutton-Brock, J. 1974. The Buhen Horse. *Journal of Archaeological Science* 1:89-100.

Danilenko, V.M., and M.M. Shmagli. 1972. Pro odin povorotnii moment v istorii eneolitichnogo naselennia Pivdennoi Evropi. *Arkheologiia* (Kiev) (6):3-20.

Davis, S.J. 1987. *The Archaeology of Animals.* Yale University Press, New Haven and London.

Levine, M.A. 1990. The Beginnings of Horse Domestication in Central Eurasia. Paper presented at the Sixth International Conference of the International Council for Archaeozoology (ICAZ), Washington, D.C.

Lichardus, J. 1980. Zur Funktion der Geweihspitzen des typus Ostorf: Verberlegungen zu einer vorbronzezeitlichen Pferdeschirrung. *Germania* 58:1-24.

Littauer, M.A. 1969. Bits and Pieces. *Antiquity* 43:289-300.

Littauer, M.A., and J.H. Crouwel. 1979. *Wheeled Vehicles and Ridden Animals in the Ancient Near East.* E.J. Brill, Leiden.

Mezlumjan, S.K. 1990. The Domesticated Horse in Ancient Armenia. Paper presented at the Sixth International Conference of the International Council for Archaeozoology (ICAZ), Washington, D.C.

Mohr, E. 1971. *The Asiatic Wild Horse. Equus przevalskii Pliakoff*, trans. D.M. Goodall. J.A. Allen, London. Originally published 1881.

Moszolics, A. 1953. Mors en bois de cerf sur le territoire du bassin des Carpathes. *Acta Archaeologiia Hungarica* 3:69-109.

Munchaev, R.M. 1975. *Kavkaz na Zare Bronzovogo Veka.* Akademiia Nauk, Moscow.

Olsen, S.L. 1988. Applications of Scanning Electron Microscopy in Archaeology. *Advances in Electronics and Electron Physics* 71:357-380.

Nobis, G. 1971. *Vom Wildpferd zum Hauspferd. Fundamenta Reihe B*, Band 6. Bohlau-Verlag, Köln and Wien.

Payne, S. In press. The KY Tumulus Equids. In *Gordion II: The Lesser Tumuli. Part I: The Inhumations*, ed. E.L. Kohler. The University Museum, Philadelphia.

Piggott, S. 1962. Heads and Hoofs. *Antiquity* 36:110-118.

Redding, R.W. 1981. The Faunal Remains. In *An Early Town on the Deh Luran Plain: Excavations at Tepe Farukhabad*, ed. H.T. Wright, pp. 233-261. Memoirs No. 13. Museum of Anthropology, University of Michigan, Ann Arbor.

Rose, J.J. 1983. A Replication Technique for Scanning Electron Microscopy: Applications for Anthropologists. *American Journal of Physical Anthropology* 62:255-261.

Silver, I.A. 1970. The Ageing of Domestic Animals. In *Science in Archaeology*, ed. D.R. Brothwell and E. Higgs, pp. 283-302. Praeger, New York.

Smirnov, K.F. 1961. Arkheologicheskie dannye o drevnikh vsadniakh Povolzhsko-Ural'skikh stepei. *Sovietskaia Arkheologiia* (3):1-14.

Teaford, M. 1988. A Review of Dental Microwear and Diet in Modern Mammals. *Scanning Microscopy* 2(2):1149-1166.

Telegin, D.Y. 1959. Eneoliticheskoe poselenie i mogil'nik u Khutora Aleksandriia. *Kratkie Soobshcheniia Instituta Arkheologii* (Kiev) 9:10-20.

_____ 1973. *Seredno-Stogivska Kul'tura Epokhi Midi.* Naukova Dumka, Kiev.

_____ 1986. *Dereivka: A Settlement and Cemetery of Copper Age Horse-keepers on the Middle Dnieper.* BAR International Series No. 287, Cambridge.

Telegin, D.Y., and D. Anthony. 1987. On the Yamna Culture. *Current Anthropology* 28(3):357-358.

Yakar, J. 1985. *The Later Prehistory of Anatolia. The Late Chalcolithic and Early Bronze Age.* BAR International Series No. 268, Cambridge.

Zarins, J. 1978. The Domesticated Equidae of Third Millennium B.C. Mesopotamia. *Journal of Cuneiform Studies* 30:317.

Zeder, M.A. 1986. The Equid Remains from Tal-e Malyan, Southern Iran. In *Equids in the Ancient World*, ed. R.H. Meadow and H.-P. Uerpmann, pp. 365-412. Ludwig Reichert Verlag, Wiesbaden.

_____ 1988. Understanding Urban Process through the Study of Specialized Subsistence Economy in the Near East. *Journal of Anthropological Archaeology* 7:1-55.

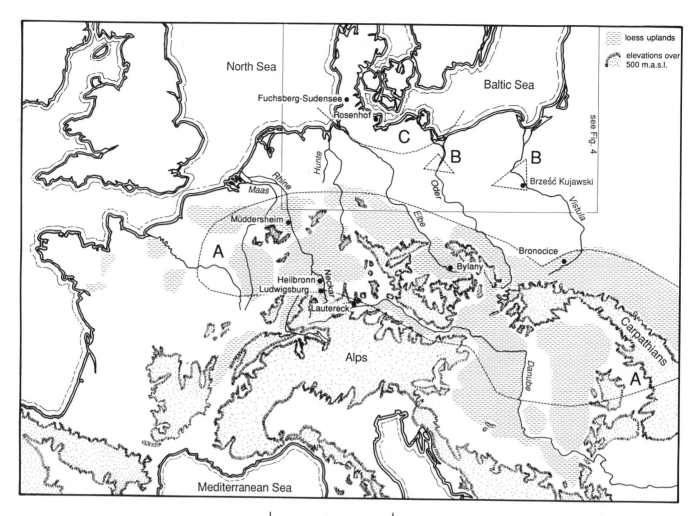

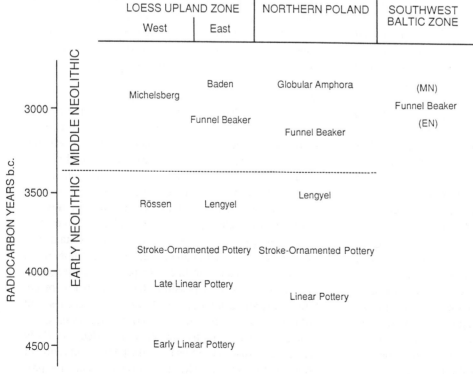

LOESS UPLAND ZONE		NORTHERN POLAND	SOUTHWEST BALTIC ZONE
West	East		

Fig. 1:
Map of Central Europe showing major regions and sites discussed in text. Key: A—zone of initial Neolithic colonization of Central Europe, corresponding largely to the distribution of loess soil and Linear Pottery sites; B—areas of Linear Pottery settlement beyond the loess, on the North European Plain; C—zone of distribution of initial agricultural communities in northern continental Europe.

Fig. 2:
Highly simplified chronological chart of areas discussed in text. Under the heading of "loess upland zone," "west" refers to West Germany, Holland, Belgium, and France, while "east" refers to East Germany, Czechoslovakia, and southern Poland. Dotted line marks the separation of "Early Neolithic" and "Middle Neolithic" mentioned in the text.

THE EXPLOITATION OF DOMESTIC ANIMALS IN NEOLITHIC CENTRAL EUROPE

Peter Bogucki

Forbes College, Princeton University, Princeton, NJ 08544-4000

Remembrances

I am included in the list of contributors for this volume because I was a student of Richard Meadow whose mentor was Dexter Perkins. Although I met Dexter on several occasions in the old Student Lounge on the fifth floor of the Peabody Musem, our contact was decidedly informal and outside the realm of faunal analysis. Clearly, however, the instruction that I received in faunal analysis from Richard reflected Dexter's concerns for the use of faunal analysis for the study of past human culture rather than the study of mammalian osteology using remains from archaeological sites. This perspective has served me well in approaching my research, and I am honored by having an opportunity to contribute to this volume.

Introduction

The expansion of food production as an economic strategy across temperate Europe between 6000 and 5000 years ago marked one of the major events in human adaptation in later prehistory. This paper evaluates the economic importance of domestic animals in these new adaptations of the first farming communities of north-central Europe (4500-2500 b.c. [all dates given in unrecalibrated radiocarbon years]). Poor bone preservation on many sites has yielded a general impression that animal husbandry played an ancillary role in this process. It now seems clear, however, that the utilization of domestic animals permitted the economic security and diversity required for the expansion of the first farming communities across north-central Europe and the diffusion of this novel economic strategy to indigenous foraging peoples on the North European Plain.

Since my own research is focused on north central and eastern Europe—primarily in Poland—in this article I will deal with developments in early animal domestication north of the Carpathians and Alps, along an east-west axis, between 4500 and 2500 b.c. During these two millennia, food production was introduced to central Europe, a process initiated by the colonization of the loess uplands of Czechoslovakia, Germany, the southern part of the Neth-

erlands and Belgium, and southern Poland by the Linear Pottery culture (zone A on Fig. 1). This colonization zone was later extended into eastern France. In addition, localized areas of Linear Pottery settlement are found off the loess on the lowlands of the North European Plain in northern Poland (zone B on Fig. 1). The Linear Pottery culture and its successors, the Stroke-Ornamented Pottery, Rössen, and Lengyel cultures, are termed "Early Neolithic" below (Fig. 2). They are succeeded by the Michelsberg culture in the western part of this area and the Funnel Beaker culture in the east. These locally developed agrarian cultures are termed "Middle Neolithic" below. Meanwhile, on the North European Plain, this period saw the adoption of agriculture and stockbreeding by local hunter-gatherer groups (zone C on Fig 1). These nascent agricultural communities are conventionally linked with the Funnel Beaker culture as well but are divided into "EN" and "MN" stages (Fig. 2). The nomenclature of the Neolithic in central Europe can be quite confusing, and it is important to be explicit about the geographical zone under discussion at any given moment.

Question of sample size and context

A fundamental problem lies in the unevenness of the corpus of data on Neolithic subsistence. Interest in the systematic collection of subsistence data has arisen only recently, although the basic complex of Early Neolithic domesticates has been known since the early part of this century. Flotation and wet-sieving as a means of recovering small bones have been employed on comparatively few Early Neolithic sites. Rather, there has been a reliance on trench-collected bones and seeds, with a resultant bias toward the larger mammalian species. Fish, amphibians, reptiles, and small mammals are poorly represented in most collections. It is possible that such taxa were not widely exploited by Early Neolithic communities, but without more comprehensive recovery techniques, we shall never know. Another gap in our knowledge of Early Neolithic subsistence stems from the poor preservation of bones in loessic soil. This condition is especially pronounced in sites where the archaeological remains lie fairly high in the soil profile, in the zone where decalcification has occurred. For instance, at the well-known Linear Pottery settlement of Bylany in Bohemia, the quality of bone preservation was abysmal. Poplin (1975:180) estimated that if there had been good bone preservation at Bylany, there should have been 500,000 to 1,000,000 recovered specimens! The total number of specimens identified by Clason (1967), however, was only 587, of which 354 were tooth fragments more resistant to the acidic loess. Deeper sites and those not situated on loess have better preservation of faunal materials, leading to further bias in the knowledge of Early Neolithic faunal exploitation.

Another factor affecting the presence of animal bone on European Neolithic sites is the presence of dogs in Neolithic settlements. Guilday (1971) has estimated that the very existence of domestic dogs in a prehistoric settlement could result in over 95% bone attrition. When carnivore gnawing is coupled with the acidic loess and generally poor recovery techniques, the recovery of *any* bone from Neolithic sites in temperate Europe is surprising. It may be more appropriate to reflect on why bones are preserved on these sites, particularly on the loess.

For the most part, animal bones on temperate European Neolithic sites are found in one type of context, the rubbish-filled pit. (There is not the variety of rooms and middens that one encounters on sites in the Near East and Southeast Europe.) "Sheet midden," as the term is used in American archaeology, is also very rare at sites on the loess, for post-Neolithic erosion has stripped away much of the general surface refuse from these sites (Modderman 1976). In the lowland zone, and in the lake basins of the Alpine Foreland, erosion is less of a factor, which partially accounts for the richer faunal assemblages found in these areas. Moreover, it is possible to assume that in many rubbish pits there was fairly rapid burial of the discarded animal bones by additional refuse disposal, washed-in soil, and blown-in leaves. It would have been in the interest of the inhabitants of these sites to bury the animal bones as quickly as possible, to discourage carnivores from the surrounding forests from making scavenging-forays into the settlements. Thus, it is reasonable to infer that in these rubbish pits a sample of the deposited bones was inaccessible to dogs. At loess sites, the rubbish pit environment could have promoted the preservation of some animal bones by buffering the chemical effects of the surrounding acidic soil.

Approaches to quantification in Neolithic zooarchaeology

Not only are there different standards of recovery and degree of identification from site to site, but the methods of reporting the primary data also vary from researcher to

researcher concerned with the analysis of fauna from Neolithic sites. In the first half of this century, animal bones from Neolithic sites were submitted to zoologists with the goal of generating "laundry lists" of identified species which were appended to site reports. This approach was sometimes the only approach possible with the handful of identifiable specimens that survived six millennia in the acidic loess and then the trauma of excavation. Relatively infrequently, counts of identified specimens were given. The result was a bias toward the larger mammalian species and those which have more elements per individual.

It is important to realize that central European faunal analysis was then, and still is to a large degree, the domain of zoologists whose interest is the osteological development of domestic species over time rather than the cultural context of the animal bones. It is thus not surprising that there has not been a widespread effort to refine methods of quantification on data from European Neolithic sites. Nonetheless, it is more than a historical aside that in 1932 the Polish palaeontologist Edward Lubicz-Niezabitowski used the "minimum numbers of individuals" (MNI) method in his quantification of the faunal assemblage from the Early Neolithic site of Poznan-Debiec. This use of MNI predates by over 20 years the appearance of White's 1953 paper, generally believed to be the occasion of the transfer of MNI from palaeontology to archaeological faunal analysis (see, for example, Grayson 1984:27). Since then, MNIs have occasionally appeared alongside fragment counts, often embedded in the text of Neolithic faunal reports.

Some researchers have attempted to convert bone weights and MNI into biomass and compare the figures so derived to ascertain the relative economic importance of different species. The "weight method," first proposed by Kubasiewicz (1956), using bone weights to estimate biomass, has a number of serious drawbacks (Casteel 1978). In particular, the ratio of bone weight to meat weight is not constant from animal to animal and from species to species. Moreover, it also assumes that meat was the sole reason why domesticated stock was kept, ignoring the economic value of products like milk and wool. The same difficulties apply to attempts to convert MNI into "kilograms of available meat" (e.g. Milisauskas 1978).

The most common denominator among Early Neolithic faunal reports from central European sites is that counts of identified specimens (NISP) are usually presented alongside other methods of quantification. Therefore, in spite of the inherent difficulties with NISP, the most widely applicable basis of comparison of these assemblages would be based on such counts. Some have argued (e.g. Gautier 1984) that when animal size classes are taken into account, fragment counts are perhaps the most generally acceptable approach to the quantification of faunal assemblages. Since most European faunal data are reported in terms of NISP, it is the only common measure of relative species abundance that can be realistically used in a synthesis of this sort.

Local domestication?

It is generally agreed that the main four domestic taxa found in Neolithic temperate Europe were domesticated for the first time elsewhere. Sheep and goat, of course, are not found wild in the central European forests, and there is no question that they were domesticated first in the Near East. Cattle and pigs have their conspecific wild counterparts in temperate Europe, but chronologically the earliest cases of the domestication of these taxa appear to have been in Anatolia or Thessaly a millennium or more prior to the expansion of a food-producing economy into temperate Europe. The existence of wild cattle and pig in north-central Europe, however, has led to a discussion about further local domestication of these species, based primarily on osteometric grounds.

The most forceful exponent of local European domestication of cattle has been Sandor Bökönyi, who has written of a "fever of domestication" across much of Neolithic Europe during a period generally within that covered in this paper (Bökönyi 1962, 1969, 1975). Bökönyi argues that the presence of transitional specimens, between the "wild" and "domestic" measurement ranges, shows the occurrence of local domestication. Thus, a marked gap between the two ranges or the total absence of either wild- or domestic-sized specimens indicates that local domestication was absent, while a continuum of measurements is taken as evidence for local domestication. Bökönyi also attaches great importance to the age and sex profiles of the wild sample. If older males make up a large proportion of the wild sample, Bökönyi believes that this indicates an effort to domesticate wild individuals. The basis for this reasoning is that the older males would have attempted to protect the younger animals and females from capture and would have been killed in the process (Bökönyi 1971:645).

As with all problems that involve the ability to distinguish one population from another, it is important to base arguments on samples large enough to permit statistical inference and not on isolated specimens (Bökönyi and Bartosiewicz 1987). Postglacial aurochs finds reflect considerable variability, and, as Grigson (1969:280) points out, this variability is aggravated by sexual dimorphism. In a small sample, there might be a sharp distinction between small, arguably domestic, and large, arguably wild, specimens which may simply reflect a sample without representative proportions of different species and sizes. The continuous size distributions that Bökönyi interprets as indicating local hybridization and thus domestication are more likely to occur in large samples, such as those found on Hungarian Neolithic sites. Unfortunately, on Neolithic sites in north-central Europe, it is unlikely that samples as large as those studied by Bökönyi would occur. In large

samples, however, the variability that is inherent in the aurochs and domestic cattle populations comes into play. How small can the aurochs cows be, and how large can particularly robust domestic bulls be? The faunal remains from consumption refuse are a composite death assemblage and may arrive in archaeological deposits via different taphonomic pathways; thus, there is the possibility that a large archaeological assemblage might contain a broad representative sample of both a hunted aurochs population and the domestic population slaughtered within the settlement. A continuous distribution of sizes can be attributable to the variation found in these two populations and the overlap of the size ranges, rather than to crossing. This may be another manifestation in zooarchaeology of the problems inherent in attempts to compare assemblages with varying sample sizes (termed "sample-size effect"—see Grayson 1984; Rhode 1988).

In regions where sample sizes are large, the argument for local domestication based on a continuous distribution of specimen sizes can be considered as a hypothesis. North of the Carpathians and the Danube, however, such sample sizes are not found on most Neolithic sites. In these areas, isolated specimens are often the focus of such discussions. The most notable case for local cattle domestication has been made by Nobis (1962, 1975) for sites in Schleswig-Holstein. At Rosenhof and Fuchsberg-Südensee, isolated specimens fall between the wild and domestic ranges, and while they do not cause the distribution to become continuous, these specimens are claimed to represent the crossing of wild and domestic populations. Rowley-Conwy (1985:189) points out, however, that in northern continental Europe, "it has become clear that neolithic domestic bulls and wild females are in fact of similar sizes." Rowley-Conwy goes on to note (1985:190) that the well-defined size differences between wild and domestic females and between wild and domestic males, when specimens are of known sex, "would argue against the local domestication of aurochs." In the absence of conclusive evidence to the contrary, it seems apparent that domestic cattle arrived on the North European Plain in a fully domesticated form.

Early Neolithic faunal remains in temperate Europe

Animal bone assemblages from Early Neolithic sites in central Europe tend to be small and do not approach the size of coeval collections from southeast Europe. This is especially true of the loess belt. As a result, one must generate a composite picture of the distribution of animal taxa on these sites rather than generalize from the data from any single site. In order to synthesize these data as economically as possible, the focus here will be on two main aspects of these data. The first is the relative proportions of bones from domestic and wild animals, while the second is the relative numbers of bones from the four main domestic subsistence species—cattle, sheep, goat, and pig.

When the proportions of wild and domestic fauna on most Early Neolithic sites in the loess belt are compared, a strikingly consistent pattern appears across central Europe: the bones of wild mammals are very rare in Early Neolithic contexts especially when fragment counts are the basis of quantification (Bogucki 1988:figure 4.2). Of course, a major problem exists when one analyst's aurochs or wild boar becomes another's cow or domestic pig. The point of separation between the domesticates which are indigenous to central Europe and their wild relatives has long been a disputed point (see, Grigson 1969; Clason 1972; Boessneck 1977, among others). The situation of the aurochs/domestic cattle bones from Müddersheim is a case in point. The original analysis by Stampfli (1965) indicated that 28.8% of the 201 identified mammal bones belonged to wild animals, based on his assessment that 33 were aurochs (*Bos primigenius*). This observation was incorporated into the argument by some that the Early Neolithic communities along the lower Rhine and Maas engaged in a greater amount of hunting than elsewhere in Europe (e.g. Newell 1970). Clason's reinterpretation of the Müddersheim cattle bones indicated that only two were aurochs and that the proportion of wild to domestic specimens was not much different from that found at other Early Neolithic sites in central Europe.

Not only are the bones of wild mammals relatively rare in Early Neolithic contexts, but those of reptiles, amphibians, and fish are also scarce. Much of this can be attributed to recovery practices, since the proportions of such species rise markedly in sieved samples (see, Meadow 1976; Clason and Prummel 1977). Another factor to account for the scarcity of such bones may lie in the way in which the meat from such animals is handled. Often, the entire animal would have been cooked, bones and all. The cooked bones would have been discarded at the location of consumption, not of preparation, and because of their small size, they do not lend themselves to systematic collection and disposal by the inhabitants of a prehistoric settlement. A fish vertebra is much easier to tread into a dirt floor than a cow femur. The cooked bones would also be more susceptible to weathering and decay than the bones of larger mammals which were either uncooked or shielded from the heat by a thicker layer of muscle and fat. It is possible that faunal samples from Early Neolithic sites in temperate Europe do not contain the bones of non-mammalian wild species in a quantity commensurate with the degree to which these species were exploited. A hint of the problems created by differential disposal of the bones of different taxa on open sites comes from the Lautereck rock shelter in southern Germany (Taute 1966). Here, Early Neolithic occupation areas were spatially restricted by the confines of the rock shelter, and a comprehensive sample of faunal remains was obtained which included fish bones. Arguably, they were found because all bones were discarded within the same confined space. At the same time, however, it may also be argued that this was a special-purpose exploitation camp which would not reflect larger trends in faunal exploitation.

The second striking regularity among Early Neolithic faunal assemblages is found in the relative frequency of the three main domesticates: cattle, sheep/goat (considered together due to the difficulty of separating them osteologically), and pig. The data from 22 Early Neolithic sites with faunal assemblages larger than 100 identified specimens are summarized graphically in Fig. 3.

A consistent pattern is readily apparent: virtually everywhere domestic cattle form the major component of the faunal assemblages. The only exception to this occurs in several of the larger assemblages reported by Müller (1964) from Saxo-Thuringia, where sheep/goat outnumber the cattle (nos. 6, 16, and 17 on Fig. 3). If, however, all 71 assemblages studied by Müller are considered together, cattle outweigh sheep/goat by a ratio of 1.7:1, since the smaller assemblages which do not respond singly to quantitative comparison are comprised largely of cattle bones.

Since the only useful products of the pig (meat, skin, lard, and bone) require the death and dismemberment of the animal before they are available, the number of pig bones on a site should, barring problems of preservation and disposal practices, be a relatively accurate reflection of the economic importance of this species to the inhabitants of the site. The relative abundance of cattle and sheep/goat bones, on the other hand, may *underrepresent* the economic importance of these taxa, due to the products such as milk, blood, and wool which can be taken from living animals. The bones of these species represent the final utilization of slaughtered animals for meat, but the utility of living cattle, sheep, and goats results in these creatures having longer "useful lives" than pigs.

It is difficult to interpret the data which bear on the sex and age composition of Early Neolithic faunal assemblages, especially for the cattle bones. This problem is directly related to the small size of the assemblages, and when they are lumped together, any vestige of statistical reliability vanishes completely. Moreover, the relative sizes of males, castrates, and females can be consistent within local populations but can vary widely across geographical zones. Frequently, the argument has been made that the kill-off patterns observed in archaeological faunal assemblages can indicate the uses to which the living populations of animals were put (e.g. Payne 1973). Unfortunately, this approach may work only when large assemblages which can be reliably separated into males and females are available. Such is not the case on Early Neolithic sites, and only general kill-off patterns have been reported from a few sites (e.g. Bogucki 1982). Even when such data are available, their interpretation is often ambiguous. It is important to remember that an archaeological faunal assemblage represents a collection of dead animals, not a living herd. The best data on kill-off patterns of Early Neolithic cattle come from the Polish Lowlands (Bogucki 1982) and East Germany (Müller 1964). At Brześć Kujawski, over 90% of the cattle from Linear Pottery contexts were slaughtered beyond their 18th month and 70% survived their 36th month and lived to an advanced age. There are very few juvenile cattle bones represented in this assemblage. On the East German sites, however, Müller found 60.5% adult, 11.5% subadult, and 28% juvenile individuals (on the basis of an estimated minimum of 143 individuals from these sites). These data suggest a higher degree of calf slaughter than found at Brześć Kujawski. In both cases, however, there is little evidence of an emphasis on the slaughter of animals in the 48-month age group, the age at which cattle reach their optimal meat weight (Higham and Message 1969).

The considerably smaller numbers of sheep/goat and pig bones on Early Neolithic sites do not permit any similar observations of sex and age distribution. In the case of the pig bones, however, the majority are usually those of juvenile individuals, reflecting a standard kill-off pattern for domestic pigs found in both prehistoric and modern times. Finally, the wild animals represented on Early Neolithic sites are too few in number to even begin to investigate sex and age distributions, and it is therefore not possible to reach any conclusions about systematic culling of wild animal populations.

The author has made the case in several publications for the role of dairy production in the Linear Pottery economy (Bogucki 1984b, 1986). The development of a tolerance for lactose through the continuation of lactase production into adulthood has been generally thought to be a relatively late evolutionary development, and hence it has been believed that the milking of domestic livestock emerged at a similarly late date in prehistory. There are ways, however, to process raw milk to obviate the effects of lactose intolerance, by separating the milk into its

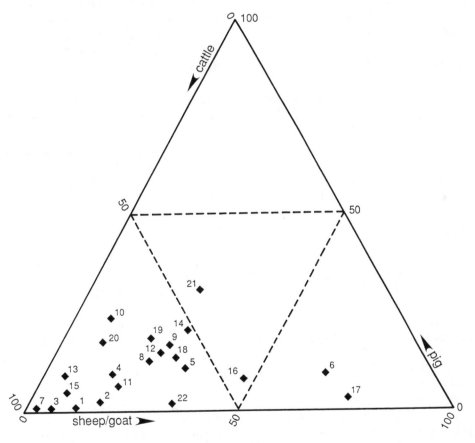

Fig. 3:
Triaxial graph of the relative proportions of cattle, sheep/goat, and pig fragments on Linear Pottery sites with large faunal assemblages (after Bogucki 1984b). Key: **1**—Brześć Kujawski 3 (n=82); **2**—Brześć Kujawski 4 (n=514); **3**—Strzelce (n=77); **4**—Łojewo (n=594); **5**—Barleben-Schweinemasterei (n=223); **6**—Barleben-Hühnenfarm (n=168); **7**—Eitzum (n=46); **8**—Armeau (n=928); **9**—Cuiry-lès-Chaudardes (n=501, data to 1976); **10**—Samborzec (n=384); **11**—Gniechowice (n=158); **12**—Jelení louka (n=532); **13**—Bylany (n=540, all Linear Pottery periods); **14**—Gatersleben (n=252); **15**—Halle-Trothe (n=357); **16**—Trobsdorf (n=345); **17**—Dammersdorf (n=199); **18**—Hohlstedt (n=351); **19**—Hienheim (n=72); **20**—Müddersheim (n=184, according to Clason 1972); **21**—Reichstett (n=125); **22**—Miechowice (n=1449).

components and permitting bacterial agents to alter the chemical structure of the milk sugars. Cheese and yogurt are the products of such processes.

The kill-off patterns in faunal remains from Early Neolithic sites in temperate Europe are ambiguous about the issue of dairy versus meat production, as in fact are most samples of domestic faunal remains from sites in the Old World.[1] A stronger argument can be made on the basis of the economics of small-scale cattle raising. Since cattle require 42 to 48 months to reach their optimal meat weight, the investment of labor, time, and energy over this period would probably outweigh the 300-400 kgs of usable meat available from each head.[2] Given the uniparous nature of cattle, and the potential for the loss of animals to predators and disease, Neolithic communities would have needed to maintain a large reserve of surplus animals or risk seriously affecting the viability of the herd as a reproductive population. It instead appears that cattle served a variety of purposes in the Early Neolithic economy and were slaughtered when they were no longer economically useful.[3]

Another line of evidence is the existence of ceramic sieves on Linear Pottery and Rössen sites (Bogucki 1984b, 1986; Jürgens 1978/79). Sherds of these are often found on smaller sites, not in very great quantities. It can be argued credibly on the basis of similar examples from later European history, modern European ethnography, and even from 19th century Vermont, that the function of these was for the straining of curds from the whey in cheese manufac-ture. Thus the evidence of the clay sieves and the predominance of domestic cattle bones in the faunal samples indicate that there is a high probability that milking and the use of dairy products such as cheese were known by the earliest Neolithic inhabitants of temperate Europe.

Early Neolithic adaptations beyond the loess

An important dimension of the earliest agricultural settlement of central Europe is its extension from the loess belt to the North European Plain (see Fig. 1). Here, early farming communities encountered landforms and soils different from those they had previously seen in the loess belt. The flat, glacially-derived topography of the lowlands contrasted strikingly with the rolling uplands of the loess belt, as did the morainic clays and sands. There are several main foci of early agricultural settlement on the North European Plain by the cultures that colonized the loess belt: the lake belt of Kuyavia in central Poland;[4] the area near the town of Chelmno along the lower Vistula; and the triangle formed by the Polish town of Pyrzyce and the East German towns of Angermünde and Prenzlau along the lower Oder (Fig. 4). Sites related to the Early Neolithic communities of the loess belt are also found around the Dümmersee in Lower Saxony.

The first tentative settlement by communities with domestic livestock on the North European Plain had already taken place by the early phases of the Linear Pottery culture, perhaps as early as 4400 b.c. (unrecalibrated).[5] The

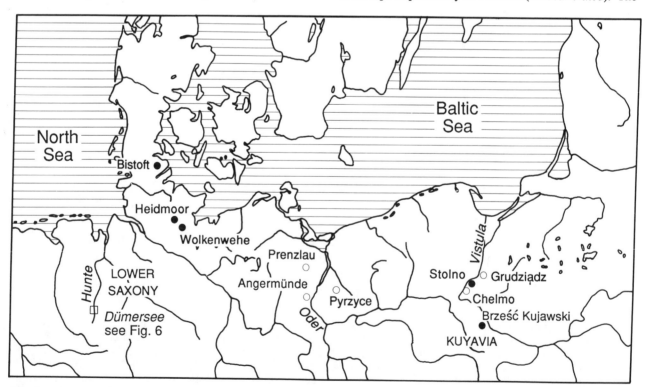

Fig. 4:
Map of the North European Plain, showing regions and sites discussed in text.

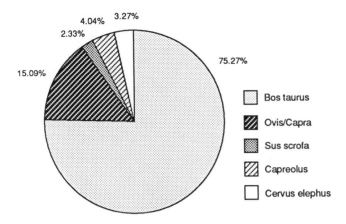

Fig. 5a:
Species ratios in faunal sample from Linear Pottery features at Brześć Kujawski.

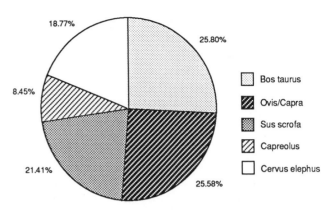

Fig. 5b:
Species ratios in faunal sample from Lengyel features at Brześć Kujawski.

lowland Linear Pottery sites do not have the appearance of long-term farming occupations, due to their relatively small size, the general absence of the same kind of longhouse architecture as found on the loess, and the pronounced predominance of domestic cattle in many of the faunal assemblages (see Fig. 5a). An exception to this almost-universal pattern of a high proportion of cattle bones is the recently-reported assemblage from Stolno, site 2, composed of 47.5% sheep/goat bones and 44.2% cattle among the domestic species (Makowiecki 1987:262). The author has hypothesized that these sites represent a specialized sort of Linear Pottery adaptation exploiting the forest grazing resources of the lowlands (Bogucki 1982). This hypothesis has aroused a measure of interest and healthy skepticism (e.g. Whittle 1987), and much work needs to be done to test it. It is worth noting that sieve sherds are very widely distributed on Linear Pottery sites in the lower Vistula and Oder drainages.

The establishment of long-term agricultural settlements on parts of the North European Plain did not really occur until about 3600/3500 b.c. In the lowlands of north-central Poland, one finds settlements of the Brześć Kujawski Group of the Lengyel Culture, characterized by permanent residential bases with longhouses, similar in many respects to the earlier Linear Pottery longhouse settlements of the loess belt. The faunal remains from Brześć Kujawski have been studied by the author since 1976 (Bogucki 1982, 1984a), and smaller assemblages are also available from several other coeval sites (Sobocinski 1979). Wet-screening at Brześć Kujawski has yielded a large sample of fish, bird, and turtle bones. Instead of the overwhelming reliance on domestic cattle that characterized many of the Early Neolithic settlements of central Europe, faunal samples from sites of the Brześć Kujawski Group show that a broader range of livestock was kept (Fig. 5b). Sheep, goats, and pigs are significantly represented in the faunal

assemblages, although the proportions of these taxa vary from site to site. In addition, wild herbivores such as red deer and roe deer were exploited, as were turtles, fish, and shellfish. The last occupation phase at Brześć Kujawski, in particular, shows a considerable increase in the use of aquatic resources.

Further west, in the glacial outwash plains of Lower Saxony, a complex of sites with similar characteristics is found. The importance of the glacial lakes on the northwest German outwash plain for the transition from foraging to farming in this area has only recently been recognized. Very few early food-producing sites have been excavated, although numerous Mesolithic sites are known from this area. One lake basin, the Dümmer, appears to be of particular significance on the basis of the research which has been done there in the last two decades (Fig. 4). The Dümmersee is the second largest lake in Lower Saxony, currently having a surface area of 15 km². It is both fed and drained by the Hunte river. In the early Holocene, the lake was clearly larger, and a perimeter of Mesolithic sites marks what must have been its shoreline during the Atlantic period (Fig. 6; Fansa and Kampffmeyer 1985:109). The Neolithic sites lie considerably closer to the present lake margins. Between 1961 and 1967, 1,100 sq. m were excavated at the site of Hüde I, and the preservation of organic material was exceptionally good. There were several occupation layers at Hüde I, although it was difficult to differentiate them. It appears that there are three main occupation phases: 4200-3700 b.c., 3700-3200 b.c., and 2950-2700 b.c.

The faunal and botanical samples from the latest two settlement phases are difficult to separate completely, and the published discussions generally treat them as a single sample. From over 30,000 faunal specimens, 10,600 mammal, 1001 fish, and 275 bird bones could be identified (Boessneck 1978; Hübner 1980; Saur 1980; Hüster 1983).

At the moment, it is difficult to assess the relative importance of the various species present, since detailed quantification has not been available. On the basis of numbers of identified specimens, the major taxa represented are cattle (36.8%), pig (21.5%), and beaver (12.8%). The same three species are also shown to be of major importance on the basis of minimum numbers of individuals. A minimum of 250 individual mammals are represented in the Hüde I assemblage, with beaver accounting for 20%, cattle for 17.1%, and pig for 16.7%. Other mammalian taxa represented include wolf, fox, bear, otter, weasel, wild cat, wild horse, red deer, roe deer, sheep/goat, and dog. The majority of the pig bones are believed to come from wild individuals, and most of the cattle bones are thought to be those of aurochs, although in light of the debate over the degree of precision possible in the separation of wild and domestic forms of the same species, these assessments may be somewhat problematic. In any event, however, it seems clear that the representation of domestic taxa in the Neolithic faunal assemblage from Hüde I is markedly less than that of wild species.

Kampffmeyer (1983:127) attaches particular importance to the large number of beaver and other fur-bearing mammal bones in the Hüde I assemblage, although it does not appear that the only function of the site was the exploitation of these species. Rather, the Hüde I site seems to have been devoted to the acquisition of a broad spectrum of wild resources whose ranges overlapped at the lake shore. The analysis of the age profiles indicates that the site was seasonally occupied in late summer and fall (Fansa and Kampffmeyer 1985:110), and the model proposed is a pattern of autumn hunting to supplement an otherwise agrarian economy. Fansa and Kampffmeyer point out that the establishment of food production on the lowlands of northwestern Germany was a risky proposition, and it may have been necessary to treat the Dümmer basin as a reserve, especially in lean years. In any event, the sites around the Dümmersee are perhaps the tip of an iceberg. The prehistoric settlement system in this area between about 4000 and 3000 b.c. may shed considerable light on the transition from foraging to farming on the lowlands of northwest Germany if it is fully investigated.

The exploitation of wild fauna, both terrestrial and lacustrine, in the Lengyel component at Brześć Kujawski, and the large proportion of wild animals in the faunal sample from Hüde I bear a similarity to the Mesolithic exploitation pattern on the North European Plain (e.g. Price 1981). In both the Mesolithic and Neolithic cases, there is a concentration on "harvestable" meat sources, such as deer and pigs, which can be culled fairly heavily without depleting population levels, along with the use of small-scale resources such as fish, shellfish, and turtles. It would be wrong, however, to use this similarity to infer an "ethnic" affiliation between the indigenous foragers of the

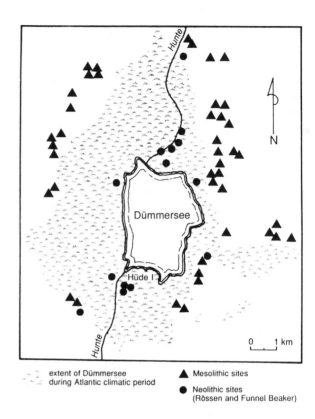

Fig. 6:
The Dümmer basin in northern Germany (see Fig. 4 for location), comparing the present extent of the Dümmersee with its extent during the Atlantic climatic period (after Bogucki 1988).

North European Plain and the Neolithic inhabitants of Brześć Kujawski and Hüde I. For instance, Reitz (1985), in her comparison of faunal samples from aboriginal Spanish colonial sites in Florida, discovered that "Spanish deposits have a very aboriginal appearance" in their range and relative abundance of species. On the basis of Reitz' study and others with similar results, Crabtree (1989) concludes that "species ratios are not necessarily good indicators of ethnic affiliation." Furthermore, the parallels between faunal samples from colonial settlements in North America and those from Brześć Kujawski and Hüde I would lend further support to the notion that "different ethnic groups may exploit the same geographic area in broadly similar ways" (Crabtree 1989).

Neolithic husbandry after the initial colonization

In the loess belt, the period between 3200 and 2500 b.c. is known as the "Middle Neolithic" across much of central Europe. As with any chronological term, it is not universally accepted, and some still prefer to call this period the "Early Eneolithic," despite the fact that copper finds on loess belt sites during this period are relatively infrequent. The empirical data on subsistence for the Middle Neolithic

126

are somewhat more difficult to synthesize than those for the Early Neolithic. Although many sites have yielded botanical and faunal remains, there are very few regional syntheses of these data which draw them together in a coherent way. There are, of course, some exceptions to this generalization (e.g. Lüttschwager 1967; Kruk 1980), but in general they are more limited in scope and quantity of data than those for the earlier Neolithic phases. There appears to be a general assumption that trends in subsistence which began during the Early Neolithic simply continued a millennium later. In the loess belt, this observation appears to be supported by the evidence to some degree, but on the North European Plain, different patterns appear.

The Loess Belt

The most comprehensive tabulation of faunal data from Middle Neolithic sites in the loess belt is Kruk's (1980:figure 33), and data recovered since 1980 have not substantially altered the pattern. As was the case in the Early Neolithic, domestic cattle constitute the major component of virtually all of the loess belt faunal assemblages of this period, but now usually on the order of between 50 and 70% of the identified specimens (Fig. 7). The relative decrease in the proportion of cattle bones in the entire assemblage is due to the perceptible increase in the number of bones from smaller domestic stock, particularly pigs. While pig bones are scarce in Early Neolithic faunal samples, and probably not for reasons of poor preservation or recovery, they are

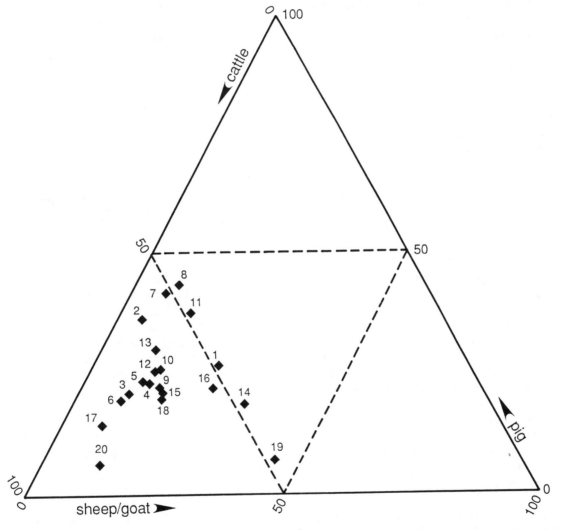

Fig. 7:
Triaxial graph of the relative proportions of cattle, sheep/goat, and pig fragments on Funnel Beaker and Michelsberg sites from the loess zone (after Bogucki 1988). Key: 1—Nosocice (n=778); 2—Janówek (n=87); 3—Tomice (n=468); 4—Gródek Nadbużny (n=1970); 5—Ćmielów (n=2480); 6—Zawarza (n=682); 7—Klementowice (n=123); 8—Książnice Wielkie (n=312); 9—Kamien Łukawski (n=2661); 10—Gniechowice (n=189); 11—Ludwigsburg "im Schlösslesfeld" (n=666); 12—Reusten (Michelsberg component) (n=103); 13—Reusten (Schussenreid component) (n=66); 14—Bronocice (Funnel Beaker component) (n=850); 15—Bronocice (Lublin-Volhynian component) (n=440); 16—Niedzwiedz (n=1338); 17—Makotřasy (n=2206); 18—Zawichost (n=1867); 19—Heilbronn (n=3344); 20—Weissenfels (n=357).

more frequent in Middle Neolithic assemblages. The greater proportion of pig bones is most apparent in Czech and Polish samples, usually constituting in the vicinity of 15-20% of the number of identified specimens.

There are several Middle Neolithic faunal assemblages in which sheep and goat, rather than pig, form the second major taxon behind domestic cattle. These include the large samples from the Funnel Beaker component at Bronocice (no. 14 on Fig. 7; Milisauskas and Kruk 1984; Hensel and Milisauskas 1985) and the Michelsberg site of Hetzenberg near Heilbronn (no. 19 on Fig. 7; Beyer 1972) (see Fig. 1). It is difficult, however, to make regional generalizations on the basis of these isolated samples. For example, the Bronocice assemblage (with a relatively constant 28% sheep/goat throughout the Funnel Beaker occupation) differs in this respect from samples from other Funnel Beaker sites in the vicinity (where pig bones are more abundant) and from the Lublin-Volynian component at Bronocice itself (no. 15 on Fig. 7; Kruk and Milisauskas 1985). The Hetzenberg faunal sample contrasts with that from the roughly coeval Schussenried settlement at Ludwigsburg "Im Schlösslesfeld" (Nobis 1977), also in the Neckar valley (see Fig. 1), where pig bones account for 36% of the faunal assemblage (compared with 46% cattle and 11% sheep/goat).

The decrease in the relative numbers of cattle bones in Middle Neolithic contexts must not be interpreted as a decrease in the number of animals in living herds or a decrease in the economic importance of cattle. It does, however, indicate a greater role in the economy for the smaller domestic animals, particularly pigs. Pigs, of course, have no major economic function other than as rapid-growing meat producers, and their increase in Middle Neolithic contexts reflects a greater diversification in the sources of animal protein in the agrarian economy. Sheep and goats, on the other hand, also yield "secondary products"—milk and wool—and thus add yet another economic dimension.[6] The overall picture is one of a stable and integrated agrarian economy with a diversified "portfolio" of livestock and crops, with households and communities buffered from shortfalls by avoiding overreliance on any single species.

Age and sex data for domestic stock are frustratingly rare in the published analyses of faunal samples from Middle Neolithic loess sites. Some basic data are available for the Lublin-Volynian component at Bronocice (Kruk and Milisauskas 1985:91) which suggest that the pattern for cattle is similar to that found at Early Neolithic loess sites. The majority of the aged cattle specimens (68%) were from individuals older than 30 months. Unfortunately, the use of a 30 month age as a division between subadult and adult categories is not useful in assessing kill-off patterns, for cattle are still growing until they reach 42-48 months when they attain their maximum meat weight.

The data from Bronocice are thus ambiguous about the extent to which meat production played a role in herd management. At Ludwigsburg "Im Schlösslesfeld," although the actual number of individuals in the sample is not reported, there are a greater number of immature specimens, including a number of bones from calves aged 5-6 months (Nobis 1977:83).

An interesting feature of the Bronocice pig bone sample is that 76% of the aged specimens were older than 24 months, which suggests that the kill-off rate for this species was not as rapid as that often found in pig bone samples from prehistoric sites. The Bronocice age data (as hitherto published) are not fine-grained enough to permit the detailed study of kill-off rates, however, and until such studies are available for this and other Middle Neolithic faunal samples, it will be difficult to draw further conclusions about slaughter patterns and their economic implications. At Ludwigsburg "Im Schlösslesfeld," by contrast, pigs were generally killed at 9-10 months (Nobis 1977:84), more in keeping with patterns of pig slaughter found from prehistoric to modern times.

In the loess belt samples, relatively few bones of wild animals are found, continuing a pattern first seen in the Early Neolithic of this area. In fact, if one considers only loess belt samples, there appears to be no significant difference in the relative proportions of wild and domestic bones between the Early and Middle Neolithic samples. Again, this relative scarcity of wild animal bones may reflect the ecological constraints of the loess-belt habitat and the fact that even a minimal amount of hunting in the vicinity of a settlement may have depressed populations of wild herbivores to the extent that this activity was not worthwhile. The relative absence of bones of birds, reptiles, amphibians, and fish from loess belt sites, on the other hand, may be due more to preservation conditions and to recovery methods, since the lighter bones of these taxa would be more prone to decomposition in a decalcified loess matrix. Valves of freshwater molluscs (*Unio sp.*) have been found on a number of sites (Wislanski 1979:217).

The North European Plain

Around 3200 b.c., the settlements of the Early Neolithic cultures on the North European Plain derived from cultures of the loess belt were replaced by agrarian communities derived from indigenous foraging populations. For much of this area, save for the small enclaves where Linear Pottery and Lengyel settlements are found, these local farming communities represent the earliest populations with domesticated livestock and plants. This is especially true in northern Germany and Denmark. There, these communities are tagged with the abbreviation "EN," for "Early Neolithic," although they have little in common with the Early Neolithic settlements of the loess belt. Thus, in order to avoid confusion with the loess belt sites, the

Table 1. Percentages of wild and domestic taxa among identified faunal specimens from Neolithic settlements in Poland, northern Germany, and Denmark. Chronological designations are those conventionally used in the respective regions. EN: Early Neolithic (ca. 3200-2700 b.c.); MN: Middle Neolithic (ca. 2700-2400 b.c.). Data from Johansson (1979:100) and Wiślański (1979:217).

Settlement	Period	No. of Specimens	Wild %	Domestic %
Rosenhof	Mesolithic/EN	358	87	13
Koustrup	EN/MN	118	87	13
Stinthorst	Mesolithic/EN	312	84	16
Sølager	EN/MN	854	82	18
Heidmoor	EN	6,427	66	34
Szlachcin	Wiórek	213	60	40
Wolkenwehe	EN	7,469	57	43
Bistoft	EN	518	52	48
Neustadt/ Marienbad	Mesolithic/EN	168	42	58
Ustowo	Luboń	1,173	35	65
Fuchsberg/ Sudensee	EN	925	15	85
Süssau	MN	790	5	95
Bundsø	MN	10,000+	2	98
Lodsø	MN	938	2	98

abbreviation "EN" will be used below to refer to these first indigenous farming communities of the North European Plain and southern Scandinavia (see Fig. 2).

In contrast to the samples from the loess belt, there is a much higher proportion of wild species represented in the earliest Neolithic lowland faunal assemblages. This is true across the entire plain, particularly in northern Poland and Germany (Lüttschwager 1967; Wislanski 1979; Johansson 1979). One caveat, however, is that the percentage of wild animal bones varies with the type of site. Table 1 presents the relative proportions of wild and domestic taxa from a number of EN faunal samples from northern Poland, Germany, and Denmark.

A dimension of the higher percentages of wild animal bones found at these sites is the number of pig bones in the samples. There is a great degree of ambiguity over what constitutes domestic and wild pigs from an osteological standpoint. The usual procedure is to establish a threshold based on overall size of the specimen above which a bone is classified as wild and below which it is domestic,

assuming that domestication produces a diminution in size. The problem is that this procedure may obscure other factors which can account for size variation, such as sexual dimorphism. It is not unlikely that in many faunal samples with pig bones, some large "domesticated" males may be classed as "wild" and some small "wild" females are considered to be "domesticated." The question that needs to be asked is whether such a distinction makes sense. In light of the fact that "domesticated" pigs probably would have been permitted to forage rather widely in the forests of the North European Plain, there would have been ample opportunity for them to encounter and mate with their conspecific counterparts. There would have been relatively little human control over their breeding.

It would seem more appropriate, then, to consider the EN faunal samples as having three categories of mammalian bones: domestic (including cattle and sheep/goat), wild (all hunted mammal species except for pigs), and pigs (both wild and domestic). When considered from this perspective, they take on a character markedly different

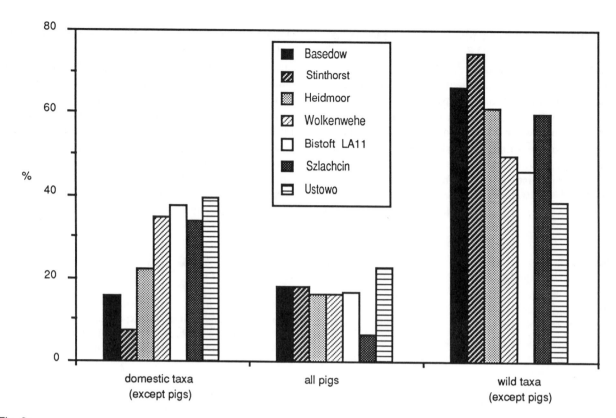

Fig. 8:
Histogram of relative proportions of pigs and other domestic and wild taxa from seven sites in northwest Poland and northern Germany, showing significant representation of unequivocally wild taxa and the mixed wild and domestic sample of pigs.

from both the Early and Middle Neolithic faunal samples from the loess belt in which the overall numbers of wild mammal bones were quite low (Fig. 8). The question is not just one of the relative proportions of hunting versus stockherding, but rather of a quite different approach to the management of the animal component of the economy from that of coeval loess-belt settlements. The pig population would have provided a harvestable meat resource of considerable productivity close at hand, which with wild species, particularly herbivores, would have had the effect of a "walking supermarket" in the surrounding forests. In the forests, small fields of grain would have been attractive for wild herbivores, and it is possible that the many bones of hunted species in the samples reflect the results of a "garden hunting" strategy, similar to that proposed by Linares (1976) for the American tropics, in which a certain amount of crop loss is compensated by the wild game lured within easy range of the hunters. The domestic cattle and the small number of sheep/goat at North European Plain sites would have probably served more for variety and for "secondary products" than as primary meat sources.

Along with the broad spectra of mammalian taxa represented in the faunal samples, the lowland EN sites have yielded significant numbers of bird bones, although well-analyzed assemblages are relatively rare. At Bistoft

LA 11, one of the better studied sites, the majority of the bird bones were from mallards (*Anas platyrynchos*) and other waterfowl (Johansson 1979:105). Fish bones have also been recovered at most sites, but they are generally not analyzed in any degree of detail. It must be noted that in virtually all cases, the deposits have not been sieved, and thus the chances for the recovery of small specimens such as fish and bird bones are minimized. In spite of this, several EN sites in northern Germany (see Fig. 4) have yielded large assemblages of fish bones which have been analyzed recently. At Bistoft LA 11, Heidmoor, and Wolkenwehe (Heinrich and Lepiksaar 1979; Mueller 1983), over 65% of the identified fish specimens belonged to pike (*Esox lucius*). At Heidmoor and Wolkenwehe, the European giant catfish (*Siluris glanis*), was also a major component of the fish bone sample.[7]

Conclusion

Any discussion of early animal husbandry in temperate Europe must acknowledge the environmental diversity in the region and its impact on cultural practices, including incorporation of domestic animals in the subsistence economy. Two major zones have been discussed in this paper, the belt of loess deposits through the middle of central Europe and the lowlands of the North European Plain. The establishment of agrarian communities proceeded in different ways in each region. The process in the loess belt was essentially one of colonization, whereas on the North European Plain, the establishment of early farming communities by non-indigenous groups was followed by the adoption of food production by the local hunter-gatherers.

As was the case in coeval communities in Southeast Europe and the Near East, cattle, sheep/goat, and pigs are the primary domestic taxa of temperate Europe throughout most of later prehistory. They were exploited to different degrees and in different proportions from the way they were used in other parts of the Old World between 4500 and 2500 b.c. First, the importance of sheep and goat is markedly lower in Neolithic central Europe than it is in Southeast Europe or the Near East. Although they are ubiquitous, sheep and goat form a major part of the faunal sample at only a few sites in central Europe. Second, domestic cattle seem to have been the most significant domestic taxon, almost to the exclusion of other species during the earliest Neolithic colonization of the loess belt and continuing in importance throughout the following millennium. Neolithic cattle appear to have been used in a mixed exploitation strategy that sought both meat and milk but did not specialize in either. There is good evidence for dairy production from the very beginning of the Neolithic in the loess belt, rather than it being a secondary phenomenon later in the Neolithic. Nonetheless, around 3000 b.c., there appears to have been an intensification in the exploitation of "secondary products" such as wool, milk, and animal traction.

The most interesting change in animal exploitation in central Europe during this period is that involving pigs, both domestic and wild. Pig bones are very rare on sites of the earliest Neolithic colonists of the loess belt, surprising in light of the apparent suitability of this species for the floodplain forests. As the agrarian communities of the loess belt became established, however, pigs increased in importance significantly, although never surpassing cattle as the main domestic species. The rapid growth and high meat yield of pigs probably permitted a degree of economic security in the agrarian economy, allowing it to weather crop losses and other uncertainties. In contrast, on the North European Plain, the earliest Neolithic faunal samples contain very large numbers of pigs, in a size range that includes both the pre-existing wild population and the smaller domestic pigs. If one assumes that the pigs were allowed to roam in search of pannage, then one cannot speak of distinct "domestic" and "wild" breeding populations, but rather of a continuum in which a single pig population constitutes a harvestable meat source in the forested ecosystem.

For central Europe, the initial domestication of livestock species has ceased to be a central issue. Of far greater interest are questions about economic changes, both *in situ* and introduced from outside. One important direction of future research will be on the ways in which indigenous hunter-gathers acquired domestic stock as they became agriculturalists. Various mechanisms can be proposed, including symbiotic relationships between foragers and farmers (e.g. Bogucki 1987) and the hunting and capture of feral domestic stock (as has recently been suggested by Davidson [1988] to explain a similar development in Spain). It is only by addressing these and similar questions within a broad comparative ethnological framework that zooarchaeology can begin to contribute to the study of Neolithic cultural change.

Notes

1. The small sample sizes are the prime culprit, but animal production systems in traditional societies are rarely so specialized as to reveal clear differences. The expectation is that a female bias in the adult cull and a high neonatal cull, presumably of male calves, can be taken as an indication of a dairy economy.

2. The specialized development of modern cattle-based meat production systems on range environments (e.g., the central United States and Argentina) is a comparatively recent phenomenon, created in response to the demands of a world economy capable of supporting it.

3. For most males, either as calves or when they had reached their maximum meat weight; and for females when they had ceased to produce milk or calves.

4. Since 1976, the author has participated in archaeological research at Brześć Kujawski, located about 150 kms northwest of Warsaw in the Kujavy region of Poland (Bogucki and Grygiel 1983). This site had also been excavated over six seasons between 1933 and 1939 by the late Konrad Jażdżewski (Jażdżewski 1938), for a total of 15 seasons of fieldwork.

5. Sites with ceramics that correspond to those of the earliest phases of the Linear Pottery culture on the loess are found as far north as the area near Grudziądz in northern Poland (visited by the author in the summer of 1988).

6. The much-discussed "Secondary Products Revolution" (Sherratt 1983) really is not a "revolution" at all, for the exploitation of many so-called "secondary" products actually appears to date to the earlier part of the Neolithic. The antiquity of dairying is a prime example (Bogucki 1984b, 1986). Rather, what appears to have happened around 3000 b.c. is the intensification of the use of domestic livestock for products other than meat in an effort by individual households to maximize the productivity of their herds (Bogucki 1988). The use of animals for traction and plough agriculture, for instance, would have increased the amount of work possible by an individual household whose productivity was constrained by the time and labor of its human members.

7. The consistent appearance of pike as a major component of these assemblages appears significant. Heinrich and Lepiksaar (1979:113) have identified two patterns of pike utilization at Bistoft LA 11. In the part of the settlement along the lake shore, the unburnt bones of very large pike were found. They estimate that these fish ranged in length from 53 to 96 cm, possibly longer, and believe that they were butchered upon landing. In hearths in the interior of the settlement, however, burnt bones of smaller pike, most under 50 cm in length, were found. These fish were apparently cooked whole. With the exploitation of the pike and large catfish, there was a clear focus on large species which would yield the most meat rather than the smaller members of the carp family.

References

Beyer, A.J. 1972. *Das Erdwerk der Michelsberger Kultur auf dem Hetzenberg bei Heilbronn-Neckargartach. Teil II: Die Tierknochenfunde.* Müller and Graaf (Forschungen und Berichte zur Vor- und Frühgeschichte in Baden-Württemburg 3/II), Stuttgart.

Bökönyi, S. 1962. Zur Naturgeschichte des Ures in Ungarn und das Problem der Domestikation des Hausrindes. *Acta Archaeologica Hungarica* 14:175-214.

_____ 1969. Archaeological Problems and Methods of Recognizing Animal Domestication. In *The Domestication and Exploitation of Plants and Animals*, ed. P. Ucko and G. Dimbleby, pp. 219-229. Duckworth, London.

_____ 1971. The Development and History of Domestic Animals in Hungary: The Neolithic through the Middle Ages. *American Anthropologist* 73:640-674.

_____ 1975. *History of Domestic Animals in Central and Eastern Europe.* Akadémiai Kiado, Budapest.

Bökönyi, S., and L. Bartosiewicz. 1987. Domestication and Variation. *Archaeozoologia* 1:161-170.

Boessneck, J. 1977. Die Tierknochen aus der Siedlung der Rössener Kultur von Schoningen, Kreis Helmstedt, Eichendorfstrasse und die Probleme ihrer Ausdeutung. *Neue Ausgrabungen und Forschungen in Niedersachsen* 11:153-158.

_____ 1978. Die Vogelknochen aus der Moorsiedlung Hüde I am Dümmer, Kreis Grafschaft Diepholz. *Neue Ausgrabungen und Forschungen in Lower Saxony* 12:155-169.

Bogucki, P. 1982. *Early Neolithic Subsistence and Settlement in the Polish Lowlands.* BAR International Series No. 150, Oxford.

_____ 1984a. Patterns of Animal Exploitation in the Early Neolithic of the Polish Lowlands. In *Animals and Archaeology. 4: Husbandry in Europe*, ed. J. Clutton-Brock and C. Grigson, pp. 35-44. BAR International Series No. 227, Oxford.

_____ 1984b. Linear Pottery Ceramic Sieves and their Economic Implications. *Oxford Journal of Archaeology* 3(1):15-30.

_____ 1986. The Antiquity of Dairying in Temperate Europe. *Expedition* 28(2):51-58.

_____ 1987. The Establishment of Agrarian Communities on the North European Plain. *Current Anthropology* 28(1):1-24.

_____ 1988. *Forest Farmers and Stockherders. Early Agriculture and its Consequences in North-Central Europe.* Cambridge University Press, Cambridge.

Bogucki, P., and R. Grygiel. 1983. Early Farmers of the North European Plain. *Scientific American* 248(4):104-112.

Brinkhuizen, D.C. 1979. On the Finds of European Catfish (*Siluris glanis* L.) in the Netherlands. In *Archaeozoology*, vol. 1, ed. M. Kubasiewicz, pp. 256-261. Agricultural Academy in Szczecin, Szczecin.

Casteel, R. 1978. Faunal Assemblages and the Weigenmethode or Weight Method. *Journal of Field Archaeology* 5:71-77.

Clason, A.T. 1967. The Animal Bones Found at the Bandkeramik Settlement of Bylany. *Archeologické Rozhledy* 19:90-96.

_____ 1972. Some Remarks on the Use and Presentation of Archaeozoological Data. *Helenium* 12:139-153.

Clason, A.T., and W. Prummel. 1977. Collecting, Sieving, and Archaeozoological Research. *Journal of Archaeological Science* 4:171-5.

Crabtree, P.J. 1989. Zooarchaeology and Complex Societies: The Use of Faunal Analysis for the Study of Trade, Status, and Ethnicity. In *Archaeological Method and Theory*, ed. M. Schiffer, in press. University of Arizona Press, Tucson.

Davidson, I. 1988. Escaped Domestic Animals and the Introduction of Agriculture to Spain. In *The Walking Larder*, ed. J. Clutton-Brock, pp. 92-111. George Allen and Unwin, London.

Degerbøl, M., and B. Fredskild. 1970. *The Urus (Bos primigenius Bojanus) and Neolithic Domesticated Cattle (Bos taurus domesticus Linne) in Denmark.* Det Kongelige Dansk Videnskabernes Selskab, biologiske skrifter 17/1.

Desse, J. 1976. La faune du site archéologique de Cuiry-lés-Chaudardes (Aisne). *Les Fouilles Protohistoriques dans la Vallée de l' Aisne*, vol. 4, pp. 187-196. University of Paris, Paris.

Fansa, M., and U. Kampffmeyer. 1985. Vom Jäger und Sammler zum Ackerbauern. In *Ausgrabungen in Niedersachsen, Archäologische Denkmalpflege 1979-*

1984, ed. K. Wilhelmi, pp. 108-111. Konrad Theiss, Stuttgart.

Gautier, A. 1984. How Do I Count You, Let me Count the Ways? Problems of Archaeozoological Quantification. In *Animals and Archaeology. 4: Husbandry in Europe*, ed. J. Clutton-Brock and C. Grigson, pp. 237-251. BAR International Series No. 227, Oxford.

Gehl, O. 1976. Die steinzeitliche Siedlung Stinthorst bei Waren/Müritz im Spiegel des Säugetierfundgutes. *Bodendenkmalpflege in Mecklenburg* 1975:39-53.

_____ 1980. Nutzung von Haus- und Wildtieren nach dem Knochenfundgut der neolithischen Siedlung bei Glasow und der Randow, Kreis Pasewalk. *Bodendenkmalpflege in Mecklenburg* 1979:39-48.

Grayson, D.K. 1979. On the Quantification of Vertebrate Archaeofaunas. In *Advances in Archaeological Method and Theory*, vol. 2, ed. M. Schiffer, pp. 200-237. Academic Press, New York.

_____ 1984. *Quantitative Zooarchaeology. Topics in the Analysis of Archaeological Faunas*. Academic Press, Orlando.

Grigson, C. 1969. The Uses and Limitations of Differences in Absolute Size in the Distinction between the Bones of Aurochs (*Bos primigenius*) and Domestic Cattle (*Bos taurus*). In *The Domestication and Exploitation of Plants and Animals*, ed. P.J. Ucko and G.W. Dimbleby, pp. 277-294. Duckworth, London.

Guilday, J. 1971. *Biological and Archaeological Analysis of Bones from a 17th Century Indian Village (46 PU 31), Putnam County, West Virginia*. Report of the Investigations No. 4. West Virginia Geological and Economic Survey, Morgantown, WV.

Heinrich, D., and J. Lepiksaar. 1979. Die Fischreste von Bistoft, LA 11. In *Socio-ekonomiska Strukturer i Tidigt Neolitikum och deras Förutsättningar*, by L. Johansson, pp. 112-117. Institute for Archaeology, University of Göteborg, Goteborg.

Hensel, W., and S. Milisauskas. 1985. *Excavations of Neolithic and Early Bronze Age Sites in South-Eastern Poland*. Ossolineum, Wrocław.

Higham, C. 1967. Stock Rearing as a Cultural Factor in Prehistoric Europe. *Proceedings of the Prehistoric Society* 33:84-106.

Higham, C., and M.A. Message. 1969. An Assessment of a Prehistoric Technique of Bovine Husbandry. In *Science in Archaeology*, ed. D. Brothwell and E. Higgs, pp. 315-330. Praeger, New York.

Hübner, K.D. 1980. *Untersuchungen an Knochen von Raubtieren und vom Biber vom vorgeschichtlichen Siedlungsplatz Hüde am Dümmer/Lower Saxony*. Unpublished Staatsexamenarbeit, University of Kiel.

Hüster, H. 1983. Die Fischknochen der neolithischen Moorsiedlung Hüde I am Dümmer, Kreis Graftschaft Diepholz. *Neue Ausgrabungen und Forschungen in Lower Saxony* 16:401-480.

Jazdzewski, K. 1938. Cmentarzyska kultury ceramiki wstegowej i zwiazane z nimi slady osadnictwa w Brzesciu Kujawskim. *Wiadomosci Archeologiczne* 15:1-105.

Johansson, F. 1979. Die Knochenfunde von Säugetieren und Vögeln von Bistoft LA 11. In *Socio-eckonomiska Strukturer i Tidigt Neolitikum och deras Förutsättningar*, by L. Johansson, pp. 98-111. Institute for Archaeology, University of Göteborg, Goteborg.

Jürgens, A. 1978/79. Rössener Siebe aus Aldenhoven. *Kölner Jahrbuch für Vor- und Frühgeschichte* 16:17-20.

Kampffmeyer, U. 1983. Die neolithische Siedlungsplatz Hüde I am Dümmer. In *Frühe Bauernkulturen in Niedersachsen*, ed. G. Wegner, pp. 119-134. Staatliches Museum für Naturkunde und Vorgeschichte, Oldenburg.

Kruk, J. 1980. *Gospodarka w Polsce Południowo-Wschodniej w V - III Tysiącleciu p.n.e.* Ossolineum, Wrocław.

Kruk, J., and S. Milisauskas. 1985. *Bronocice. Osiedle Obronne Ludności Kultury Lubelsko-Wolynskiej (2800-2700 lat p.n.e.)*. Ossolineum, Wrocław.

Kubasiewicz, M. 1956. O metodyce badań wykopaliskowych szczątkow kostnych zwierzęcych. *Materiały Zachodnio-Pomorskie* 2:235-244.

Linares, O. 1976. 'Garden Hunting' in the American Tropics. *Human Ecology* 4:331-349.

Lubicz-Niezabitowski, E. 1932. Szczatki zwierzat z osady neolitycznej w Debcu pod Poznaniem. *Z Otchlani Wiekow* 7:11-19.

Lüttschwager, H. 1967. Kurzbericht über Tierfunde aus meso- und neolithischen Moorsiedlungen in Schleswig-Holstein. *Schriften des Naturwissenschaftlichen Vereins für Schleswig-Holstein* 37:53-64.

Makowiecki, D. 1987. Zródła archeozoologiczne z epoki neolitu i początku epoki brązu z Ziemi Chełminskiej. In *Neolit i Początki Epoki Brazu na Ziemi Chełminskiej*, ed. T. Wiślański, pp. 259-273. Mikolaj Kopernik University, Toruń.

Meadow, R.H. 1976. Methodological Concerns in Zooarchaeology. In *Problèmes Ethnographiques des Vestiges Osseux (Thèmes Spécialisés)*, pp. 108-123. IXe Congrès, Union International de Sciences Préhistoriques et Protohistoriques, Nice.

Meniel, P. 1984. Les faunes du Rubané Récent de Menneville "Derriere le Village" et de Berry-au-Bac "La Croix Maigret" (Aisne). *Revue Archéologique de Picardie* 1984(1/2):87-93.

Milisauskas, S. 1978. *European Prehistory*. Academic Press, New York.

Milisauskas, S., and J. Kruk. 1984. Settlement Organization and the Appearance of Low Level Hierarchical Societies during the Neolithic in the Bronocice Microregion. *Germania* 62:1-30.

Modderman, P.J.R. 1976. Abschwemmung und neolithische Siedlungsplätze in Niederbayern. *Archäologisches Korrespondenzblatt* 6:105-108.

Mueller, B. 1983. *Untersuchungen an Fischknochen aus den neolithischen Moorsiedlungen Heidmoor (Berlin-Krs. Segeberg) und Oldesloe-Wolkenwehe (Krs. Stormarn).* Unpublished Examensarbeit zum 1, University of Kiel. Staatsexamen für Lehramt an Gymnasien.

Müller, H.-H. 1964. *Die Haustiere der Mitteldeutschen Bandkeramiker.* Deutsche Akademie der Wissenschaften, Berlin.

Newell, R.R. 1970. The Flint Industry of the Dutch Linearbandkeramik. In *Linearbandkeramik aus Elsloo und Stein,* by P.J.R. Modderman, pp. 144-183. Institute of Prehistory (Analecta Praehistorica Leidensia 3), Leiden.

Nobis, G. 1962. Die Tierreste prähistorischer Siedlungen aus den Satrupholmer Moor. *Zeitschrift für Tierzüchtung und Züchtungsbiologie* 77:16-30.

———— 1975. Zur Fauna des Ellerbekzeitlichen Wohnplatzes Rosenhof in Ostholstein I. (Grabung 1968-1973). *Schriften des Naturwissenschaftlichen Vereins für Schleswig-Holstein* 45:5-30

———— 1977. Die Fauna. In *Die Schussenrieder Siedlung "Im Schlösslesfeld," Markung Ludwigsburg,* by J. Lüning and H. Zürn, pp. 82-90. Landesdenkmalamt Baden-Württemburg (Forschungen und Berichte zur Vor- und Frühgeschichte in Baden-Württemburg, Vol. 8), Stuttgart.

Payne, S. 1973. Kill-off Patterns in Sheep and Goat: The Mandibles from Aşvan Kale. *Anatolian Studies* 23:281-303.

Poplin, F. 1975. La faune danubienne d'Armeau (Yonne, France). In *Archaeozoological Studies,* ed. A.T. Clason, pp. 179-192. North Holland/Elsevier, Amsterdam/New York.

Price, T.D. 1981. Regional Approaches to Human Adaptation in the Mesolithic of the North European Plain. In *Mesolithikum in Europa,* ed. B. Gramsch, pp. 217-234. Museum für Ur- und Frühgeschichte, Veröffentlichungen 14/15, Potsdam.

Reitz, E. 1985. Comparison of Spanish and Aboriginal Subsistence on the Atlantic Coastal Plain. *Southeastern Archaeology* 4:41-50.

Rhode, D. 1988. Measurement of Archaeological Diversity and the Sample-size Effect. *American Antiquity* 53:708-716.

Rowley-Conwy, P. 1984. The Laziness of the Short-distance Hunter: The Origins of Agriculture in Western Denmark. *Journal of Anthropological Archaeology* 3:300-324.

———— 1985. The Origin of Agriculture in Denmark: A Review of Some Theories. *Journal of Danish Archaeology* 4:188-195.

Saur, R. 1980. *Die knochenreste der Paar- und Unpaarhufe der neolithischen Moorsiedlung Hüde I am Dümmer.* Unpublished Staatsexamenarbeit, University of Kiel.

Sherratt, A.G. 1983. The Secondary Exploitation of Animals in the Old World. *World Archaeology* 15:90-104.

Sobocinski, M. 1979. Material kostny zwierzęcy z osad kultury lendzielskiej w strefie czarnoziemu Kujaw Zachodnich. *Pomerania Antiqua* 8:111-131.

Stampfli, H.R. 1965. Tierreste der Grabung Müddersheim, Kr. Düren. In *Müddersheim, eine Ansiedlung der jüngeren Bandkeramik im Rheinland,* by K. Schietzel, pp. 115-123. Böhlau, Bologne.

Taute, W. 1966. Das Felsdach Lautereck, eine mesolithisch-neolithisch-bronzezeitliche Stratigraphie an der Oberen Donau. *Palaeohistoria* 12:483-504.

White, T. 1953. A Method of Calculating the Dietary Percentage of Various Food Animals Utilized by Aboriginal Peoples. *American Antiquity* 18:396-398.

Whittle, A. 1987. Neolithic Settlement Patterns in Temperate Europe: Progress and Problems. *Journal of World Prehistory* 1:5-52.

Wiślański, T. 1979. Ksztaltowanie się miejscowych kultur rolniczo-hodowlanych. Plemiona kultury pucharow lejkowatych. In *Prahistoria Ziem Polskich II.* Neolit, ed. W. Hensel and T. Wiślański, pp. 165-260. Ossolineum, Wrocław.

Zvelebil, M., and P. Rowley-Conwy. 1984. Transition to Farming in Northern Europe: A Hunter-gatherer Perspective. *Norwegian Archaeological Review* 17:104-128.

Research Papers
in Science and Archaeology

Supplement to Volume 6, 1989

Series Editor
Kathleen Ryan

Production Editors
Helen Schenck
Jennifer Quick

Advisory Committee
Stuart Fleming, Chairman
Philip Chase
Patrick McGovern
Henry Michael
Naomi F. Miller
Vincent Pigott

Assistant Editor
Katherine Moreau

Design and Layout
Helen Schenck

The subscription price for *MASCA Research Papers in Science and Archaeology* is $20, payable in U.S. dollars. We also accept VISA/MASTERCARD. This price covers one main volume per year. In addition, we publish supplementary volumes which are offered to MASCA subscribers at a discounted price.

This is a refereed series. All material for publication and books for review should be sent to The Editor, *MASCA Research Papers in Science and Archaeology*. Subscription correspondence should be addressed to The Subscriptions Manager, MASCA, The University Museum, University of Pennsylvania, 33rd and Spruce Streets, Philadelphia, PA 19104-6324.

We gratefully acknowledge a grant from the Women's Committee of The University Museum in support of this volume.